The Dolorous Passion of Our Lord Jesus Christ

By Anne Catherine Emmerich

D0912731

Coming Soon
How I Stole 5.6 Million from Walmart
The Gods Return Loki's Trial
Zombie Squirrels

Loki's Publishing

Seattle, WA

The Dolorous Passion of Our Lord Jesus Christ

Contents

INTRODUCTION.

On the evening of the 18th of February, 1823, a friend of Sister Emmerich went up to the bed, where she was lying apparently asleep; and being much struck by the beautiful and mournful expression of her countenance, felt himself inwardly inspired to raise his heart fervently to God, and offer the Passion of Christ to the Eternal Father, in union with the sufferings of all those who have carried their cross after him. While making this short prayer, he chanced to fix his eyes for a moment upon the stigmatised hands of Sister Emmerich. She immediately hid them under the counterpane, starting as if someone had given her a blow. He felt surprised at this, and asked her, 'What has happened to you?' 'Many things,' she answered in an expressive tone. Whilst he was considering what her meaning could be, she appeared to be asleep. At the end of about a quarter of an hour, she suddenly started up with all the eagerness of a person having a violent struggle with another, stretched out both her arms, clenching her hand, as if to repel an enemy standing on the left side of her bed, and exclaimed in an indignant voice: 'What do you mean by this contract of Magdalum?' Then she continued to speak with the warmth of a person who is being questioned during a quarrel—'Yes, it is that accursed spirit—the liar from the beginning—Satan, who is reproaching him about the Magdalum contract, and other things of the same nature, and says that he spent all that money upon himself.' When asked, 'Who has spent money? Who is being spoken to in that way?' she replied, 'Jesus, my adorable Spouse, on Mount Olivet.' Then she again turned to the left, with menacing gestures, and exclaimed, 'What meanest thou, O father of lies, with thy Magdalum contract? Did he not deliver twenty-seven poor prisoners at Thirza, with the money derived from the sale of Magdalum? I saw him, and thou darest to say that he has brought confusion into the whole estate, driven out its inhabitants, and squandered the money for which it was sold? But thy time is come, accursed spirit! Thou wilt be chained, and his heel will crush thy head.'

Here she was interrupted by the entrance of another person; her friends thought that she was in delirium, and pitied her. The following morning she owned that the previous night she had imagined herself to be following our Saviour to the Garden of Olives, after the institution of the Blessed Eucharist, but that just at that moment someone having looked at the stigmas on her hands with a degree of veneration, she felt so horrified at this being done in the presence of our Lord, that she hastily hid them, with a feeling of pain. She then related her vision of what took place in the Garden of Olives, and as she continued her narrations the following days, the friend who was listening to her was enabled to connect the different scenes of the Passion together. But as, during Lent, she was also celebrating the combats of our Lord with Satan in the desert, she had to endure in her own person many sufferings and temptations. Hence there were a few pauses in the history of the Passion, which were, however, easily filled up by means of some later communications.

She usually spoke in common German, but when in a state of ecstasy, her language became much purer, and her narrations partook at once of child-like simplicity and dignified inspiration. Her friend wrote down all that she had said, directly he returned to his own apartments; for it was seldom that he could so much as even take notes in her presence. The Giver of all good gifts bestowed upon him memory, zeal, and strength to bear much trouble and fatigue, so that he has been enabled to bring this work to a conclusion. His conscience tells him that he has done his best, and he humbly begs the reader, if satisfied with the result of his labours, to bestow upon him the alms of an occasional prayer.

CHAPTER I.

Jesus in the Garden of Olives.

When Jesus left the supper-room with the eleven Apostles, after the institution of the Adorable Sacrament of the Altar, his soul was deeply oppressed and his sorrow on the increase. He led the eleven, by an unfrequented path, to the Valley of Josaphat. As they left the house, I saw the moon, which was not yet quite at the full, rising in front of the mountain.

Our Divine Lord; as he wandered with his Apostles about the valley, told them that here he should one day return to judge the world, but not in a state of poverty and humiliation, as he then was, and that men would tremble with fear, and cry: 'Mountains, fall upon us!' His disciples did not understand him, and thought, by no means for the first time that night, that weakness and exhaustion had affected his brain. He said to them again: 'All you shall be scandalised in me this night. For it is written: I WILL STRIKE THE SHEPHERD, AND THE SHEEP OF THE FLOCK SHALL BE DISPERSED. But after I shall be risen again, I will go before you into Galilee.'

The Apostles were still in some degree animated by the spirit of enthusiasm and devotion with which their reception of the Blessed Sacrament and the solemn and affecting words of Jesus had inspired them. They eagerly crowded round him, and expressed their love in a thousand different ways, earnestly protesting that they would never abandon him. But as Jesus continued to talk in the same strain, Peter exclaimed: 'Although all shall be scandalised in thee, I will never be scandalised!' and our Lord answered him: 'Amen, I say to thee, that in this night, before the cock crow, thou wilt deny me thrice.' But Peter still insisted, saying: 'Yea, though I should die with thee, I will not deny thee.' And the others all said the same. They walked onward and stopped, by turns, for the sadness of our Divine Lord continued to increase. The Apostles tried to comfort him by human arguments, assuring him that what he foresaw would not come to pass. They tired themselves in these vain efforts, began to doubt, and were assailed by temptation.

They crossed the brook Cedron, not by the bridge where, a few hours later, Jesus was taken prisoner, but by another, for they had left the direct road. Gethsemani, whither they were going, was about a mile and a half distant from the supper-hall, for it was three quarters of a mile from the supper-hall to the Valley of Josaphat, and about as far from thence to Gethsemani. The place called Gethsemani (where latterly Jesus had several times passed the night with his disciples) was a large garden, surrounded by a hedge, and containing only some fruit trees and flowers, while outside there stood a few deserted unclosed buildings.

The Apostles and several others persons had keys of this garden, which was used sometimes as a pleasure ground, and sometimes as a place of retirement for prayer. Some arbours made of leaves and branches had been raised there, and eight of the Apostles remained in them, and were later joined by others of the disciples. The Garden of Olives was separated by a road from that of Gethsemani, and was open, surrounded only by an earthern wall, and smaller than the Garden of Gethsemani. There were caverns, terraces, and many olive-trees to be seen in this garden, and it was easy to find there a suitable spot for prayer and meditation. It was to the wildest part that Jesus went to pray.

It was about nine o'clock when Jesus reached Gethsemani with his disciples. The moon had risen, and already gave light in the sky, although the earth was still dark. Jesus was most sorrowful, and told his Apostles that danger was at hand. The disciples felt uneasy, and he told eight of those who were following him, to remain in the Garden of Gethsemani whilst he went on to pray. He took with him Peter, James, and John, and going on a little further, entered into the Garden of Olives. No words can describe the sorrow which then oppressed his soul, for the time of trial was near. John asked him how it was that he, who had hitherto always consoled them, would now be so dejected? 'My soul is sorrowful even unto death,' was his reply. And he beheld sufferings and temptations surrounding him on all sides, and drawing nearer and nearer, under the forms of frightful figures borne on clouds. Then it was that he said to the three Apostles: 'Stay you here and watch with me. Pray, lest ye enter into temptation.' Jesus went a few steps to the left, down a hill, and concealed himself beneath a rock, in a grotto about six feet deep, while the Apostles remained in a species of hollow above. The earth sank gradually the further you entered this grotto, and the plants which were hanging from the rock screened its interior like a curtain from persons outside.

When Jesus left his disciples, I saw a number of frightful figures surrounding him in an ever-narrowing circle.

His sorrow and anguish of soul continued to increase, and he was trembling all over when he entered the grotto to pray, like a wayworn traveller hurriedly seeking shelter from a sudden storm, but the awful visions pursued him even there, and became more and more clear and distinct. Alas! this small cavern appeared to contain the awful picture of all the sins which had been or were to be committed from the fall of Adam to the end of the world, and of the punishment which they deserved. It was here, on Mount Olivet, that Adam and Eve took refuge when drive out of Paradise to wander homeless on earth, and they had wept and bewailed themselves in this very grotto.

I felt that Jesus, in delivering himself up to Divine Justice in satisfaction for the sins of the world, caused his divinity to return, in some sort, into the bosom of the Holy Trinity, concentrated himself, so to speak, in his pure, loving and innocent humanity, and strong only in his ineffable love, gave it up to anguish and suffering.

He fell on his face, overwhelmed with unspeakable sorrow, and all the sins of the world displayed themselves before him, under countless forms and in all their real deformity. He took them all upon himself, and in his prayer offered his own adorable Person to the justice of his Heavenly Father, in payment for so awful a debt. But Satan, who was enthroned amid all these horrors, and even filled with diabolical joy at the sight of them, let loose his fury against Jesus, and displayed before the eyes of his soul increasingly awful visions, at the same time addressing his adorable humanity in words such as these: 'Takest thou even this sin upon thyself? Art thou willing to bear its penalty? Art thou prepared to satisfy for all these sins?'

And now a long ray of light, like a luminous path in the air descended from Heaven; it was a procession of angels who came up to Jesus and strengthened and re-invigorated him. The remainder of the grotto was filled with frightful visions of our crimes; Jesus took them all upon himself, but that adorable Heart, which was so filled with the most perfect love for God and man, was flooded with anguish, and overwhelmed beneath the weight of so many abominable crimes. When this huge mass of iniquities, like the waves of a fathomless ocean, has passed over his soul, Satan brought forward innumerable temptations, as he had formerly done in the desert, even daring to adduce various accusations against him. 'And takest thou all these things upon thyself,' he exclaimed, 'thou who art not unspotted thyself?' then he laid to the charge of our Lord, with infernal impudence, a host of imaginary crimes. He reproached him with the faults of his disciples, the scandals which they had caused, and the disturbances which he had occasioned in the world by giving up ancient customs. No Pharisee, however wily and severe, could have surpassed Satan on this occasion; he reproached Jesus with having been the cause of the massacre of the Innocents, as well as of the sufferings of his parents in Egypt, with not having saved John the Baptist from death, with having brought disunion into families, protected men of despicable character, refused to cure various sick persons, injured the inhabitants of Gergesa by permitting men possessed by the devil to overturn their vats,[1] and demons to make swine cast themselves into the sea; with having deserted his family, and squandered the property of others; in one word Satan, in the hopes of causing Jesus to waver, suggested to him every thought by which he would have tempted at the hour of death an ordinary mortal who might have performed all these actions without a superhuman intention; for it was hidden from him that Jesus was the Son of God, and he tempted him only as the most just of men. Our Divine Saviour permitted his humanity thus to preponderate over his divinity, for he was pleased to endure even those temptations with which holy souls are assailed at the hour of death concerning the merit of their good works. That he might drink the chalice of suffering even to the dregs, he permitted the evil spirit to tempt his sacred humanity, as he would have tempted a man who should wish to attribute to his good works some special value in themselves, over and above what they might have by their union with the merits of our Saviour. There was not an action out of which he did not contrive to frame some accusation, and he reproached Jesus, among other things, with having spent the price of the property of Mary Magdalen at Magdalum, which he had received from Lazarus.

---

[1] On the 11th of December 1812, in her visions of the public life of Jesus, she saw our Lord permit the devils whom he had expelled from the men of Gergesa to enter into a herd of swine, she also saw, on this particular occasion that the possessed men first overturned a large vat filled with some fermented liquid.

The Dolorous Passion of Our Lord Jesus Christ

Among the sins of the world which Jesus took upon himself, I saw also my own; and a stream, in which I distinctly beheld each of my faults, appeared to flow towards me from out of the temptations with which he was encircled. During this time my eyes were fixed upon my Heavenly Spouse; with him I wept and prayed, and with him I turned towards the consoling angels. Ah, truly did our dear Lord writhe like a worm beneath the weight of his anguish and sufferings!

Whilst Satan was pouring forth his accusations against Jesus, it was with difficulty that I could restrain my indignation, but when he spoke of the sale of Magdalen's property, I could no longer keep silence, and exclaimed: 'How canst thou reproach him with the sale of this property as with a crime? Did I not myself see our Lord spend the sum which was given him by Lazarus in works of mercy, and deliver twenty-eight debtors imprisoned at Thirza?'

At first Jesus looked calm, as he kneeled down and prayed, but after a time his soul became terrified at the sight of the innumerable crimes of men, and of their ingratitude towards God, and his anguish was so great that the trembled and shuddered as he exclaimed: 'Father, if it is possible, let this chalice pass from me! Father, all things are possible to thee, remove this chalice from me!' But the next moment he added: 'Nevertheless, not my will but thine be done.' His will and that of his Father were one, but now that his love had ordained that he should be left to all the weakness of his human nature, he trembled at the prospect of death.

I saw the cavern in which he was kneeling filled with frightful figures; I saw all the sins, wickedness, vices, and ingratitude of mankind torturing and crushing him to the earth; the horror of death and terror which he felt as man at the sight of the expiatory sufferings about to come upon him, surrounded and assailed his Divine Person under the forms of hideous spectres. He fell from side to side, clasping his hands; his body was covered with a cold sweat, and he trembled and shuddered. He then arose, but his knees were shaking and apparently scarcely able to support him; his countenance was pale, and quite altered in appearance, his lips white, and his hair standing on end. It was about half-past ten o'clock when he arose from his knees, and, bathed in a cold sweat, directed his trembling, weak footsteps towards his three Apostles. With difficulty did he ascend the left side of the cavern, and reach a spot where the ground was level, and where they were sleeping, exhausted with fatigue, sorrow and anxiety. He came to them, like a man overwhelmed with bitter sorrow, whom terror urges to seek his friends, but like also to a good shepherd, who, when warned of the approach of danger, hastens to visit his flock, the safety of which is threatened; for he well knew that they also were being tried by suffering and temptation. The terrible visions never left him, even while he was thus seeking his disciples. When he found that they were asleep, he clasped his hands and fell down on his knees beside them, overcome with sorrow and anxiety, and said: 'Simon, sleepest thou?' They awoke, and raised him up, and he, in his desolation of spirit, said to them: 'What? Could you not watch one hour with me?' When they looked at him, and saw him pale and exhausted, scarcely able to support himself, bathed in sweat, trembling and shuddering,—when they heard how changed and almost inaudible his voice had become, they did not know what to think, and had he not been still surrounded by a well-known halo of light, they would never have recognised him as Jesus. John said to him: 'Master, what has befallen thee? Must I call the other disciples? Ought we to take to flight?' Jesus answered him: 'Were I to live, teach, and perform miracles for thirty-three years longer, that would not suffice for the accomplishment of what must be fulfilled before this time tomorrow. Call not the eight; I did not bring them hither, because they could not see me thus agonising without being scandalised; they would yield to temptation, forget much of the past, and lose their confidence in me. But you, who have seen the Son of Man transfigured, may also see him under a cloud, and in dereliction of spirit; nevertheless, watch and pray, lest ye fall into temptation, for the spirit indeed is willing, but the flesh is weak.'

By these words he sought at once to encourage them to persevere, and to make known to them the combat which his human nature was sustaining against death, together with the cause of his weakness. In his overwhelming sorrow, he remained with them nearly a quarter of an hour, and spoke to them again. He then returned to the grotto, his mental sufferings being still on the increase, while his disciples, on their part, stretched forth their hands towards him, wept, and embraced each other, asking, 'What can it be? What is happening to him? He appears to be in a state of complete desolation.' After this, they covered their heads, and began to pray, sorrowfully and anxiously.

About an hour and a half had passed since Jesus entered the Garden of Olives. It is true that Scripture tells us he said, 'Could you not watch one hour with me?' but his words should not be taken literally, nor according to our way of counting time. The three Apostles who were with Jesus had prayed at first, but then they had fallen asleep, for temptation had come upon them by reason of their want of trust in God. The other eight, who had remained outside the garden, did not sleep, for our Lord's last words, so expressive of suffering and sadness, had filled their hearts with sinister forebodings, and they wandered about Mount Olivet, trying to find some place of refuge in case of danger.

The town of Jerusalem was very quiet; the Jews were in their houses, engaged in preparing for the feast, but I saw, here and there, some of the friends and disciples of Jesus walking to and fro, with anxious countenances, conversing earnestly together, and evidently expecting some great event. The Mother of our Lord, Magdalen, Martha, Mary of Cleophas, Mary Salome, and Salome had gone from the supper-hall to the house of Mary, the mother of Mark. Mary was alarmed at the reports which were spreading, and wished to return to the town with her friends, in order to hear something of Jesus. Lazarus, Nicodemus, Joseph of Arimathea, and some relations from Hebron, came to see and endeavour to tranquillise her, for as they were aware, either from their own knowledge or from what the disciples had told them, of the mournful predictions which Jesus had made in the supper-room, they had made inquiries of some Pharisees of their acquaintance, and had not been able to hear that any conspiracy was on foot for the time against our Lord. Being utterly ignorant of the treason of Judas, they assured Mary that the danger could not yet be very great, and that the enemies of Jesus would not make any attempt upon his person, at least until the festival was over. Mary told them how restless and disturbed in mind Judas had latterly appeared, and how abruptly he had left the supper-room. She felt no doubt of his having gone to betray our Lord, for she had often warned him that he was a son of perdition. The holy women then returned to the house of Mary, the mother of Mark.

When Jesus, unrelieved of all the weight of his sufferings, returned to the grotto, he fell prostrate, with his face on the ground and his arms extended, and prayed to his Eternal Father; but his soul had to sustain a second interior combat, which lasted three-quarters of an hour. Angels came and showed him, in a series of visions, all the sufferings that he was to endure in order to expiate sin; how great was the beauty of man, the image of God, before the fall, and how that beauty was changed and obliterated when sin entered the world. He beheld how all sins originated in that of Adam, the signification and essence of concupiscence, its terrible effect on the powers of the soul, and likewise the signification and essence of all the sufferings entailed by concupiscence. They showed him the satisfaction which he would have to offer to Divine Justice, and how it would consist of a degree of suffering in his soul and body which would comprehend all the sufferings due to the concupiscence of all mankind, since the debt of the whole human race had to be paid by that humanity which alone was sinless—the humanity of the Son of God. The angels showed him all these things under different forms, and I felt what they were saying, although I heard no voice. No tongue can describe what anguish and what horror overwhelmed the soul of Jesus at the sight of so terrible an expiation—his sufferings were so great, indeed, that a bloody sweat issued forth from all the pores of this sacred body.

Whilst the adorable humanity of Christ was thus crushed to the earth beneath this awful weight of suffering, the angels appeared filled with compassion; there was a pause, and I perceived that they were earnestly desiring to console him, and praying to that effect before the throne of God. For one instant there appeared to be, as it were, a struggle between the mercy and justice of God and that love which was sacrificing itself. I was permitted to see an image of God, not, as before, seated on a throne, but under a luminous form. I beheld the divine nature of the Son in the Person of the Father, and, as it were, withdrawn in his bosom; the Person of the Holy Ghost proceeded from the Father and the Son, it was, so to speak, between them, and yet the whole formed only one God—but these things are indescribable.

All this was more an inward perception than a vision under distinct forms, and it appeared to me that the Divine Will of our Lord withdrew in some sort into the Eternal Father, in order to permit all those sufferings which his human will besought his Father to spare him, to weigh upon his humanity alone. I saw this at the time when the angels, filled with compassion, were desiring to console Jesus, who, in fact, was slightly relieved at that moment. Then all disappeared, and the angels retired from our Lord, whose soul was about to sustain fresh assaults.

Anne Catherine Emmerich

When our Redeemer, on Mount Olivet, was pleased to experience and overcome that violent repugnance of human nature to suffering and death which constitutes a portion of all sufferings, the tempter was permitted to do to him what he does to all men who desire to sacrifice themselves in a holy cause. In the first portion of the agony, Satan displayed before the eyes of our Lord the enormity of that debt of sin which he was going to pay, and was even bold and malicious enough to seek faults in the very works of our Saviour himself. In the second agony, Jesus beheld, to its fullest extent and in all its bitterness, the expiatory suffering which would be required to satisfy Divine Justice. This was displayed to him by angels; for it belongs not to Satan to show that expiation is possible, and the father of lies and despair never exhibits the works of Divine Mercy before men. Jesus having victoriously resisted all these assaults by his entire and absolute submission to the will of his Heavenly Father, a succession of new and terrifying visions were presented before his eyes, and that feeling of doubt and anxiety which a man on the point of making some great sacrifice always experiences, arose in the soul of our Lord, as he asked himself the tremendous question: 'And what good will result from this sacrifice?' Then a most awful picture of the future was displayed before his eyes and overwhelmed his tender heart with anguish.

When God had created the first Adam, he cast a deep sleep upon him, opened his side, and took one of his ribs, of which he made Eve, his wife and the mother of all the living. Then he brought her to Adam, who exclaimed: 'This now is bone of my bones, and flesh of my flesh… Wherefore a man shall leave father and mother, and shall cleave to his wife, and they shall be two in one flesh.' That was the marriage of which it is written: 'This is a great Sacrament. I speak in Christ and in the Church.' Jesus Christ, the second Adam, was pleased also to let sleep come upon him—the sleep of death on the cross, and he was also pleased to let his side be opened, in order that the second Eve, his virgin Spouse, the Church, the mother of all the living, might be formed from it. It was his will to give her the blood of redemption, the water of purification, and his spirit—the three which render testimony on earth—and to bestow upon her also the holy Sacraments, in order that she might be pure, holy, and undefiled; he was to be her head, and we were to be her members, under submission to the head, the bone of his bones, and the flesh of his flesh. In taking human nature, that he might suffer death for us, he had also left his Eternal Father, to cleave to his Spouse, the Church, and he became one flesh with her, by feeding her with the Adorable Sacrament of the Altar, in which he unites himself unceasingly with us. He had been pleased to remain on earth with his Church, until we shall all be united together by him within her fold, and he has said: 'The gates of hell shall never prevail against her.' To satisfy his unspeakable love for sinners, our Lord had become man and a brother of these same sinners, that so he might take upon himself the punishment due to all their crimes. He had contemplated with deep sorrow the greatness of this debt and the unspeakable sufferings by which it was to be acquitted. Yet he had most joyfully given himself up to the will of his Heavenly Father as a victim of expiation. Now, however, he beheld all the future sufferings, combats, and wounds of his heavenly Spouse; in one word, he beheld the ingratitude of men.

The soul of Jesus beheld all the future sufferings of his Apostles, disciples, and friends; after which he saw the primitive Church, numbering but few souls in her fold at first, and then in proportion as her numbers increased, disturbed by heresies and schisms breaking out among her children, who repeated the sin of Adam by pride and disobedience. He saw the tepidity, malice and corruption of an infinite number of Christians, the lies and deceptions of proud teachers, all the sacrileges of wicked priests, the fatal consequences of each sin, and the abomination of desolation in the kingdom of God, in the sanctuary of those ungrateful human beings whom he was about to redeem with his blood at the cost of unspeakable sufferings.

The scandals of all ages, down to the present day and even to the end of the world—every species of error, deception, mad fanaticism, obstinacy and malice—were displayed before his eyes, and he beheld, as it were floating before him, all the apostates, heresiarchs, and pretended reformers, who deceive men by an appearance of sanctity. The corrupters and the corrupted of all ages outraged and tormented him for not having been crucified after their fashion, or for not having suffered precisely as they settled or imagined he should have done. They vied with each other in tearing the seamless robe of his Church; many illtreated, insulted, and denied him, and many turned contemptuously away, shaking their heads at him, avoiding his compassionate embrace, and hurrying on to the abyss where they were finally swallowed up. He saw countless numbers of other men who did not dare openly to deny him, but who passed on in disgust at the sight of the wounds of his Church, as the Levite passed by the poor man who had fallen among robbers. Like unto cowardly and faithless children, who desert their mother in the middle of the night, at the sight of the thieves and robbers to whom their negligence or their malice has opened the door, they fled from his wounded Spouse. He beheld all these men, sometimes separated from the True Vine, and taking their rest amid the wild fruit trees, sometimes like lost sheep, left to the mercy of the wolves, led by base hirelings into bad pasturages, and refusing to enter the fold of the Good Shepherd who gave his life for his sheep. They were wandering homeless in the desert in the midst of the sand blown about by the wind, and were obstinately determined not to see his City placed upon a hill, which could not be hidden, the House of his Spouse, his Church built upon a rock, and with which he had promised to remain to the end of ages. They built upon the sand wretched tenements, which they were continually pulling down and rebuilding, but in which there was neither altar nor sacrifice; they had weathercocks on their roofs, and their doctrines changed with the wind, consequently they were for ever in opposition one with the other. They never could come to a mutual understanding, and were forever unsettled, often destroying their own dwellings and hurling the fragments against the Corner-Stone of the Church, which always remained unshaken.

As there was nothing but darkness in the dwelling of these men, many among them, instead of directing their steps towards the Candle placed on the

Candlestick in the House of the Spouse of Christ, wandered with closed eyes around the gardens of the Church, sustaining life only by inhaling the sweet odours which were diffused from them far and near, stretching forth their hands towards shadowy idols, and following wandering stars which led them to wells where there was no water. Even when on the very brink of the precipice, they refused to listen to the voice of the Spouse calling them, and, though dying with hunger, derided, insulted, and mocked at those servants and messengers who were sent to invite them to the Nuptial Feast. They obstinately refused to enter the garden, because they feared the thorns of the hedge, although they had neither wheat with which to satisfy their hunger nor wine to quench their thirst, but were simply intoxicated with pride and self-esteem, and being blinded by their own false lights, persisted in asserting that the Church of the Word made flesh was invisible. Jesus beheld them all, he wept over them, and was pleased to suffer for all those who do not see him and who will not carry their crosses after him in his City built upon a hill—his Church founded upon a rock, to which he has given himself in the Holy Eucharist, and against which the gates of Hell will never prevail.

Bearing a prominent place in these mournful visions which were beheld by the soul of Jesus, I saw Satan, who dragged away and strangled a multitude of men redeemed by the blood of Christ and sanctified by the unction of his Sacrament. Our Divine Saviour beheld with bitterest anguish the ingratitude and corruption of the Christians of the first and of all succeeding ages, even to the end of the world, and during the whole of this time the voice of the tempter was incessantly repeating: 'Canst thou resolve to suffer for such ungrateful reprobates?' while the various apparitions succeeded each other with intense rapidity, and so violently weighed down and crushed the soul of Jesus, that his sacred humanity was overwhelmed with unspeakable anguish. Jesus—the Anointed of the Lord—the Son of Man struggled and writhed as he fell on his knees, with clasped hands, as it were annihilated beneath the weight of his suffering. So violent was the struggle which then took place between his human will and his repugnance to suffer so much for such an ungrateful race, that from every pore of his sacred body there burst forth large drops of blood, which fell trickling on to the ground. In his bitter agony, he looked around, as though seeking help, and appeared to take Heaven, earth, and the stars of the firmament to witness of his sufferings.

Jesus, in his anguish of spirit, raised his voice, and gave utterance to several cries of pain. The three Apostles awoke, listened, and were desirous of approaching him, but Peter detained James and John, saying: 'Stay you here; I will join him.' Then I saw Peter hastily run forward and enter the grotto. 'Master,' he exclaimed, 'what has befallen thee?' But at the sight of Jesus, thus bathed in his own blood, and sinking to the ground beneath the weight of mortal fear and anguish, he drew back, and paused for a moment, overcome with terror. Jesus made him no answer, and appeared unconscious of his presence. Peter returned to the other two, and told them that the Lord had not answered him except by groans and sighs. They became more and more sorrowful after this, covered their heads, and sat down to weep and pray.

The Dolorous Passion of Our Lord Jesus Christ

I then returned to my Heavenly Spouse in his most bitter agony. The frightful visions of the future ingratitude of the men whose debt to Divine Justice he was taking upon himself, continued to become more and more vivid and tremendous. Several times I heard him exclaim: 'O my Father, can I possibly suffer for so ungrateful a race? O my Father, if this chalice may not pass from me, but I must drink it, thy will be done!'

Amid all these apparitions, Satan held a conspicuous place, under various forms, which represented different species of sins. Sometimes he appeared under the form of a gigantic black figure, sometimes under those of a tiger, a fox, a wolf, a dragon, or a serpent. Not, however, that he really took any of these shapes, but merely some one of their characteristics, joined with other hideous forms. None of these frightful apparitions entirely resembled any creature, but were symbols of abomination, discord, contradiction, and sin—in one word, were demoniacal to the fullest extent. These diabolical figures urged on, dragged, and tore to pieces, before the very eyes of Jesus, countless numbers of those men for whose redemption he was entering upon the painful way of the Cross. At first I but seldom saw the serpent: soon, however, it made its appearance, with a crown upon its head. This odious reptile was of gigantic size, apparently possessed of unbounded strength, and led forward countless legions of the enemies of Jesus in every age and of every nation. Being armed with all kinds of destructive weapons, they sometimes tore one another in pieces, and then renewed their attacks upon our Saviour with redoubled rage. It was indeed an awful sight; for they heaped upon him the most fearful outrages, cursing, striking, wounding, and tearing him in pieces. Their weapons, swords, and spears flew about in the air, crossing and recrossing continually in all directions, like the flails of threshers in an immense barn; and the rage of each of these fiends seemed exclusively directed against Jesus—that grain of heavenly wheat descended to the earth to die there, in order to feed men eternally with the Bread of Life.

Thus exposed to the fury of these hellish bands, some of which appeared to me wholly composed of blind men, Jesus was as much wounded and bruised as if their blows had been real. I saw him stagger from side to side, sometimes raising himself up, and sometimes falling again, while the serpent, in the midst of the crowds whom it was unceasingly leading forward against Jesus, struck the ground with its tail, and tore to pieces or swallowed all whom it thus knocked to the ground.

It was made known to me that these apparitions were all those persons who in divers ways insult and outrage Jesus, really and truly present in the Holy Sacrament. I recognised among them all those who in any way profane the Blessed Eucharist. I beheld with horror all the outrages thus offered to our Lord, whether by neglect, irreverence, and omission of what was due to him; by open contempt, abuse, and the most awful sacrileges; by the worship of worldly idols; by spiritual darkness and false knowledge; or, finally, by error, incredulity, fanaticism, hatred, and open persecution. Among these men I saw many who were blind, paralysed, deaf, and dumb, and even children;—blind men who would not see the truth; paralytic men who would not advance, according to its directions, on the road leading to eternal live; deaf men who refused to listen to its warnings and threats; dumb men who would never use their voices in its defence; and, finally, children who were led astray by following parents and teachers filled with the love of the world and forgetfulness of God, who were fed on earthly luxuries, drunk with false wisdom, and loathing all that pertained to religion. Among the latter, the sight of whom grieved me especially, because Jesus so loved children, I saw many irreverent, ill-behaved acolytes, who did not honour our Lord in the holy ceremonies in which they took a part. I beheld with terror that many priests, some of whom even fancied themselves full of faith and piety, also outraged Jesus in the Adorable Sacrament. I saw many who believed and taught the doctrine of the Real Presence, but did not sufficiently take it to heart, for they forgot and neglected the palace, throne, and seat of the Living God, that is to say, the church, the altar, the tabernacle, the chalice, the monstrance, the vases and ornaments; in one word, all that is used in his worship, or to adorn his house.

Entire neglect reigned everywhere, all things were left to moulder away in dust and filth, and the worship of God was, if not inwardly profaned, at least outwardly dishonoured. Nor did this arise from real poverty, but from indifference, sloth, preoccupation of mind about vain earthly concerns, and often also from egotism and spiritual death; for I saw neglect of this kind in churches the pastors and congregations of which were rich, or at east tolerably well off. I saw many others in which worldly, tasteless, unsuitable ornaments had replaced the magnificent adornments of a more pious age.

I saw that often the poorest of men were better lodged in their cottages than the Master of heaven and earth in his churches. Ah, how deeply did the inhospitality of men grieve Jesus, who had given himself to them to be their Food! Truly, there is no need to be rich in order to receive him who rewards a hundredfold the glass of cold water given to the thirsty; but how shameful is not our conduct when in giving drink to the Divine Lord, who thirst for our souls, we give him corrupted water in a filthy glass! In consequence of all this neglect, I saw the weak scandalised, the Adorable Sacrament profaned, the churches deserted, and the priests despised. This state of impurity and negligence extended even to the souls of the faithful, who left the tabernacle of their hearts unprepared and uncleansed when Jesus was about to enter them, exactly the same as they left his tabernacle on the altar.

Were I to speak for an entire year, I would never detail all the insults offered to Jesus in the Adorable Sacrament which were made known to me in this way. I saw their authors assault Jesus in bands, and strike him with different arms, corresponding to their various offences. I saw irreverent Christians of all ages, careless or sacrilegious priests, crowds of tepid and unworthy communicants, wicked soldiers profaning the sacred vessels, and servants of the devil making use of the Holy Eucharist in the frightful mysteries of hellish worship. Among these bands I saw a great number of theologians, who had been drawn into heresy by their sins, attacking Jesus in the Holy Sacrament of his Church, and snatching out of his Heart, by their seductive words and promises, a number of souls for whom he had shed his blood. Ah! it was indeed an awful sight, for I saw the Church as the body of Christ; and all these bands of men, who were separating themselves from the Church, mangled and tore off whole pieces of his living flesh. Alas! he looked at them in the most touching manner, and lamented that they should thus cause their own eternal loss. He had given his own divine Self to us for our Food in the Holy Sacrament, in order to unite in one body—that of the Church, his Spouse—men who were to an infinite extent divided and separated from each other; and now he beheld himself torn and rent in twain in that very body; for his principal work of love, the Holy Communion, in which men should have been made wholly one, was become, by the malice of false teachers, the subject of separation. I beheld whole nations thus snatched out of his bosom, and deprived of any participation in the treasure of graces left to the Church. Finally, I saw all who were separated from the Church plunged into the depths of infidelity, superstition, heresy, and false worldly philosophy; and they gave vent to their fierce rage by joining together in large bodies to attack the Church, being urged on by the serpent which was disporting itself in the midst of them. Alas! it was as though Jesus himself had been torn in a thousand pieces!

So great was my horror and terror, that my Heavenly Spouse appeared to me, and mercifully placed his hand upon my heart, saying: 'No one has yet seen all these things, and thy heart would burst with sorrow if I did not give thee strength.'

I saw the blood flowing in large drops down the pale face of our Saviour, his hair matted together, and his beard bloody and entangled. After the vision which I have last described, he fled, so to speak, out of the cave, and returned to his disciples. But he tottered as he walked; his appearance was that of a man covered with wounds and bending beneath a heavy burden, and he stumbled at every step.

When he came up to the three Apostles, they were not lying down asleep as they had been the first time, but their heads were covered, and they had sunk down on their knees, in an attitude often assumed by the people of that country when in sorrow or desiring to pray. They had fallen asleep, overpowered by grief and fatigue. Jesus, trembling and groaning, drew nigh to them, and they awoke.

But when, by the light of the moon, they saw him standing before them, his face pale and bloody, and his hair in disorder, their weary eyes did not at the first moment recognise him, for he was indescribably changed. He clasped his hands together, upon which they arose and lovingly supported him in their arms, and he told them in sorrowful accents that the next day he should be put to death,—that in one hour's time he should be seized, led before a tribunal, maltreated, outraged, scourged, and finally put to a most cruel death. He besought them to console his Mother, and also Magdalen. They made no reply, for they knew not what to say, so greatly had his appearance and language alarmed them, and they even thought his mind must be wandering. When he desired to return to the grotto, he had not strength to walk. I saw John and

James lead him back, and return when he had entered the grotto. It was then about a quarter-past eleven.

During this agony of Jesus, I saw the Blessed Virgin also overwhelmed with sorrow and anguish of soul, in the house of Mary, the mother of Mark. She was with Magdalen and Mary in the garden belonging to the house, and almost prostrate from grief, with her whole body bowed down as she knelt. She fainted several times, for she beheld in spirit different portions of the agony of Jesus. She had sent some messengers to make inquiries concerning him, but her deep anxiety would not suffer her to await their return, and she went with Magdalen and Salome as far as the Valley of Josaphat. She walked along with her head veiled, and her arms frequently stretched forth towards Mount Olivet; for she beheld in spirit Jesus bathed in a bloody sweat, and her gestures were as though she wished with her extended hands to wipe the face of her Son. I saw these interior movements of her soul towards Jesus, who thought of her, and turned his eyes in her direction, as if to seek her assistance. I beheld the spiritual communication which they had with each other, under the form of rays passing to and fro between them. Our Divine Lord thought also of Magdalen, was touched by her distress, and therefore recommended his Apostles to console her; for he knew that her love for his adorable Person was greater than that felt for him by any one save his Blessed Mother, and he foresaw that she would suffer much for his sake, and never offend him more.

About this time, the eight Apostles returned to the arbour of Gethsemani, and after talking together for some time, ended by going to sleep. They were wavering, discouraged, and sorely tempted. They had each been seeking for a place of refuge in case of danger, and they anxiously asked one another, 'What shall we do when they have put him to death? We have left all to follow him; we are poor and the offscouring of the world, we gave ourselves up entirely to his service, and now he is so sorrowful and so defected himself, that he can afford us no consolation.' The other disciples had at first wandered about in various directions, but then, having heard something concerning the awful prophecies which Jesus had made, they had nearly all retired to Bethphage.

I saw Jesus still praying in the grotto, struggling against the repugnance to suffering which belonged to human nature, and abandoning himself wholly to the will of this Eternal Father. Here the abyss opened before him, and he had a vision of the first part of Limbo. He saw Adam and Eve, the patriarchs, prophets, and just men, the parents of his Mother, and John the Baptist, awaiting his arrival in the lower world with such intense longing, that the sight strengthened and gave fresh courage to his loving heart. His death was to open Heaven to these captives,—his death was to deliver them out of that prison in which they were languishing in eager hope! When Jesus had, with deep emotion, looked upon these saints of antiquity, angels presented to him all the bands of saints of future ages, who, joining their labours to the merits of his Passion, were, through him, to be united to his Heavenly Father. Most beautiful and consoling was this vision, in which he beheld the salvation and sanctification flowing forth in ceaseless streams from the fountain of redemption opened by his death.

The Dolorous Passion of Our Lord Jesus Christ

The Apostles, disciples, virgins, and holy women, the martyrs, confessors, hermits, popes, and bishops, and large bands of religious of both sexes—in one word, the entire army of the blessed—appeared before him. All bore on their heads triumphal crowns, and the flowers of their crowns differed in form, in colour, in odour, and in perfection, according to the difference of the sufferings, labours and victories which had procured them eternal glory. Their whole life, and all their actions, merits, and power, as well as all the glory of their triumph, came solely from their union with the merits of Jesus Christ.

The reciprocal influence exercised by these saints upon each other, and the manner in which they all drank from one sole Fountain—the Adorable Sacrament and the Passion of our Lord—formed a most touching and wonderful spectacle. Nothing about them was devoid of deep meaning,—their works, martyrdom, victories, appearance, and dress,—all, though indescribably varied, was confused together in infinite harmony and unity; and this unity in diversity was produced by the rays of one single Sun, by the Passion of the Lord, of the Word made flesh, in whom was life, the light of men, which shined in darkness, and the darkness did not comprehend it.

The army of the future saints passed before the soul of our Lord, which was thus placed between the desiring patriarchs, and the triumphant band of the future blessed, and these two armies joining together, and completing one another, so to speak, surrounded the loving Heart of our Saviour as with a crown of victory. This most affecting and consoling spectacle bestowed a degree of strength and comfort upon the soul of Jesus. Ah! He so loved his brethren and creatures that, to accomplish the redemption of one single soul, he would have accepted with joy all the sufferings to which he was now devoting himself. As these visions referred to the future, they were diffused to a certain height in the air.

But these consoling visions faded away, and the angels displayed before him the scenes of his Passion quite close to the earth, because it was near at hand. I beheld every scene distinctly portrayed, from the kiss of Judas to the last words of Jesus on the cross, and I saw in this single vision all that I see in my meditations on the Passion. The treason of Judas, the flight of the disciples, the insults which were offered our Lord before Annas and Caiphas, Peter's denial, the tribunal of Pilate, Herod's mockery, the scourging and crowning with thorns, the condemnation to death, the carrying of the cross, the linen cloth presented by Veronica, the crucifixion, the insults of the Pharisees, the sorrows of Mary, of Magdalen, and of John, the wound of the lance in his side, after death;—in one word, every part of the Passion was shown to him in the minutest detail. He accepted all voluntarily, submitting to everything for the love of man. He saw also and felt the sufferings endured at that moment by his Mother, whose interior union with his agony was so entire that she had fainted in the arms of her two friends.

When the visions of the Passion were concluded, Jesus fell on his face like one at the point of death; the angels disappeared, and the bloody sweat became more copious, so that I saw it had soaked his garment. Entire darkness reigned in the cavern, when I beheld an angel descent to Jesus. This angel was of higher stature than any whom I had before beheld, and his form was also more distinct and more resembling that of a man. He was clothed like a priest in a long floating garment, and bore before him, in his hands, a small vase, in shape resembling the chalice used at the Last Supper. At the top of this chalice, there was a small oval body, about the size of a bean, and which diffused a reddish light. The angel, without touching the earth with his feet, stretched forth his right hand to Jesus, who arose, when he placed the mysterious food in his mouth, and gave him to drink from the luminous chalice. Then he disappeared.

Jesus having freely accepted the chalice of his sufferings, and received new strength, remained some minutes longer in the grotto, absorbed in calm meditation, and returning thanks to his Heavenly Father. He was still in deep affliction of spirit, but supernaturally comforted to such a degree as to be able to go to his disciples without tottering as he walked, or bending beneath the weight of his sufferings. His countenance was still pale and altered, but his step was firm and determined. He had wiped his face with a linen cloth, and rearranged his hair, which hung about his shoulders, matted together and damp with blood.

When Jesus came to his disciples, they were lying, as before, against the wall of the terrace, asleep, and with their heads covered. Our Lord told them that then was not the time for sleep, but that they should arise and pray: 'Behold the hour is at hand, and the Son of Man shall be betrayed into the hand of sinners,' he said: 'Arise, let us go, behold he is at hand that will betray me. It were better for him, if that man had not been born.' The Apostles arose in much alarm, and looked round with anxiety. When they had somewhat recovered themselves, Peter said warmly: 'Lord, I will call the others, that so we may defend thee.' But Jesus pointed out to them at some distance in the valley, on the other side of the Brook of Cedron, a band of armed men, who were advancing with torches, and he said that one of their number had betrayed him. He spoke calmly, exhorted them to console his Mother, and said: 'Let us go to meet them—I shall deliver myself up without resistance into the hands of my enemies.' He then left the Garden of Olives with the three Apostles, and went to meet the archers on the road which led from that garden to Gethsemani.

When the Blessed Virgin, under the care of Magdalen and Salome, recovered her senses, some disciples, who had seen the soldiers approaching, conducted her back to the house of Mary, the mother of Mark. The archers took a shorter road than that which Jesus followed when he left the supper-room.

The grotto in which Jesus had this day prayed was not the one where he usually prayed on Mount Olivet. He commonly went to a cabin at a greater distance off, where, one day, after having cursed the barren fig-tree, he had prayed in great affliction of spirit, with his arms stretched out, and leaning against a rock.

The traces of his body and hands remained impressed on the stone, and were honoured later. But it was not known on what occasion the miracle had taken place. I have several times seen similar impressions left upon the stone, either by the Prophets of the Old Testament, or by Jesus, Mary, or some of the Apostles, and I have also seen those made by the body of St. Catherine on Mount Sinai. These impressions do not seem deep, but resemble what would be made upon a thick piece of dough, if a person leaned his hand upon it.

CHAPTER II.

Judas and his band.

Judas had not expected that his treason would have produced such fatal results. He had been anxious to obtain the promised reward, and to please the Pharisees by delivering up Jesus into their hands, but he had never calculated on things going so far, or thought that the enemies of his Master would actually bring him to judgment and crucify him; his mind was engrossed with the love of gain alone, and some astute Pharisees and Sadducees, with whom he had established an intercourse, had constantly urged him on to treason by flattering him. He was sick of the fatiguing, wandering, and persecuted life which the Apostles led. For several months past he had continually stolen from the alms which were consigned to his care, and his avarice, grudging the expenses incurred by Magdalen when she poured the precious ointment on the feet of our Lord, incited him to the commission of the greatest of crimes. He had always hoped that Jesus would establish a temporal kingdom, and bestow upon him some brilliant and lucrative post in it, but finding himself disappointed, he turned his thoughts to amassing a fortune. He saw that sufferings and persecutions were on the increase for our Lord and his followers, and he sought to make friends with the powerful enemies of our Saviour before the time of danger, for the saw that Jesus did not become a king, whereas the actual dignity and power of the High Priest, and of all who were attached to his service, made a very strong impression upon his mind.

He began to enter by degrees into a close connection with their agents, who were constantly flattering him, and assuring him in strong terms that, in any case, an end would speedily be put to the career of our Divine Lord. He listened more and more eagerly to the criminal suggestions of his corrupt heart, and he had done nothing during the last few days but go backwards and forwards in order to induce the chief priests to come to some agreement. But they were unwilling to act at once, and treated him with contempt. They said that sufficient time would not intervene before the festival day, and that there would be a tumult among the people. The Sanhedrin alone listened to his proposals with some degree of attention. After Judas had sacrilegiously received the Blessed Sacrament, Satan took entire possession of him, and he went off at once to complete his crime. He in the first place sought those persons who had hitherto flattered and entered into agreements with him, and who still received him with pretended friendship. Some others joined the party, and among the number Annas and Caiphas, but the latter treated him with considerable pride and scorn. All these enemies of Christ were extremely undecided and far from feeling any confidence of success, because they mistrusted Judas.

I saw the empire of Hell divided against itself; Satan desired the crime of the Jews, and earnestly longed for the death of Jesus, the Converter of souls, the holy Teacher, the Just Man, who was so abhorrent to him; but at the same time he felt an extraordinary interior fear of the death of the innocent Victim, who would not conceal himself from his persecutors. I saw him then, on the one hand, stimulate the hatred and fury of the enemies of Jesus, and on the other, insinuate to some of their number that Judas was a wicked; despicable character, and that the sentence could not be pronounced before the festival, or a sufficient number of witnesses against Jesus be gathered together.

Everyone proposed something different, and some questioned Judas, saying: 'Shall we be able to take him? Has he not armed men with him?' And the traitor replied: 'No, he is alone with eleven disciples; he is greatly depressed, and the eleven are timid men.' He told them that now or never was the time to get possession of the person of Jesus, that later he might no longer have it in his power to give our Lord up into their hands, and that perhaps he should never return to him again, because for several days past it had been very clear that the other disciples and Jesus himself suspected and would certainly kill him if he returned to them. He told them likewise that if they did not at once seize the person of Jesus, he would make his escape, and return with an army of his partisans, to have himself proclaimed King. These threats of Judas produced some effect, his proposals were acceded to, and he received the price of this treason—thirty pieces of silver. These pieces were oblong, with holes in their sides, strung together by means of rings in a kind of chain, and bearing certain impressions.

Judas could not help being conscious that they regarded him with contempt and distrust, for their language and gestures betrayed their feelings, and pride suggested to him to give back the money as an offering for the Temple, in order to make them suppose his intentions to have been just and disinterested. But they rejected his proposal, because the price of blood could not be offered in the Temple. Judas saw how much they despised him, and his rage was excessive. He had not expected to reap the bitter fruits of his treason even before it was accomplished, but he had gone so far with these men that he was in their power, and escape was no longer possible. They watched him carefully, and would not let him leave their presence, until he had shown them exactly what steps were to be taken in order to secure the person of Jesus. Three Pharisees accompanied him when he went down into a room where the soldiers of the Temple (some only of whom were Jews, and the rest of various nations) were assembled. When everything was settled, and the necessary number of soldiers gathered together, Judas hastened first to the supper-room, accompanied by a servant of the Pharisees, for the purpose of ascertaining whether Jesus had left, as they would have seized his person there without difficulty, if once they had secured the doors. He agreed to send them a messenger with the required information.

A short time before when Judas had received the price of this treason, a Pharisee had gone out, and sent seven slaves to fetch wood with which to prepare the Cross for our Saviour, in case he should be judged, because the next day there would not be sufficient time on account of the commencement of the Paschal festivity. They procured this wood from a spot about three-quarters of a mile distant, near a high wall, where there was a great quantity of other wood belonging to the Temple, and dragged it to a square situated behind the tribunal of Caiphas. The principal piece of the Cross came from a tree formerly growing in the Valley of Josaphat, near the torrent of Cedron, and which, having fallen across the stream, had been used as a sort of bridge. When Nehemias hid the sacred fire and the holy vessels in the pool of Bethsaida, it had been thrown over the spot, together with other pieces of wood,—then later taken away, and left on one side. The Cross was prepared in a very peculiar manner, either with the object of deriding the royalty of Jesus, or from what men might term chance. It was composed of five pieces of wood, exclusive of the inscription. I saw many other things concerning the Cross, and the meaning of different circumstances was also made known to me, but I have forgotten all that. Judas returned, and said that Jesus was no longer in the supper-room, but that he must certainly be on Mount Olivet, in the spot where he was accustomed to pray. He requested that only a small number of men might be sent with him, lest the disciples who were on the watch should perceive anything and raise a sedition. Three hundred men were to be stationed at the gates and in the streets of Ophel, a part of the town situated to the south of the Temple, and along the valley of Millo as far as the house of Annas, on the top of Mount Sion, in order to be ready to send reinforcements if necessary, for, he said, all the people of the lower class of Ophel were partisans of Jesus. The traitor likewise bade them be careful, lest he should escape them—since he, by mysterious means, had so often hidden himself in the mountain, and made himself suddenly invisible to those around. He recommended them, besides, to fasten him with a chain, and make use of certain magical forms to prevent his breaking it. The Jews listened to all these pieces of advice with scornful indifference, and replied, 'If we once have him in our hands, we will take care not to let him go.'

Judas next began to make his arrangements with those who were to accompany him. He wished to enter the garden before them, and embrace and salute Jesus as if he were returning to him as his friend and disciple, and then for the soldiers to run forward and seize the person of Jesus. He was anxious that it should be thought they had come there by chance, that so, when they had made their appearance, he might run away like the other disciples and be no more heard of. He likewise thought that, perhaps, a tumult would ensue, that the Apostles might defend themselves, and Jesus pass through the midst of his enemies, as he had so often done before. He dwelt upon these thoughts especially, when his pride was hurt by the disdainful manner of the Jews in his regard; but he did not repent, for he had wholly given himself up to Satan. It was his desire also that the soldiers following him should not carry chains and cords, and his accomplices pretended to accede to all his wishes, although in reality they acted with him as with a traitor who was not to be trusted, but to be cast off as soon as he had done what was wanted. The soldiers received orders to keep close to Judas, watch him carefully, and not let him escape until Jesus was seized, for he had received his reward, and it was feared that he might run off with the money, and Jesus not be taken after all, or another be taken in his place. The band of men chosen to accompany Judas was composed of twenty soldiers, selected from the Temple guard and from others of the military who were under the orders of Annas and Caiphas. They were dressed very much like the Roman soldiers, had morions (crested metal helmets) like them, and wore hanging straps round their thighs, but their beards were long, whereas the Roman soldiers at Jerusalem had whiskers only, and shaved their chins and upper lips. They all had swords, some of them being also armed with spears, and they carried sticks with lanterns and torches; but when they set off they only lighted one. It had at first been intended that Judas should be accompanied by a more numerous escort, but he drew their attention to the fact that so large a number of men would be too easily seen, because Mount Olivet commanded a view of the whole valley. Most of the soldiers remained, therefore, at Ophel, and sentinels were stationed on all sides to put down any attempt which might be made to release Jesus. Judas set off with the twenty soldiers, but he was followed at some distance by four archers, who were only common bailiffs, carrying cords and chains, and after them came the six agents with whom Judas had been in communication for some time. One of these was a priest and a confidant of Annas, a second was devoted to Caiphas, the third and fourth were Pharisees, and the other two Sadducees and Herodians. These six men were courtiers of Annas and Caiphas, acting in the capacity of spies, and most bitter enemies of Jesus.

The soldiers remained on friendly terms with Judas until they reached the spot where the road divides the Garden of Olives from the Garden of Gethsemani, but there they refused to allow him to advance alone, and entirely changed their manner, treating him with much insolence and harshness.

CHAPTER III.

Jesus is arrested.

Jesus was standing with his three Apostles on the road between Gethsemani, and the Garden of Olives, when Judas and the band who accompanied him made their appearance. A warm dispute arose between Judas and the soldiers, because he wished to approach first and speak to Jesus quietly as if nothing was the matter, and then for them to come up and seize our Saviour, thus letting him suppose that he had no connection with the affair. But the men answered rudely, 'Not so, friend, thou shalt not escape from our hands until we have the Galilean safely bound,' and seeing the eight Apostles who hastened to rejoin Jesus when they heard the dispute which was going on, they (notwithstanding the opposition of Judas) called up four archers, whom they had left at a little distance, to assist. When by the light of the moon Jesus and the three Apostles first saw the band of armed men, Peter wished to repel them by force of arms, and said: 'Lord, the other eight are close at hand, let us attack the archers,' but Jesus bade him hold his peace, and then turned and walked back a few steps. At this moment four disciples came out of the garden, and asked what was taking place. Judas was about to reply, but the soldiers interrupted, and would not let him speak. These four disciples were James the Less, Philip, Thomas, and Nathaniel; the last named, who was a son of the aged Simeon, had with a few others joined the eight Apostles at Gethsemani, being perhaps sent by the friends of Jesus to know what was going on, or possibly simply incited by curiosity and anxiety. The other disciples were wandering to and fro, on the look out, and ready to fly at a moment's notice.

Jesus walked up to the soldiers and said in a firm and clear voice, 'Whom seek ye?' The soldiers answered, 'Jesus of Nazareth.' Jesus said to them, 'I am he.' Scarcely had he pronounced these words than they all fell to the ground, as if struck with apoplexy. Judas, who stood by them, was much alarmed, and as he appeared desirous of approaching, Jesus held out his hand and said: 'Friend, whereto art thou come?' Judas stammered forth something about business which had brought him. Jesus answered in few words, the sense of which was: 'It were better for thee that thou hadst never been born;' however, I cannot remember the words exactly. In the mean time, the soldiers had risen, and again approached Jesus, but they waited for the sign of the kiss, with which Judas had promised to salute his Master that they might recognise him. Peter and the other disciples surrounded Judas, and reviled him in unmeasured terms, calling him thief and traitor; he tried to mollify their wrath by all kinds of lies, but his efforts were vain, for the soldiers came up and offered to defend him, which proceeding manifested the truth at once.

Jesus again asked, 'Whom seek ye?' They replied: 'Jesus of Nazareth.' Jesus made answer, 'I have told you that I am he,' 'if therefore you seek me, let these go their way.' At these words the soldiers fell for the second time to the ground, in convulsions similar to those of epilepsy, and the Apostles again surrounded Judas and expressed their indignation at his shameful treachery. Jesus said to the soldiers, 'Arise,' and they arose, but at first quite speechless from terror. They then told Judas to give them the signal agreed upon instantly, as their orders were to seize upon no one but him whom Judas kissed. Judas therefore approached Jesus, and gave him a kiss, saying, 'Hail Rabbi.' Jesus replied, 'What, Judas, dost thou betray the Son of Man with a kiss?' The soldiers immediately surrounded Jesus, and the archers laid hands upon him. Judas wished to fly, but the Apostles would not allow it, they rushed at the soldiers and cried out, 'Master, shall we strike with the sword?' Peter, who was more impetuous than the rest, seized the sword, and struck Malchus, the servant of the high priest, who wished to drive away the Apostles, and cut off his right ear; Malchus fell to the ground, and a great tumult ensued.

The archers had seized upon Jesus, and wished to bind him; while Malchus and the rest of the soldiers stood around. When Peter struck the former, the rest were occupied in repulsing those among the disciples who approached too near, and in pursuing those who ran away. Four disciples made their appearance in the distance, and looked fearfully at the scene before them; but the soldiers were still too much alarmed at their late fall to trouble themselves much about them, and besides they did not wish to leave our Saviour without a certain number of men to guard him. Judas fled as soon as he had given the traitorous kiss, but was met by some of the disciples, who overwhelmed him with reproaches. Six Pharisees, however, came to his rescue, and he escaped whilst the archers were busily occupied in pinioning Jesus.

When Peter struck Malchus, Jesus said to him, 'Put up again thy sword into its place; for all that take the sword shall perish with the sword. Thinkest thou that I cannot ask my Father, and he will give me presently more than twelve legions of angels? How then shall the Scriptures be fulfilled, that so it must be done?' Then he said, 'Let me cure this man;' and approaching Malchus, he touched his ear, prayed, and it wad healed. The soldiers who were standing near, as well as the archers and the six Pharisees, far from being moved by this miracle, continued to insult our Lord, and said to the bystanders, 'It is a trick of the devil, the powers of witchcraft made the ear appear to be cut off, and now the same power gives it the appearance of being healed.'

Then Jesus again addressed them, 'You are come out as it were to a robber, with swords and clubs, to apprehend me. I sat daily with you teaching in the Temple, and you laid not hands upon me, but this is your hour and the power of darkness.' The Pharisees ordered him to be bound still more strongly, and made answer in a contemptuous tone, 'Ah! Thou couldst not overthrow us by thy witchcraft.' Jesus replied, but I do not remember his words, and all the disciples fled. The four archers and the six Pharisees did not fall to the ground at the words of Jesus, because, as was afterwards revealed to me, they as well as Judas, who likewise did not fall, were entirely in the power of Satan, whereas all those who fell and rose again were afterwards converted, and became Christians; they had only surrounded Jesus, and not laid hands upon him. Malchus was instantly converted by the cure wrought upon him, and during the time of the Passion his employment was to carry messages backwards and forwards to Mary and the other friends of our Lord.

The archers, who now proceeded to pinion Jesus with the greatest brutality, were pagans of the lowest extraction, short, stout, and active, with sandy complexions, resembling those of Egyptian slaves, and bare legs, arms, and neck.

They tied his hands as tightly as possible with hard new cords, fastening the right-hand wrist under the left elbow, and the left-hand wrist under the right elbow. They encircled his waist with a species of belt studded with iron points, and to this collar were appended two leathern straps, which were crossed over his chest like a stole and fastened to the belt. They then fastened four ropes to different parts of the belt, and by means of these ropes dragged our Blessed Lord from side to side in the most cruel manner. The ropes were new; I think they were purchased when the Pharisees first determined to arrest Jesus. The Pharisees lighted fresh torches, and the procession started. Ten soldiers walked in front, the archers who held the ropes and dragged Jesus along, followed, and the Pharisees and ten other soldiers brought up the rear. The disciples wandered about at a distance, and wept and moaned as if beside themselves from grief. John alone followed, and walked at no great distance from the soldiers, until the Pharisees, seeing him, ordered the guards to arrest him. They endeavoured to obey, but he ran away, leaving in their hands a cloth with which he was covered, and of which they had taken hold when they endeavoured to seize him. He had slipped off his coat, that he might escape more easily from the hands of his enemies, and kept nothing on but a short under garment without sleeves, and the long band which the Jews usually wore, and which was wrapped round his neck, head, and arms. The archers behaved in the most cruel manner to Jesus as they led him along; this they did to curry favour with the six Pharisees, who they well knew perfectly hated and detested our Lord. They led him along the roughest road they could select, over the sharpest stones, and through the thickest mire; they pulled the cords as tightly as possible; they struck him with knotted cords, as a butcher would strike the beast he is about to slaughter; and they accompanied this cruel treatment with such ignoble and indecent insults that I cannot recount them. The feet of Jesus were bare; he wore, besides the ordinary dress, a seamless woollen garment, and a cloak which was thrown over all. I have forgotten to state that when Jesus was arrested, it was done without any order being presented or legal ceremony taking place; he was treated as a person without the pale of the law.

The procession proceeded at a good pace; when they left the road which runs between the Garden of Olives and that of Gethsemani, they turned to the right, and soon reached a bridge which was thrown over the Torrent of Cedron. When Jesus went to the Garden of Olives with the Apostles, he did not cross this bridge, but went by a private path which ran through the Valley of Josaphat, and led to another bridge more to the south. The bridge over which the soldiers led Jesus was long, being thrown over not only the torrent, which was very large in this part, but likewise over the valley, which extends a considerable distance to the right and to the left, and is much lower than the bed of the river. I saw our Lord fall twice before he reached the bridge, and these falls were caused entirely by the barbarous manner in which the soldiers dragged him; but when they were half over the bridge they gave full vent to their brutal inclination, and struck Jesus with such violence that they threw him off the bridge into the water, and scornfully recommended him to quench his thirst there. If God had not preserved him, he must have been killed by this fall; he fell first on his knee, and then on his face, but saved himself a little by stretching out his hands, which, although so tightly bound before, were loosened, I know not whether by miracle, or whether the soldiers had cut the cords before they threw him into the water. The marks of his feet, his elbows, and his fingers were miraculously impressed on the rock on which he fell, and these impressions were afterwards shown for the veneration of Christians. These stones were less hard than the unbelieving hearts of the wicked men who surrounded Jesus, and bore witness at this terrible moment to the Divine Power which had touched them.

I had not seen Jesus take anything to quench the thirst which had consumed him ever since his agony in the garden, but he drank when he fell into the Cedron, and I heard him repeat these words from the prophetic Psalm, 'In his thirst he will drink water from the torrent' (Psalm 108).

The archers still held the ends of the ropes with which Jesus was bound, but it would have been difficult to drag him out of the water on that side, on account of a wall which was built on the shore; they turned back and dragged him quite through the Cedron to the shore, and then made him cross the bridge a second time, accompanying their every action with insults, blasphemies, and blows. His long woollen garment, which was quite soaked through, adhered to his legs, impeded every movement, and rendered it almost impossible for him to walk, and when he reached the end of the bridge he fell quite down. They pulled him up again in the most cruel manner, struck him with cords, and fastened the ends of his wet garment to the belt, abusing him at the same time in the most cowardly manner. It was not quite midnight when I saw the four archers inhumanly dragging Jesus over a narrow path, which was choked up with stones, garments of rock, thistles, and thorns, on the opposite shore of the Cedron. The six brutal Pharisees walked as close to our Lord as they could, struck him constantly with thick pointed sticks, and seeing that his bare and bleeding feet were torn by the stones and briars, exclaimed scornfully: 'His precursor, John the Baptist, has certainly not prepared a good path for him here;' or, 'The words of Malachy, "Behold, I send my angel before thy face, to prepare the way before thee," do not exactly apply now.' Every jest uttered by these men incited the archers to greater cruelty.

The enemies of Jesus remarked that several persons made their appearance in the distance; they were only disciples who had assembled when they heard that their Master was arrested, and who were anxious to discover what the end would be; but the sight of them rendered the Pharisees uneasy, lest any attempt should be made to rescue Jesus, and they therefore sent for a reinforcement of soldiers. At a very short distance from an entrance opposite to the south side of the Temple, which leads through a little village called Ophel to Mount Sion, where the residences of Annas and Caiphas were situated, I saw a band of about fifty soldiers, who carried torches, and appeared ready for anything; the demeanour of these men was outrageous, and they gave loud shouts, both to announce their arrival, and to congratulate their comrades upon the success of the expedition. This caused a slight confusion among the soldiers who were leading Jesus, and Malchus and a few others took advantage of it to depart, and fly towards Mount Olivet.

When the fresh band of soldiers left Ophel, I saw those disciples who had gathered together disperse; some went one way, and some another. The Blessed Virgin and about nine of the holy women, being filled with anxiety, directed their steps towards the Valley of Josaphat, accompanied by Lazarus, John the son of Mark, the son of Veronica, and the son of Simon. The last-named was at Gethsemani with Nathaniel and the eight Apostles, and had fled when the soldiers appeared. He was giving the Blessed Virgin the account of all that had been done, when the fresh band of soldiers joined those who were leading Jesus, and she then heard their tumultuous vociferations, and saw the light of the torches they carried. This sight quite overcame her; she became insensible, and John took her into the house of Mary, the mother of Mark.

The fifty soldiers who were sent to join those who had taken Jesus, were a detachment from a company of three hundred men posted to guard the gates and environs of Ophel; for the traitor Judas had reminded the High Priests that the inhabitants of Ophel (who were principally of the labouring class, and whose chief employment was to bring water and wood to the Temple) were the most attached partisans of Jesus, and might perhaps make some attempts to rescue him. The traitor was aware that Jesus had both consoled, instructed, assisted, and cured the diseases of many of these poor workmen, and that Ophel was the place where he halted during his journey from Bethania to Hebron, when John the Baptist had just been executed. Judas also knew that Jesus had cured many of the masons who were injured by the fall of the Tower of Siloe. The greatest part of the inhabitants of Ophel were converted after the death of our Lord, and joined the first Christian community that was formed after Pentecost, and when the Christians separated from the Jews and erected new dwellings, they placed their huts and tents in the valley which is situated between Mount Olivet and Ophel, and there St. Stephen lived. Ophel was on a hill to the south of the Temple, surrounded by walls, and its inhabitants were very poor. I think it was smaller than Dulmen.[2]

The slumbers of the good inhabitants of Ophel were disturbed by the noise of the soldiers; they came out of their houses and ran to the entrance of the village to ask the cause of the uproar; but the soldiers received them roughly, ordered them to return home, and in reply to their numerous questions, said, 'We have just arrested Jesus, your false prophet—he who has deceived you so grossly; the High Priests are about to judge him, and he will be crucified.' Cries and lamentations arose on all sides; the poor women and children ran

---

[2] Dulmen is a small town in Westphalia, where Sister Emmerich lived at this time.

backwards and forwards, weeping and wringing their hands; and calling to mind all the benefits they had received from our Lord, they cast themselves on their knees to implore the protection of Heaven. But the soldiers pushed them on one side, struck them, obliged them to return to their houses, and exclaimed, 'What farther proof is required? Does not the conduct of these persons show plainly that the Galilean incites rebellion?'

They were, however, a little cautious in their expressions and demeanour for fear of causing an insurrection in Ophel, and therefore only endeavoured to drive the inhabitants away from those parts of the village which Jesus was obliged to cross.

When the cruel soldiers who led our Lord were near the gates of Ophel he again fell, and appeared unable to proceed a step farther, upon which one among them, being moved to compassion, said to another, 'You see the poor man is perfectly exhausted, he cannot support himself with the weight of his chains; if we wish to get him to the High Priest alive we must loosen the cords with which his hands are bound, that he may be able to save himself a little when he falls.' The band stopped for a moment, the fetters were loosened, and another kind-hearted soldier brought some water to Jesus from a neighbouring fountain. Jesus thanked him, and spoke of the 'fountains of living water,' of which those who believed in him should drink; but his words enraged the Pharisees still more, and they overwhelmed him with insults and contumelious language. I saw the heart of the soldier who had caused Jesus to be unbound, as also that of the one who brought him water, suddenly illuminated by grace; they were both converted before the death of Jesus, and immediately joined his disciples.

The procession started again, and reached the gate of Ophel. Here Jesus was again saluted by the cries of grief and sympathy of those who owed him so much gratitude, and the soldiers had considerable difficulty in keeping back the men and women who crowded round from all parts. They clasped their hands, fell on their knees, lamented, and exclaimed, 'Release this man unto us, release him! Who will assist, who will console us, who will cure our diseases? Release him unto us!' It was indeed heart-rending to look upon Jesus; his face was white, disfigured, and wounded, his hair dishevelled, his dress wet and soiled, and his savage and drunken guards were dragging him about and striking him with sticks like a poor dumb animal led to the slaughter. Thus was he conducted through the midst of the afflicted inhabitants of Ophel, and the paralytic whom he had cured, the dumb to whom he had restored speech, and the blind whose eyes he had opened, united, but in vain, in offering supplications for his release.

Many persons from among the lowest and most degraded classes had been sent by Annas, Caiphas, and the other enemies of Jesus, to join the procession, and assist the soldiers both in ill-treating Jesus, and in driving away the inhabitants of Ophel. The village of Ophel was seated upon a hill, and I saw a great deal of timber placed there ready for building. The procession had to proceed down a hill, and then pass through a door made in the wall. On one side of this door stood a large building erected originally by Solomon, and on the other the pool of Bethsaida. After passing this, they followed a westerly direction down a steep street called Millo, at the end of which a turn to the south brought them to the house of Annas. The guards never ceased their cruel treatment of our Divine Saviour, and excused such conduct by saying that the crowds who gathered together in front of the procession compelled them to severity. Jesus fell seven times between Mount Olivet and the house of Annas.

The inhabitants of Ophel were still in a state of consternation and grief, when the sight of the Blessed Virgin who passed through the village accompanied by the holy women and some other friends on her way from the Valley of Cedron to the house of Mary the mother of Mark, excited them still more, and they made the place re-echo with sobs and lamentations, while they surrounded and almost carried her in their arms. Mary was speechless from grief, and did not open her lips after she reached the house of Mary the mother of Mark, until the arrival of John, who related all he had seen since Jesus left the supper-room; and a little later she was taken to the house of Martha, which was near that of Lazarus. Peter and John, who had followed Jesus at a distance, went in haste to some servants of the High Priest with whom the latter was acquainted, in order to endeavour by their means to obtain admittance into the tribunal where their Master was to be tried. These servants acted as messengers, and had just been ordered to go to the houses of the ancients, and other members of the Council, to summon them to attend the meeting which was convoked. As they were anxious to oblige the Apostles, but foresaw much difficulty in obtaining their admittance into the tribunal, they gave them cloaks similar to those they themselves wore, and made them assist in carrying messages to the members in order that afterwards they might enter the tribunal of Caiphas, and mingle, without being recognised, among the soldiers and false witnesses, as all other persons were to be expelled. As Nicodemus, Joseph of Arimathea, and other well-intentioned persons were members of this Council, the Apostles undertook to let them know what was going to be done in the Council, thus securing the presence of those friends of Jesus whom the Pharisees had purposely omitted to invite. In the mean time Judas wandered up and down the steep and wild precipices at the south of Jerusalem, despair marked on his every feature, and the devil pursuing him to and fro, filling his imagination with still darker visions, and not allowing him a moment's respite.

CHAPTER IV.

Means employed by the enemies of Jesus for carrying out their designs against him.

No sooner was Jesus arrested than Annas and Caiphas were informed, and instantly began to arrange their plans with regard to the course to be pursued. Confusion speedily reigned everywhere—the rooms were lighted up in haste, guards placed at the entrances, and messengers dispatched to different parts of the town to convoke the members of the Council, the scribes, and all who were to take a part in the trial. Many among them had, however, assembled at the house of Caiphas as soon as the treacherous compact with Judas was completed, and had remained there to await the course of events. The different classes of ancients were likewise assembled, and as the Pharisees, Sadducees, and Herodians were congregated in Jerusalem from all parts of the country for the celebration of the festival, and had long been concerting measures with the Council for the arrest of our Lord, the High Priests now sent for those whom they knew to be the most bitterly opposed to Jesus, and desired them to assemble the witnesses, gather together every possible proof, and bring all before the Council. The proud Sadducees of Nazareth, of Capharnaum, of Thirza, of Gabara, of Jotapata, and of Silo, whom Jesus had so often reproved before the people, were actually dying for revenge. They hastened to all the inns to seek out those persons whom they knew to be enemies of our Lord, and offered them bribes in order to secure their appearance. But, with the exception of a few ridiculous calumnies, which were certain to be disproved a soon as investigated, nothing tangible could be brought forward against Jesus, excepting, indeed, those foolish accusations which he had so often refuted in the synagogue.

The enemies of Jesus hastened, however, to the tribunal of Caiphas, escorted by the scribes and Pharisees of Jerusalem, and accompanied by many of those merchants whom our Lord drove out of the Temple when they were holding market there; as also by the proud doctors whom he had silenced before all the people, and even by some who could not forgive the humiliation of being convicted of error when he disputed with them in the Temple at the age of twelve. There was likewise a large body of impenitent sinners whom he had refused to cure, relapsed sinners whose diseases had returned, worldly young men whom he would not receive as disciples, avaricious persons whom he had enraged by causing the money which they had been in hopes of possessing to be distributed in alms. Others there were whose friends he had cured, and who had thus been disappointed in their expectations of inheriting property; debauchees whose victims he had converted; and many despicable characters who made their fortunes by flattering and fostering the vices of the great.

All these emissaries of Satan were overflowing with rage against everything holy, and consequently with an indescribable hatred of the Holy of Holies. They were farther incited by the enemies of our Lord, and therefore assembled in crowds round the palace of Caiphas, to bring forward all their false accusations and to endeavour to cover with infamy that spotless Lamb, who took upon himself the sins of the world, and accepted the burden in order to reconcile man with God.

Whilst all these wicked beings were busily consulting as to what was best to be done, anguish and anxiety filled the hearts of the friends of Jesus, for they were ignorant of the mystery which was about to be accomplished, and they wandered about, sighing, and listening to every different opinion. Each word they uttered gave raise to feelings of suspicion on the part of those who they addressed, and if they were silent, their silence was set down as wrong. Many well-meaning but weak and undecided characters yielded to temptation, were scandalised, and lost their fait; indeed, the number of those who persevered was very small indeed. Things were the same then as they oftentimes are now, persons were willing to serve God if they met with no opposition from their fellowcreatures, but were ashamed of the Cross if held in contempt by others. The hearts of some were, however, touched by the patience displayed by our Lord in the midst of his sufferings, and they walked away silent and sad.

CHAPTER V.

A Glance at Jerusalem.

The customary prayers and preparations for the celebration of the festival being completed, the greatest part of the inhabitants of the densely-populated city of Jerusalem, as also the strangers congregated there, were plunged in sleep after the fatigues of the day, when, all at once, the arrest of Jesus was announced, and everyone was aroused, both his friends and foes, and numbers immediately responded to the summons of the High Priest, and left their dwellings to assemble at his court. In some parts the light of the moon enabled them to grope their way in safety along the dark and gloomy streets, but in other parts they were obliged to make use of torches. Very few of the houses were built with their windows looking on the street, and, generally speaking, their doors were in inner courts, which gave the streets a still more gloomy appearance than is usual at this hour. The steps of all were directed towards Sion, and an attentive listener might have heard persons stop at the doors of their friends, and knock, in order to awaken them—then hurry on, then again stop to question others, and, finally, set off anew in haste towards Sion. Newsmongers and servants were hurrying forward to ascertain what was going on; in order that they might return and give the account to those who remained at home; and the bolting and barricading of doors might be plainly heard, as many persons were much alarmed and feared an insurrection, while a thousand different propositions were made and opinions given, such as the following:— 'Lazarus and his sisters will soon know who is this man in whom they have placed such firm reliance. Johanna Chusa, Susannah, Mary the mother of Mark, and Salome will repent, but too late, the imprudence of their conduct; Seraphia, the wife of Sirach, will be compelled to make an apology to her husband now, for he has so often reproached her with her partiality for the Galilean. The partisans of this fanatical man, this inciter of rebellion, pretended to be filled with compassion for all who looked upon things in a different light from themselves, and now they will not know where to hide their heads. He will find no one now to cast garments and strew olive-branches at his feet. Those hypocrites who pretended to be so much better than other persons will receive their deserts, for they are all implicated with the Galilean. It is a much more serious business than was at first thought. I should like to know how Nicodemus and Joseph of Arimathea will get out of it; the High Priests have mistrusted them for some time; they made common cause with Lazarus: but they are extremely cunning. All will now, however, be brought to light.'

Speeches such as these were uttered by persons who were exasperated, not only against the disciples of Jesus, but likewise with the holy women who had supplied his temporal wants, and had publicly and fearlessly expressed their veneration for his doctrines, and their belief in his Divine mission.

But although many persons spoke of Jesus and his followers in this contemptuous manner, yet there were others who held very different opinions, and of these some were frightened, and others, being overcome with sorrow, sought friends to whom they might unburden their hearts, and before whom they could, without fear, give vent to their feelings; but the number of those sufficiently daring openly to avow their admiration for Jesus was but small.

Nevertheless, it was in parts only of Jerusalem that these disturbances took place—in those parts where the messengers had been sent by the High Priests and the Pharisees, to convoke the members of the Council and to call together the witnesses. It appeared to me that I saw feelings of hatred and fury burst forth in different parts of the city, under the form of flames, which flames traversed the streets, united with others which they met, and proceeded in the direction of Sion, increasing every moment, and at last came to a stop beneath the tribunal of Caiphas, where they remained, forming together a perfect whirlwind of fire.

The Roman soldiers took no part in what was going on; they did not understand the excited feelings of the people, but their sentinels were doubled, their cohorts drawn up, and they kept a strict look out; this, indeed, was customary at the time of the Paschal solemnity, on account of the vast number of strangers who were then assembled together. The Pharisees endeavoured to avoid the neighbourhood of the sentinels, for fear of being questioned by them, and of contracting defilement by answering their questions. The High Priests had sent a message to Pilate intimating their reasons for stationing soldiers round Ophel and Sion; but he mistrusted their intentions, as much ill-feeling existed between the Romans and the Jews. He could not sleep, but walked about during the greatest part of the night, hearkening to the different reports and issuing orders consequent on what he heard; his wife slept, but her sleep was disturbed by frightful dreams, and she groaned and wept alternately.

In no part of Jerusalem did the arrest of Jesus produce more touching demonstrations of grief than among the poor inhabitants of Ophel, the greatest part of whom were daylabourers, and the rest principally employed in menial offices in the service of the Temple. The news came unexpectedly upon them; for some time they doubted the truth of the report, and wavered between hope and fear; but the sight of their Master, their Benefactor, their Consoler, dragged through the streets, torn, bruised, and ill-treated in every imaginable way, filled them with horror; and their grief was still farther increased by beholding his afflicted Mother wandering about from street to street, accompanied by the holy women, and endeavouring to obtain some intelligence concerning her Divine Son. These holy women were often obliged to hide in corners and under door-ways for fear of being seen by the enemies of Jesus; but even with these precautions they were oftentimes insulted, and taken for women of bad character—their feelings were frequently harrowed by hearing the malignant words and triumphant expressions of the cruel Jews, and seldom, very seldom, did a word of kindness or pity strike their ears. They were completely exhausted before reaching their place of refuge, but they endeavoured to console and support one another, and wrapped thick veils over their heads. When at last seated, they heard a sudden knock at the door, and listened breathlessly—the knock was repeated, but softly, therefore they made certain that it was no enemy, and yet they opened the door cautiously, fearing a stratagem. It was indeed a friend, and they issued forth and walked about for a time, and then again returned to their place of refuge—still more heartbroken than before.

The majority of the Apostles, overcome with terror, were wandering about among the valleys which surround Jerusalem, and at times took refuge in the caverns beneath Mount Olivet. They started if they came in contact with one another, spoke in trembling tones, and separated on the least noise being heard. First they concealed themselves in one cave and then in another, next they endeavoured to return to the town, while some of their number climbed to the top of Mount Olivet and cast anxious glances at the torches, the light of which they could see glimmering at and about Sion; they listened to every distant sound, made a thousand different conjectures, and then returned to the valley, in hopes of getting some certain intelligence.

The streets in the vicinity of Caiphas's tribunal were brightly illuminated with lamps and torches, but, as the crowds gathered around it, the noise and confusion continued to increase. Mingling with these discordant sounds might be heard the bellowing of the beasts which were tethered on the outside of the walls of Jerusalem, and the plaintive bleating of the lambs. There was something most touching in the bleating of these lambs, which were to be sacrificed on the following day in the Temple,—the one Lamb alone who was about to be offered a willing sacrifice opened not his mouth, like a sheep in the hands of the butcher, which resists not, or the lamb which is silent before the shearer; and that Lamb was the Lamb of God—the Lamb without spot—the true Paschal Lamb—Jesus Christ himself.

The sky looked dark, gloomy, and threatening—the moon was red, and covered with livid spots; it appeared as if dreading to reach its full, because its Creator was then to die.

Next I cast a glance outside the town, and, near the south gate, I beheld the traitor, Judas Iscariot, wandering about, alone, and a prey to the tortures of his guilty conscience; he feared even his own shadow, and was followed by many devils, who endeavoured to turn his feelings of remorse into black despair. Thousands of evil spirits were busying themselves in all parts, tempting men first to one sin and then to another. It appeared as if the gates of hell were flung open, and Satan madly striving and exerting his whole energies to increase the heavy load of iniquities which the Lamb without spot had taken upon himself. The angels wavered between joy and grief; they desired ardently to fall prostrate before the throne of God, and to obtain permission to assist Jesus; but at the same time they were filled with astonishment, and could only adore that miracle of Divine justice and mercy which had existed in Heaven for all eternity, and was now about to be accomplished; for the angels believe, like us, in God, the Father Almighty, Creator of Heaven and Earth, and in Jesus Christ, his only Son, our Lord, who was conceived by the Holy Ghost, born of the Virgin Mary, who began on this night to suffer under Pontius Pilate, and the next day was to be crucified; to die, and be buried; descend into hell, rise again on the third day, ascent into Heaven, be seated at the right hand of God the Father Almighty, and from thence come to judge the living and the dead; they likewise believe in the Holy Ghost, the Holy Catholic Church, the communion of Saints, the forgiveness of sins, the resurrection of the body, and life everlasting.

CHAPTER VI.

Jesus before Annas.

It was towards midnight when Jesus reached the palace of Annas, and his guards immediately conducted him into a very large hall, where Annas, surrounded by twentyeight councillors, was seated on a species of platform, raised a little above the level of the floor, and placed opposite to the entrance. The soldiers who first arrested Jesus now dragged him roughly to the foot of the tribunal. The room was quite full, between soldiers, the servants of Annas, a number of the mob who had been admitted, and the false witnesses who afterwards adjourned to Caiphas's hall.

Annas was delighted at the thought of our Lord being brought before him, and was looking out for his arrival with the greatest impatience. The expression of his countenance was most repulsive, as it showed in every lineament not only the infernal joy with which he was filled, but likewise all the cunning and duplicity of this heart. He was the president of a species of tribunal instituted for the purpose of examining persons accused of teaching false doctrines; and if convicted there, they were then taken before the High Priest.

Jesus stood before Annas. He looked exhausted and haggard; his garments were covered with mud, his hands manacled, his head bowed down, and he spoke not a word. Annas was a thin ill-humoured-looking old man, with a scraggy beard. His pride and arrogance were great; and as he seated himself he smiled ironically, pretending that he knew nothing at all, and that he was perfectly astonished at finding that the prisoner, whom he had just been informed was to be brought before him, was no other than Jesus of Nazareth. 'Is it possible,' said he, 'is it possible that thou art Jesus of Nazareth? Where are thy disciples, thy numerous followers? Where is thy kingdom? I fear affairs have not turned out as thou didst expect. The authorities, I presume, discovered that it was quite time to put a stop to thy conduct, disrespectful as it was towards God and his priests, and to such violations of the Sabbath. What disciples hast thou now? Where are they all gone? Thou are silent! Speak out, seducer! Speak out, thou inciter of rebellion! Didst thou not eat the Paschal lamb in an unlawful manner, at an improper time, and in an improper place? Dost thou not desire to introduce new doctrines? Who gave thee the right of preaching? Where didst thou study? Speak, what are the tenets of thy religion?'

Jesus then raised his weary head, looked at Annas, and said, 'I have spoken openly to the world; I have always taught in the synagogue, and in the Temple, whither all the Jews resort; and in secret I have spoken nothing. Why askest thou me? Ask them who have heard what I have spoken unto them; behold, they know what thing I have said.'

At this answer of Jesus the countenance of Annas flushed with fury and indignation. A base menial who was standing near perceived this, and he immediately struck our Lord on the face with his iron gauntlet, exclaiming at the same moment, 'Answerest thou the High Priest so?' Jesus was so nearly prostrated by the violence of the blow, that when the guards likewise reviled and struck him, he fell quite down, and blood trickled from his face on to the floor. Laughter, insults, and bitter words resounded through the hall. The archers dragged him roughly up again, and he mildly answered, 'If I have spoken evil, give testimony of the evil; but if well, why strikest thou me?'

Annas became still more enraged when he saw the calm demeanour of Jesus, and, turning to the witnesses, he desired them to bring forward their accusations. They all began to speak at once:—'He has called himself king; he says that God is his Father; that the Pharisees are an adulterous generation. He causes insurrection among the people; he cures the sick by the help of the devil on the Sabbath-day. The inhabitants of Ophel assembled round him a short time ago, and addressed him by the titles of Saviour and Prophet. He lets himself be called the Son of God; he says that he is sent by God; he predicts the destruction of Jerusalem. He does not fast; he eats with sinners, with pagans, and with publicans, and associates with women of evil repute. A short time ago he said to a man who gave him some water to drink at the gates of Ophel, "that he would give unto him the water of eternal life, after drinking which he would thirst no more." He seduces the people by words of double meaning,' etc., etc.

These accusations were all vociferated at once; some of the witnesses stood before Jesus and insulted him while they spoke by derisive gestures, and the archers went so far as even to strike him, saying at the same time, 'Speak; why dost thou not answer?' Annas and his adherents added mockery to insult, exclaiming at every pause in the accusations, 'This is thy doctrine, then, is it? What canst thou answer to this? Issue thy orders, great King; man sent by God, give proofs of thy mission.' 'Who art thou?' continued Annas, in a tone of cutting contempt; 'by whom art thou sent? Art thou the son of an obscure carpenter, or art thou Elias, who was carried up to heaven in a fiery chariot? He is said to be still living, and I have been told that thou canst make thyself invisible when thou pleasest. Perhaps thou art the prophet Malachy, whose words thou dost so frequently quote. Some say that an angel was his father, and that he likewise is still alive. An impostor as thou art could not have a finer opportunity of taking persons in than by passing thyself off as this prophet. Tell me, without farther preamble, to what order of kings thou dost belong? Thou art greater than Solomon,—at least thou pretendest so to be, and dost even expect to be believed. Be easy, I will no longer refuse the title and the sceptre which are so justly thy due.'

Annas then called for the sheet of parchment, about a yard in length, and six inches in width; on this he wrote a series of words in large letters, and each word expressed some different accusation which had been brought against our Lord. He then rolled it up, placed it in a little hollow tube, fastened it carefully on the top of a reed, and presented this reed to Jesus, saying at the same time, with a contemptuous sneer, 'Behold the sceptre of thy kingdom; it contains thy titles, as also the account of the honours to which thou art entitled, and thy right to the throne. Take them to the High Priest, in order that he may acknowledge thy regal dignity, and treat thee according to thy deserts. Tie the hands of this king, and take him before the High Priest.'

The hands of Jesus, which had been loosened, were then tied across his breast in such a manner as to make him hold the pretended sceptre, which contained the accusations of Annas, and he was led to the Court of Caiphas, amidst the hisses, shouts, and blows lavished upon him by the brutal mob.

The house of Annas was not more than three hundred steps from that of Caiphas; there were high walls and common-looking houses on each side of the road, which was lighted up by torches and lanterns placed on poles, and there were numbers of Jews standing about talking in an angry excited manner. The soldiers could scarcely make their way through the crowd, and those who had behaved so shamefully to Jesus at the Court of Annas continued their insults and base usage during the whole of the time sent in walking to the house of Caiphas. I saw money given to those who behaved the worst to Jesus by armed men belonging to the tribunal, and I saw them push out of the way all who looked compassionately at him. The former were allowed to enter the Court of Caiphas.

CHAPTER VII.

The Tribunal of Caiphas.

To enter Caiphas's tribunal persons had to pass through a large court, which may be called the exterior court; from thence they entered into an inner court, which extended all round the building. The building itself was of far greater length than breadth, and in the front there was a kind of open vestibule surrounded on three sides by columns of no great height. On the fourth side the columns were higher, and behind them was a room almost as large as the vestibule itself, where the seat of the members of the Council were placed on a species of round platform raised above the level of the floor. That assigned to the High Priest was elevated above the others; the criminal to be tried stood in the centre of the halfcircle formed by the seats. The witnesses and accusers stood either by the side or behind the prisoner. There were three doors at the back of the judges' seats which led into another apartment, filled likewise with seats. This room was used for secret consultation. Entrances placed on the right and left hand sides of this room opened into the interior court, which was round, like the back of the building. Those who left the room by the door on the righthand side saw on the left-hand side of the court the gate which led to a subterranean prison excavated under the room. There were many underground prisons there, and it was in one of these that Peter and John were confined a whole night, when they had cured the lame man in the Temple after Pentecost. Both the house and the courts were filled with torches and lamps, which made them as light as day. There was a large fire lighted in the middle of the porch, on each side of which were hollow pipes to serve as chimneys for the smoke, and round this fire were standing soldiers, menial servants, and witnesses of the lowest class who had received bribes for giving their false testimony. A few women were there likewise, whose employment was to pour out a species of red beverage for the soldiers, and to bake cakes, for which services they received a small compensation. The majority of the judges were already seated around Caiphas, the others came in shortly afterwards, and the porch was almost filled, between true and false witnesses, while many other persons likewise endeavoured to come in to gratify their curiosity, but were prevented. Peter and John entered the outer court, in the dress of travellers, a short time before Jesus was led through, and John succeeded in penetrating into the inner court, by means of a servant with whom he was acquainted. The door was instantly closed after him, therefore Peter, who was a little behind, was shut out. He begged the maid-servant to open the door for him, but she refused both his entreaties and those of John, and he must have remained on the outside had not Nicodemus and Joseph of Arimathea, who came up at this moment, taken him with them. The two Apostles then returned the cloaks which they had borrowed, and stationed themselves in a place from whence they could see the judges, and hear everything that was going on. Caiphas was seated in the centre of the raised platform, and seventy of the members of the Sanhedrin were placed around him, while the public officers, the scribes, and the ancients were standing on either side, and the false witnesses behind them. Soldiers were posted from the base of the platform to the door of the vestibule through which Jesus was to enter. The countenance of Caiphas was solemn in the extreme, but the gravity was accompanied by unmistakable signs of suppressed rage and sinister intentions. He wore a long mantle of a dull red colour, embroidered in flowers and trimmed with golden fringe; it was fastened at the shoulders and on the chest, besides being ornamented in the front with gold clasps. His head-attire was high, and adorned with hanging ribbons, the sides were open, and it rather resembled a bishop's mitre. Caiphas had been waiting with his adherents belonging to the Great Council for some time, and so impatient was he that he arose several times, went into the outer court in his magnificent dress, and asked angrily whether Jesus of Nazareth was come. When he saw the procession drawing near he returned to his seat.

CHAPTER VIII.

Jesus before Caiphas.

Jesus was led across the court, and the mob received him with groans and hisses. As he passed by Peter and John, he looked at them, but without turning his head, for fear of betraying them. Scarcely had he reached the council-chamber, than Caiphas exclaimed in a loud tone, 'Thou art come, then, at last, thou enemy of God, thou blasphemer, who dost disturb the peace of this holy night!' The tube which contained the accusations of Annas, and was fastened to the pretended sceptre in the hands of Jesus, was instantly opened and read.

Caiphas made use of the most insulting language, and the archers again struck and abused our Lord, vociferating at the same time, 'Answer at once! Speak out! Art thou dumb?' Caiphas, whose temper was indescribably proud and arrogant, became even more enraged than Annas had been, and asked a thousand questions one after the other, but Jesus stood before him in silence, and with his eyes cast down. The archers endeavoured to force him to speak by repeated blows, and a malicious child pressed his thumb into his lips, tauntingly bidding him to bite. The witnesses were then called for. The first were persons of the lowest class, whose accusations were as incoherent and inconsistent as those brought forward at the court of Annas, and nothing could be made out of them; Caiphas therefore turned to the principal witnesses, the Pharisees and the Sadducees, who had assembled from all parts of the country. They endeavoured to speak calmly, but their faces and manner betrayed the virulent envy and hatred with which their hearts were overflowing, and they repeated over and over again the same accusations, to which he had already replied so many times: 'That he cured the sick, and cast out devils, by the help of devils—that he profaned the Sabbath—incited the people to rebel—called the Pharisees a race of vipers and adulterers—predicted the destruction of Jerusalem—frequented the society of publicans and sinners—assembled the people and gave himself out as a king, a prophet, and the Son of God.' They deposed 'that he was constantly speaking of his kingdom,—that he forbade divorce,—called himself the Bread of Life, and said that whoever did not eat his flesh and drink his blood would not have eternal life.'

Thus did they distort and misinterpret the words he had uttered, the instructions he had given and the parables by which he had illustrated his instructions, giving them the semblance of crimes. But these witnesses could not agree in their depositions, for one said, 'He calls himself king;' and a second instantly contradicted, saying, 'No, he allows persons to call him so; but directly they attempted to proclaim him, he fled.' Another said, 'He calls himself the Son of God,' but he was interrupted by a fourth, who exclaimed, 'No, he only styles himself the Son of God because he does the will of his Heavenly Father.' Some of the witnesses stated that he had cured them, but that their diseases had returned, and that his pretended cures were only performed by magic. They spoke likewise of the cure of the paralytic man at the pool of Bethsaida, but they distorted the facts so as to give them the semblance of crimes, and even in these accusations they could not agree, contradicting one another. The Pharisees of Sephoris, with whom he had once had a discussion on the subject of divorces, accused him of teaching false doctrines, and a young man of Nazareth, whom he had refused to allow to become one of his disciples, was likewise base enough to bear witness against him.

It was found to be utterly impossible to prove a single fact, and the witnesses appeared to come forward for the sole purpose of insulting Jesus, rather than to demonstrate the truth of their statements. Whilst they were disputing with one another, Caiphas and some of the other members of the Council employed themselves in questioning Jesus, and turning his answers into derision. 'What species of king art thou? Give proofs of thy power! Call the legions of angels of whom thou didst speak in the Garden of Olives! What hast thou done with the money given unto thee by the widows, and other simpletons whom thou didst seduce by thy false doctrines? Answer at once: speak out,—art thou dumb? Thou wouldst have been far wiser to have kept silence when in the midst of the foolish mob: there thou didst speak far too much.'

All these questions were accompanied by blows from the under-servants of the members of the tribunal, and had our Lord not been supported from above, he could not have survived this treatment. Some of the base witnesses endeavoured to prove that he was an illegitimate son; but others declared that his mother was a pious Virgin, belonging to the Temple, and that they afterwards saw her betrothed to a man who feared God. The witnesses upbraided Jesus and his disciples with not having offered sacrifice in the Temple. It is true that I never did see either Jesus or his disciples offer any sacrifice in the Temple, excepting the Paschal lamb; but Joseph and Anna used frequently during their lifetime to offer sacrifice for the Child Jesus. However, even this accusation was puerile, for the Essenians never offered sacrifice, and no one thought the less well of them for not doing so. The enemies of Jesus still continued to accuse him of being a sorcerer, and Caiphas affirmed several times that the confusion in the statements of the witnesses was caused solely by witchcraft.

Some said that he had eaten the Paschal lamb on the previous day, which was contrary to the law, and that the year before he had made different alterations in the manner of celebrating this ceremony. But the witnesses contradicted one another to such a degree that Caiphas and his adherents found, to their very great annoyance and anger, that not one accusation could be really proved. Nicodemus and Joseph of Arimathea were called up, and being commanded to say how it happened that they had allowed him to eat the Pasch on the wrong day in a room which belonged to them, they proved from ancient documents that from time immemorial the Galileans had been allowed to eat the Pasch a day earlier than the rest of the Jews. They added that every other part of the ceremony had been performed according to the directions given in the law, and that persons belonging to the Temple were present at the supper. This quite puzzled the witnesses, and Nicodemus increased the rage of the enemies of Jesus by pointing out the passages in the archives which proved the right of the Galileans, and gave the reason for which this privilege was granted. The reason was this: the sacrifices would not have been finished by the Sabbath if the immense multitudes who congregated together for that purpose had all been obliged to perform the ceremony on the same day; and although the Galileans had not always profited by this right, yet its existence was incontestably proved by Nicodemus; and the anger of the Pharisees was heightened by his remarking that the members of the Council had cause to be greatly offended at the gross contradictions in the statements of the witnesses, and that the extraordinary and hurried manner in which the whole affair had been conducted showed that malice and envy were the sole motives which induced the accusers, and made them bring the case forward at a moment when all were busied in the preparations for the most solemn feast of the year. They looked at Nicodemus furiously, and could not reply, but continued to question the witnesses in a still more precipitate and imprudent manner. Two witnesses at last came forward, who said, 'This man said, "I will destroy this Temple made with hands, and within three days I will build another not made with hands;"' however, even these witnesses did not agree in their statements, for one said that the accused wished to build a new Temple, and that he had eaten the Pasch in an unusual place, because he desired the destruction of the ancient Temple; but the other said, 'Not so: the edifice where he ate the Pasch was built by human hands, therefore he could not have referred to that.'

The wrath of Caiphas was indescribable; for the cruel treatment which Jesus had suffered, his Divine patience, and the contradiction of the witnesses, were beginning to make a great impression on many persons present, a few hisses were heard, and the hearts of some were so touched that they could not silence the voice of their consciences. Ten soldiers left the court under pretext of indisposition, but in reality overcome by their feelings. As they passed by the place where Peter and John were standing, they exclaimed, 'The silence of Jesus of Nazareth, in the midst of such cruel treatment, is superhuman: it would melt a heart of iron: the wonder is, that the earth does not open and swallow such reprobates as his accusers must be. But tell us, where must we go?' The two Apostles either mistrusted the soldiers, and thought they were only seeking to betray them, or they were fearful of being recognised by those around and denounced as disciples of Jesus, for they only made answer in a melancholy tone: 'If truth calls you, follow it, and all will come right of itself.' The soldiers instantly went out of the room, and left Jerusalem soon after. They met persons on the outskirts of the town, who directed them to the caverns which lay to the south of Jerusalem, on the other side of Mount Sion, where many of the Apostles had taken refuge. These latter were at first alarmed at seeing strangers enter their hiding-place; but the soldiers soon dispelled all fear, and gave them an account of the sufferings of Jesus.

The temper of Caiphas, which was already perturbed, became quite infuriated by the contradictory statements of the two last witnesses, and rising from his seat he approached Jesus, and said: 'Answerest thou nothing to the things which these witness against thee?'

Jesus neither raised his head nor looked at the High Priest, which increased the anger of the latter to the greatest degree; and the archers perceiving this seized our Lord by the hair, pulled his head back, and gave him blows under the chin; but he still kept his eyes cast down. Caiphas raised his hands, and exclaimed in an enraged tone: 'I adjure thee by the living God that thou tell us if thou be Christ the Messiah, the son of the living God?'

A momentary and solemn pause ensued. Then Jesus in a majestic and superhuman voice replied, 'Thou hast said it. Nevertheless I say to you, hereafter you shall see the Son of Man sitting on the right hand of the power of God, and coming in the clouds of Heaven.' Whilst Jesus was pronouncing these words, a bright light appeared to me to surround him; Heaven was opened above his head; I saw the Eternal Father; but no words from a human pen can describe the intuitive view that was then vouchsafed me of him. I likewise saw the angels, and the prayers of the just ascending to the throne of God.

At the same moment I perceived the yawning abyss of hell like a fiery meteor at the feet of Caiphas; it was filled with horrible devils; a slight gauze alone appeared to separate him from its dark flames. I could see the demoniacal fury with which his heart was overflowing, and the whole house looked to me like hell. At the moment that our Lord pronounced the solemn words, 'I am the Christ, the Son of the living God,' hell appeared to be shaken from one extremity to the other, and then, as it were, to burst forth and inundate every person in the house of Caiphas with feelings of redoubled hatred towards our Lord. These things are always shown to me under the appearance of some material object, which renders them less difficult of comprehension, and impresses them in a more clear and forcible manner on the mind, because we ourselves being material beings, facts are more easily illustrated in our regard if manifested through the medium of the senses. The despair and fury which these words produced in hell were shown to me under the appearance of a thousand terrific figures in different places. I remember seeing, among other frightful things, a number of little black objects, like dogs with claws, which walked on their hind legs; I knew at the time what kind of wickedness was indicated by this apparition, but I cannot remember now. I saw these horrible phantoms enter into the bodies of the greatest part of the bystanders, or else place themselves on their head or shoulders. I likewise at this moment saw frightful spectres come out of the sepulchres on the other side of Sion; I believe they were evil spirits. I saw in the neighbourhood of the Temple many other apparitions, which resembled prisoners loaded with chains: I do not know whether they were demons, or souls condemned to remain in some particular part of the earth, and who were then going to Limbo, which our Lord's condemnation to death had opened to them.

It is extremely difficult to explain these facts, for fear of scandalising those who have no knowledge of such things; but persons who see feel them, and they often cause the very hair to stand on end on the head. I think that John saw some of these apparitions, for I heard him speak about them afterwards. All whose hearts were not radically corrupted felt excessively terrified at these events, but the hardened were sensible of nothing but an increase of hatred and anger against our Lord.

Caiphas then arose, and, urged on by Satan, took up the end of his mantle, pierced it with his knife, and rent it from one end to the other, exclaiming at the same time, in a loud voice, 'He hath blasphemed, what further need have we of witnesses? Behold, now you have heard the blasphemy: what think you?' All who were then present arose, and exclaimed with astounding malignancy, 'He is guilty of death!'

During the whole of this frightful scene, the devils were in the most tremendous state of excitement; they appeared to have complete possession not only of the enemies of Jesus, but likewise of their partisans and cowardly followers. The powers of darkness seemed to me to proclaim a triumph over the light, and the few among the spectators whose hearts still retained a glimmering of light were filled with such consternation that, covering their heads, they instantly departed. The witnesses who belonged to the upper classes were less hardened than the others; their consciences were racked with remorse, and they followed the example given by the persons mentioned above, and left the room as quickly as possible, while the rest crowded round the fire in the vestibule, and ate and drank after receiving full pay for their services. The High Priest then addressed the archers, and said, 'I deliver this king up into your hands; render the blasphemer the honours which are his due.' After these words he retired with the members of his Council into the round room behind the tribunal, which could not be seen from the vestibule.

In the midst of the bitter affliction which inundated the heart of John, his thoughts were with the Mother of Jesus; he feared that the dreadful news of the condemnation of her Son might be communicated to her suddenly, or that perhaps some enemy might give the information in a heartless manner. He therefore looked at Jesus, and saying in a low voice, 'Lord, thou knowest why I leave thee,' went away quickly to seek the Blessed Virgin, as if he had been sent by Jesus himself. Peter was quite overcome between anxiety and sorrow, which, joined to fatigue, made him chilly; therefore, as the morning was cold, he went up to the fire where many of the common people were warming themselves. He did his best to hide his grief in their presence, as he could not make up his mind to go home and leave his beloved Master.

CHAPTER IX.

The Insults received by Jesus in the Court of Caiphas.

No sooner did Caiphas, with the other members of the Council, leave the tribunal than a crowd of miscreants—the very scum of the people—surrounded Jesus like a swarm of infuriated wasps, and began to heap every imaginable insult upon him. Even during the trial, whilst the witnesses were speaking, the archers and some others could not restrain their cruel inclinations, but pulled out handfuls of his hair and beard, spat upon him, struck him with their fists, wounded him with sharp-pointed sticks, and even ran needles into his body; but when Caiphas left the hall they set no bounds to their barbarity. They first placed a crown, made of straw and the bark of trees, upon his head, and then took it off, saluting him at the same time with insulting expressions, like the following: 'Behold the Son of David wearing the crown of his father.' 'A greater than Solomon is here; this is the king who is preparing a wedding feast for his son.' Thus did they turn into ridicule those eternal truths which he had taught under the from of parables to those whom he came from heaven to save; and whilst repeating these scoffing words, they continued to strike him with their fists and sticks, and to spit in his face. Next they put a crown of reeds upon his head, took off his robe and scapular, and then threw an old torn mantle, which scarcely reached his knees, over his shoulders; around his neck they hung a long iron chain, with an iron ring at each end, studded with sharp points, which bruised and tore his knees as he walked. They again pinioned his arms, put a reed into his hand, and covered his Divine countenance with spittle. They had already thrown all sorts of filth over his hair, as well as over his chest, and upon the old mantle. They bound his eyes with a dirty rag, and struck him, crying out at the same time in loud tones, 'Prophesy unto us, O Christ, who is he that struck thee?' He answered not one word, but sighed, and prayed inwardly for them.

After many more insults, they seized the chain which was hanging on his neck, dragged him towards the room into which the Council had withdrawn, and with their stick forced him in, vociferating at the same time, 'March forward, thou King of Straw! Show thyself to the Council with the insignia of the regal honours we have rendered unto thee.' A large body of councillors, with Caiphas at their head, were still in the room, and they looked with both delight and approbation at the shameful scene which was enacted, beholding with pleasure the most sacred ceremonies turned into derision. The pitiless guards covered him with mud and spittle, and with mock gravity exclaimed, 'Receive the prophetic unction—the regal unction.' Then they impiously parodied the baptismal ceremonies, and the pious act of Magdalen in emptying the vase of perfume on his head. 'How canst thou presume,' they exclaimed, 'to appear before the Council in such a condition? Thou dost purify others, and thou art not pure thyself; but we will soon purify thee.' They fetched a basin of dirty water, which they poured over his face and shoulders, whilst they bent their knees before him, and exclaimed, 'Behold thy precious unction, behold the spikenard worth three hundred pence; thou hast been baptised in the pool of Bethsaida.' They intended by this to throw into ridicule the act of respect and veneration shown by Magdalen, when she poured the precious ointment over his head, at the house of the Pharisee.

By their derisive words concerning his baptism in the pool of Bethsaida, they pointed out, although unintentionally, the resemblance between Jesus and the Paschal lamb, for the lambs were washed in the first place in the pond near the Probatica gate, and then brought to the pool of Bethsaida, where they underwent another purification before being taken to the Temple to be sacrificed. The enemies of Jesus likewise alluded to the man who had been infirm for thirty-eight years, and who was cured by Jesus at the pool of Bethsaida; for I saw this man either washed or baptised there; I say either washed or baptised, because I do not exactly remember the circumstances.

They then dragged Jesus round the room, before all the members of the Council, who continued to address him in reproachful and abusive language. Every countenance looked diabolical and enraged, and all around was dark, confused, and terrified. Our Lord, on the contrary, was from the moment that he declared himself to be the Son of God, generally surrounded with a halo of light. Many of the assembly appeared to have a confused knowledge of this fact, and to be filled with consternation at perceiving that neither outrages or ignominies could alter the majestic expression of his countenance.

The halo which shone around Jesus from the moment he declared himself to be the Christ, the Son of the Living God, served but to incite his enemies to greater fury, and yet it was so resplendent that they could not look at it, and I believe their intention in throwing the dirty rag over his head was to deaden its brightness.

CHAPTER X.

The Denial of St. Peter

At the moment when Jesus uttered the words, 'Thou hast said it,' and the High Priest rent his garment, the whole room resounded with tumultuous cries. Peter and John, who had suffered intensely during the scene which had just been enacted, and which they had been obliged to witness in silence, could bear the sight no longer. Peter therefore got up to leave the room, and John followed soon after. The latter went to the Blessed Virgin, who was in the house of Martha with the holy women, but Peter's love for Jesus was so great, that he could not make up his mind to leave him; his heart was bursting, and he wept bitterly, although he endeavoured to restrain and hide his tears. It was impossible for him to remain in the tribunal, as his deep emotion at the sight of his beloved Master's sufferings would have betrayed him; therefore he went into the vestibule and approached the fire, around which soldiers and common people were sitting and talking in the most heartless and disgusting manner concerning the sufferings of Jesus, and relating all that they themselves had done to him. Peter was silent, but his silence and dejected demeanour made the bystanders suspect something. The portress came up to the fire in the midst of the conversation, cast a bold glance at Peter and said, 'Thou also wast with Jesus the Galilean.' These words startled and alarmed Peter; he trembled as to what might ensue if he owned the truth before his brutal companions, and therefore answered quickly, 'Woman, I know him not,' got up, and left the vestibule. At this moment the cock crowed somewhere in the outskirts of the town. I do not remember hearing it, but I felt that is was crowing. As he went out, another maid-servant looked at him, and said to those who were with her, 'This man was also with him,' and the persons she addressed immediately demanded of Peter whether her words were true, saying, 'Art thou not one of this man's disciples?' Peter was even more alarmed than before, and renewed his denial in these words, 'I am not; I know not the man.'

He left the inner court, and entered the exterior court; he was weeping, and so great was his anxiety and grief, that he did not reflect in the least on the words he had just uttered. The exterior court was quite filled with persons, and some had climbed on to the top of the wall to listen to what was going on in the inner court which they were forbidden to enter. A few of the disciples were likewise there, for their anxiety concerning Jesus was so great that they could not make up their minds to remain concealed in the caves of Hinnom. They came up to Peter, and with many tears questioned him concerning their loved Master, but he was so unnerved and so fearful of betraying himself, that he briefly recommended them to go away, as it was dangerous to remain, and left them instantly. He continued to indulge his violent grief, while they hastened to leave the town. I recognised among these disciples, who were about sixteen in number, Bartholomew, Nathaniel, Saturninus, Judas Barsabeas, Simon, who was afterwards bishop of Jerusalem, Zacheus, and Manahem, the man who was born blind and cured by our Lord.

Anne Catherine Emmerich

Peter could not rest anywhere, and his love for Jesus prompted him to return to the inner court, which he was allowed to enter, because Joseph of Arimathea and Nicodemus had, in the first instance, taken him in. He did not re-enter the vestibule, but turned to the right and went towards the round room which was behind the tribunal, and in which Jesus was undergoing every possible insult and ignominy from his cruel enemies. Peter walked timidly up to the door, and although perfectly conscious that he was suspected by all present of being a partisan of Jesus, yet he could not remain outside; his love for his Master impelled him forward; he entered the room, advanced, and soon stood in the very midst of the brutal throng who were feasting their cruel eyes on the sufferings of Jesus. They were at that moment dragging him ignominiously backwards and forwards with the crown of straw upon his head; he cast a sorrowful and even severe glance upon Peter, which cut him to the heart, but as he was still much alarmed, and at that moment heard some of the bystanders call out, 'Who is that man?' he went back again into the court, and seeing that the persons in the vestibule were watching him, came up to the fire and remained before it for some time. Several persons who had observed his anxious troubled countenance began to speak in opprobrious terms of Jesus, and one of them said to him, 'Thou also art one of his disciples; thou also art a Galilean; thy very speech betrays thee.' Peter got up, intending to leave the room, when a brother of Malchus came up to him and said, 'Did I not see thee in the garden with him? Didst thou not cut off my brother's ear?'

Peter became almost beside himself with terror; he began to curse and to swear 'that he knew not the man,' and ran out of the vestibule into the outer court; the cock then crowed again, and Jesus, who at that moment was led across the court, cast a look of mingled compassion and grief upon his Apostle. This look of our Lord pierced Peter to the very heart,—it recalled to his mind in the most forcible and terrible manner the words addressed to him by our Lord on the previous evening: 'Before the cock crows twice, thou shalt thrice deny me.' He had forgotten all his promises and protestations to our Lord, that he would die rather than deny him—he had forgotten the warning given to him by our Lord;—but when Jesus looked at him, he felt the enormity of his fault, and his heart was nigh bursting with grief. He had denied his Lord, when that beloved Master was outraged, insulted, delivered up into the hands of unjust judges,—when he was suffering all in patience and in silence. His feelings of remorse were beyond expression; he returned to the exterior court, covered his face and wept bitterly; all fear of being recognised was over;—he was ready to proclaim to the whole universe both his fault and his repentance.

What man will dare assert that he would have shown more courage than Peter if, with his quick and ardent temperament, he were exposed to such danger, trouble, and sorrow, at a moment, too, when completely unnerved between fear and grief, and exhausted by the sufferings of this sad night? Our Lord left Peter to his own strength, and he was weak; like all who forget the words: 'Watch and pray, that ye enter not into temptation.'

CHAPTER XI.

Mary in the House of Caiphas.

The Blessed Virgin was ever united to her Divine Son by interior spiritual communications; she was, therefore, fully aware of all that happened to him— she suffered with him, and joined in his continual prayer for his murderers. But her maternal feelings prompted her to supplicate Almighty God most ardently not to suffer the crime to be completed, and to save her Son from such dreadful torments. She eagerly desired to return to him; and when John, who had left the tribunal at the moment the frightful cry, 'He is guilty of death,' was raised, came to the house of Lazarus to see after her, and to relate the particulars of the dreadful scene he had just witnessed, she, as also Magdalen and some of the other holy women, begged to be taken to the place where Jesus was suffering. John, who had only left our Saviour in order to console her whom he loved best next to his Divine Master, instantly acceded to their request, and conducted them through the streets, which were lighted up by the moon alone, and crowded with persons hastening to their home. The holy women were closely veiled; but the sobs which they could not restrain made many who passed by observe them, and their feelings were harrowed by the abusive epithets they overheard bestowed upon Jesus by those who were conversing on the subject of his arrest. The Blessed Virgin, who ever beheld in spirit the opprobrious treatment which her dear Son was receiving, continued 'to lay up all these things in her heart;' like him she suffered in silence; but more than once she became totally unconscious. Some disciples of Jesus, who were returning from the hall of Caiphas, saw her fainting in the arms of the holy women, and, touched with pity, stopped to look at her compassionately, and saluted her in these words: 'Hail! Unhappy Mother—hail, Mother of the Most Holy One of Israel, the most afflicted of all mothers!' Mary raised her head, thanked them gratefully, and continued her sad journey.

When in the vicinity of Caiphas's house, their grief was renewed by the sight of a group of men who were busily occupied under a tent, making the cross ready for our Lord's crucifixion. The enemies of Jesus had given orders that the cross should be prepared directly after his arrest, that they might without delay execute the sentence which they hoped to persuade Pilate to pass on him. The Romans had already prepared the crosses of the two thieves, and the workmen who were making that of Jesus were much annoyed at being obliged to labour at it during the night; they did not attempt to conceal their anger at this, and uttered the most frightful oaths and curses, which pierced the heart of the tender Mother of Jesus through and through; but she prayed for these blind creatures who thus unknowingly blasphemed the Saviour who was about to die for their salvation, and prepared the cross for his cruel execution.

Mary, John, and the holy women traversed the outer court attached to Caiphas's house. They stopped under the archway of a door which opened into the inner court. Mary's heart was with her Divine Son, and she desired most ardently to see this door opened, that she might again have a chance of beholding him, for she knew that it alone separated her from the prison where he was confined. The door was at length opened, and Peter rushed out, his face covered with his mantle, wringing his hands, and weeping bitterly. By the light of the torches he soon recognised John and the Blessed Virgin, but the sight of them only renewed those dreadful feelings of remorse which the look of Jesus had awakened in his breast. Mary approached him instantly, and said, 'Simon, tell me, I entreat you, what is become of Jesus, my Son?' These words pierced his very heart; he could not even look at her, but turned away, and again wrung his hands. Mary drew close to him, and said in a voice trembling with emotion: 'Simon, son of John, why dost thou not answer me?'—Mother!' exclaimed Peter, in a dejected tone, 'O, Mother, speak not to me—thy Son is suffering more than words can express: speak not to me! They have condemned him to death, and I have denied him three times.' John came up to ask a few more questions, but Peter ran out of the court as if beside himself, and did not stop for a single moment until he reached the cave at Mount Olivet—that cave on the stones of which the impression of the hands of our Saviour had been miraculously left. I believe it is the cave in which Adam took refuge to weep after his fall.

The Blessed Virgin was inexpressibly grieved at hearing of the fresh pang inflicted on the loving heart of her Divine Son, the pang of hearing himself denied by that disciple who had first acknowledged him as the Son of the Living God; she was unable to support herself, and fell down on the door-stone, upon which the impression of her feet and hands remains to the present day. I have seen the stones, which are preserved somewhere, but I cannot at this moment remember where. The door was not again shut, for the crowd was dispersing, and when the Blessed Virgin came to herself, she begged to be taken to some place as near as possible to her Divine Son. John, therefore, led her and the holy women to the front of the prison where Jesus was confined. Mary was with Jesus in spirit, and Jesus was with her; but this loving Mother wished to hear with her own ear the voice of her Divine Son. She listened and heard not only his moans, but also the abusive language of those around him. It was impossible for the holy women to remain in the court any longer without attracting attention. The grief of Magdalen was so violent that she was unable to conceal it; and although the Blessed Virgin, by a special grace from Almighty God, maintained a calm and dignified exterior in the midst of her sufferings, yet even she was recognised, and overheard harsh words, such as these: 'Is not that the Mother of the Galilean? Her Son will most certainly be executed, but not before the festival, unless, indeed, he is the greatest of criminals.'

The Blessed Virgin left the court, and went up to the fireplace in the vestibule, where a certain number of persons were still standing. When she reached the spot where Jesus had said that he was the Son of God, and the wicked Jews cried out, 'He is guilty of death,' she again fainted, and John and the holy women carried her away, in appearance more like a corpse than a living person. The bystanders said not a word; they seemed struck with astonishment, and silence, such as might have been produced in hell by the passage of a celestial being, reigned in that vestibule.

The holy women again passed the place where the cross was being prepared; the workmen appeared to find as much difficulty in completing it as the judges had found in pronouncing sentence, and were obliged to fetch fresh wood every moment, for some bits would not fit, and others split; this continued until the different species of wood were placed in the cross according to the intentions of Divine Providence. I saw angels who obliged these men to recommence their work, and who would not let them rest, until all was accomplished in a proper manner; but my remembrance of this vision is indistinct.

CHAPTER XII.

Jesus confined in the subterranean Prison.

The Jews, having quite exhausted their barbarity, shut Jesus up in a little vaulted prison, the remains of which subsist to this day. Two of the archers alone remained with him, and they were soon replaced by two others. He was still clothed in the old dirty mantle, and covered with the spittle and other filth which they had thrown over him; for they had not allowed him to put on his own clothes again, but kept his hands tightly bound together.

When our Lord entered this prison, he prayed most fervently that his Heavenly Father would accept all that he had already suffered, and all that he was about to suffer, as an expiatory sacrifice, not only for his executioners, but likewise for all who in future ages might have to suffer torments such as he was about to endure, and be tempted to impatience or anger.

The enemies of our Lord did not allow him a moment's respite, even in this dreary prison, but tied him to a pillar which stood in the centre, and would not allow him to lean upon it, although he was so exhausted from ill treatment, the weight of his chains, and his numerous falls, that he could scarcely support himself on his swollen and torn feet. Never for a moment did they cease insulting him; and when the first set were tired out, others replaced them.

It is quite impossible to describe all that the Holy of Holies suffered from these heartless beings; for the sight affected me so excessively that I became really ill, and I felt as if I could not survive it. We ought, indeed, to be ashamed of that weakness and susceptibility which renders us unable to listen composedly to the descriptions, or speak without repugnance, of those sufferings which our Lord endured so calmly and patiently for our salvation. The horror we feel is as great as that of a murderer who is forced to place his hands upon the wound he himself has inflicted on his victim. Jesus endured all without opening his mouth; and it was man, sinful man, who perpetrated all these outrages against one who was at once their Brother, their Redeemer, and their God. I, too, am a great sinner, and my sins cause these sufferings. At the day of judgment, when the most hidden things will be manifested, we shall see the share we have had in the torments endured by the Son of God; we shall see how far we have caused them by the sins we so frequently commit, and which are, in fact, a species of consent which we give to, and a participation in, the tortures which were inflicted on Jesus by his cruel enemies. If, alas! we reflected seriously on this, we should repeat with much greater fervour the words which we find so often in prayer books: 'Lord, grant that I may die, rather than ever wilfully offend thee again by sin.'

Jesus continued to pray for his enemies, and they being at last tired out left him in peace for a short time, when he leaned against the pillar to rest, and a bright light shone around him. The day was beginning to dawn,—the day of his Passion, of our Redemption,—and a faint ray penetrating the narrow vent-hole of the prison, fell upon the holy and immaculate Lamb, who had taken upon himself the sins of the world. Jesus turned towards the ray of light, raised his fettered hands, and, in the most touching manner, returned thanks to his Heavenly Father for the dawn of that day, which had been so long desired by the prophets, and for which he himself had so ardently sighed from the moment of his birth on earth, and concerning which he had said to his disciples, 'I have a baptism wherewith I am to be baptised, and how am I straitened until it be accomplished!' I prayed with him; but I cannot give the words of his prayer, for I was so completely overcome, and touched to hear him return thanks to his Father for the terrible sufferings which he had already endured for me, and for the still greater which he was about to endure. I could only repeat over and over with the greatest fervour, 'Lord, I beseech thee, give me these sufferings: they belong to me: I have deserved them in punishment for my sins.' I was quite overwhelmed with feelings of love and compassion when I looked upon him thus welcoming the first dawn of the great day of his Sacrifice, and that ray of light which penetrated into his prison might, indeed, be compared to the visit of a judge who wishes to be reconciled to a criminal before the sentence of death which he has pronounced upon him is executed.

The archers, who were dozing, woke up for a moment, and looked at him with surprise: they said nothing, but appeared to be somewhat astonished and frightened. Our Divine Lord was confined in this prison an hour, or thereabouts.

Whilst Jesus was in this dungeon, Judas, who had been wandering up and down the valley of Hinnom like a madman, directed his step towards the house of Caiphas, with the thirty pieces of silver, the reward of his treachery, still hanging to his waist. All was silent around, and he addressed himself to some of the sentinels, without letting them know who he was, and asked what was going to be done to the Galilean. 'He has been condemned to death, and he will certainly be crucified,' was the reply. Judas walked to and fro, and listened to the different conversations which were held concerning Jesus. Some spoke of the cruel treatment he had received, other of his astonishing patience, while others, again discoursed concerning the solemn trial which was to take place in the morning before the great Council. Whilst the traitor was listening eagerly to the different opinions given, day dawned; the members of the tribunal commenced their preparations, and Judas slunk behind the building that he might not be seen, for like Cain he sought to hide himself from human eyes, and despair was beginning to take possession of his soul. The place in which he took refuge happened to be the very spot where the workmen had been preparing the wood for making the cross of our Lord; all was in readiness, and the men were asleep by its side. Judas was filled with horror at the sight: he shuddered and fled when he beheld the instrument of that cruel death to which for a paltry sum of money he had delivered up his Lord and Master; he ran to and fro in perfect agonies of remorse, and finally hid himself in an adjoining cave, where he determined to await the trial which was to take place in the morning.

CHAPTER XIII.

The Morning Trial.

Caiphas, Annas, the ancients, and the scribes assembled in the morning in the great hall of the tribunal, to have a legal trial, as meetings at night were not lawful, and could only be looked upon in the light of preparatory audiences. The majority of the members had slept in the house of Caiphas, where beds had been prepared for them, but some, and among them Nicodemus and Joseph of Arimathea, had gone home, and returned at the dawn of day. The meeting was crowded, and the members commenced their operations in the most hurried manner possible. They wished to condemn Jesus to death at once, but Nicodemus, Joseph, and some others opposed their wishes and demanded that the decision should be deferred until after the festival, for fear of causing an insurrection among the people, maintaining likewise that no criminal could be justly condemned upon charges which were not proved, and that in the case now before them all the witnesses contradicted one another. The High Priests and their adherents became very angry, and told Joseph and Nicodemus, in plain terms, that they were not surprised at their expressing displeasure at what had been done, because they were themselves partisans of the Galilean and his doctrines, and were fearful of being convicted. The High Priest even went so far as to endeavour to exclude from the Council all those members who were in the lightest degree favourable to Jesus. These members protested that they washed their hands of all the future proceedings of the Council, and leaving the room went to the Temple, and from this day never again took their seats in the Council. Caiphas then ordered the guards to bring Jesus once more into his presence, and to prepare everything for taking him to Pilate's court directly he should have pronounced sentence. The emissaries of the Council hurried off to the prison, and with their usual brutality untied the hands of Jesus, dragged off the old mantle which they had thrown over his shoulders, made him put on his own soiled garment, and having fastened ropes round his waist, dragged him out of the prison. The appearance of Jesus, when he passed through the midst of the crowd who were already assembled in the front of the house, was that of a victim led to be sacrificed; his countenance was totally changed and disfigured from ill-usage, and his garments stained and torn; but the sight of his sufferings, far from exciting a feeling of compassion in the hard hearted Jews, simply filled them with disgust, and increased their rage. Pity was, indeed, a feeling unknown in their cruel breasts.

Caiphas, who did not make the slightest effort to conceal his hatred, addressed our Lord haughtily in these words: 'If thou be Christ , tell us plainly.' Then Jesus raised his head, and answered with great dignity and calmness, 'If I shall tell you, you will not believe me; and if I shall also ask you, you will not answer me, or let me go. But hereafter the Son of Man shall be sitting on the right hand of the power of God.' The High Priests looked at one another, and said to Jesus, with a disdainful laugh, 'Art thou, then, the Son of God?' And Jesus answered, with the voice of eternal truth, 'You say that I am.' At these words they all exclaimed, 'What need we any further testimony? For we ourselves have heard it from his own mouth.'

They all arose instantly and vied with each other as to who should heap the most abusive epithets upon Jesus, whom they termed a low-born miscreant, who aspired to being their Messiah, and pretended to be entitled to sit at the right hand of God. They ordered the archers to tie his hands again, and to fasten a chain round his neck (this was usually done to criminals condemned to death), and they then prepared to conduct him to Pilate's hall, where a messenger had already been dispatched to beg him to have all in readiness for trying a criminal, as it was necessary to make no delay on account of the festival day.

The Jewish Priests murmured among themselves at being obliged to apply to the Roman governor for the confirmation of their sentence, but it was necessary, as they had not the right of condemning criminals excepting for things which concerned religion and the Temple alone, and they could not pass a sentence of death. They wished to prove that Jesus was an enemy to the emperor, and this accusation concerned those departments which were under Pilate's jurisdiction. The soldiers were all standing in front of the house, surrounded by a large body of the enemies of Jesus, and of common persons attracted by curiosity. The High Priests and a part of the Council walked at the head of the procession, and Jesus, led by archers, and guarded by soldiers, followed, while the mob brought up the rear. They were obliged to descend Mount Sion, and cross a part of the lower town to reach Pilate's palace, and many priests who had attended the Council went to the Temple directly afterwards, as it was necessary to prepare for the festival.

CHAPTER XIV.

The Despair of Judas

Whilst the Jews were conducting Jesus to Pilate, the traitor Judas walked about listening to the conversation of the crowd who followed, and his ears were struck by words such as these: 'They are taking him before Pilate; the High Priests have condemned the Galilean to death; he will be crucified; they will accomplish his death; he has been already dreadfully illtreated; his patience is wonderful, he answers not; his only words are that he is the Messiah, and that he will be seated at the right hand of God; they will crucify him on account of those words; had he not said them they could not have condemned him to death. The miscreant who sold him was one of his disciples; and had a short time before eaten the Paschal lamb with him; not for worlds would I have had to do with such an act; however guilty the Galilean may be, he has not at all events sold his friend for money; such an infamous character as this disciple is infinitely more deserving of death.' Then, but too late, anguish, despair, and remorse took possession of the mind of Judas. Satan instantly prompted him to fly. He fled as if a thousand furies were at his heel, and the bag which was hanging at his side struck him as he ran, and propelled him as a spur from hell; but he took it into his hand to prevent its blows. He fled as fast as possible, but where did he fly? Not towards the crowd, that he might cast himself at the feet of Jesus, his merciful Saviour, implore his pardon, and beg do die with him,—not to confess his fault with true repentance before God, but to endeavour to unburden himself before the world of his crime, and of the price of his treachery. He ran like one beside himself into the Temple, where several members of the Council had gathered together after the judgment of Jesus. They looked at one another with astonishment; and then turned their haughty countenances, on which a smile of irony was visible, upon Judas. He with a frantic gesture tore the thirty pieces of silver from his side, and holding them forth with his right hand, exclaimed in accents of the most deep despair, 'Take back your silver—that silver with which you bribed me to betray this just man; take back your silver; release Jesus; our compact is at an end; I have sinned grievously, for I have betrayed innocent blood.' The priests answered him in the most contemptuous manner, and, as if fearful of contaminating themselves by the contact of the reward of the traitor, would not touch the silver he tended, but replied, 'What have we to do with thy sin? If thou thinkest to have sold innocent blood, it is thine own affair; we know what we have paid for, and we have judged him worthy of death. Thou hast thy money, say no more.' They addressed these words to him in the abrupt tone in which men usually speak when anxious to get rid of a troublesome person, and instantly arose and walked away. These words filled Judas with such rage and despair that he became almost frantic: his hair stood on end on his head; he rent in two the bag which contained the thirty pieces of silver, cast them down in the Temple, and fled to the outskirts of the town.

The Dolorous Passion of Our Lord Jesus Christ

I again beheld him rushing to and fro like a madman in the valley of Hinnom: Satan was by his side in a hideous form, whispering in his ear, to endeavour to drive him to despair, all the curses which the prophets had hurled upon this valley, where the Jews formerly sacrificed their children to idols.

It appeared as if all these maledictions were directed against him, as in these words, for instance: 'They shall go forth, and behold the carcases of those who have sinned against me, whose worm dieth not, and whore fires shall never be extinguished.' Then the devil murmured in his ears, 'Cain, where is thy brother Abel? What hast thou done?—his blood cries to me for vengeance: thou art cursed upon earth, a wanderer for ever.' When he reached the torrent of Cedron, and saw Mount Olivet, he shuddered, turned away, and again the words vibrated in his ear, 'Friend, whereto art thou come? Judas, dost thou betray the Son of Man with a kiss?' Horror filled his soul, his head began to wander, and the arch fiend again whispered, 'It was here that David crossed the Cedron when he fled from Absalom. Absalom put an end to his life by hanging himself. It was of thee that David spoke when he said: "And they repaid me evil for good; hatred for my love. May the devil stand at his right hand; when he is judged, may he go out condemned. May his days be few, and his bishopric let another take. May the iniquity of his father be remembered in the sight of the Lord, and let not the sin of his mother be blotted out, because he remembered not to show mercy, but persecuted the poor man and the beggar and the broken in heart, to put him to death. And he loved cursing, and it shall come unto him. And he put on cursing like a garment, and it went in like water into his entrails, and like oil into his bones. May it be unto him like a garment which covereth him; and like a girdle, with which he is girded continually." Overcome by these terrible thoughts Judas rushed on, and reached the foot of the mountain. It was a dreary, desolate spot filled with rubbish and putrid remains; discordant sounds from the city reverberated in his ears, and Satan continually repeated, 'They are now about to put him to death; thou has sold him. Knowest thou not the words of the law, "He who sells a soul among his brethren, and receives the price of it, let him die the death"? Put an end to thy misery, wretched one; put an end to thy misery.' Overcome by despair Judas tore off his girdle, and hung himself on a tree which grew in a crevice of the rock, and after death his body burst asunder, and his bowels were scattered around.

CHAPTER XV.

Jesus is taken before Pilate.

The malicious enemies of our Saviour led him through the most public part of the town to take him before Pilate. The procession wended its way slowly down the north side of the mountain of Sion, then passed through that section on the eastern side of the Temple, called Acre, towards the palace and tribunal of Pilate, which were seated on the north-west side of the Temple, facing a large square. Caiphas, Annas, and many others of the Chief Council, walked first in festival attire; they were followed by a multitude of scribes and many other Jews, among whom were the false witnesses, and the wicked Pharisees who had taken the most prominent part in accusing Jesus. Our Lord followed at a short distance; he was surrounded by a band of soldiers, and led by the archers. The multitude thronged on all sides and followed the procession, thundering forth the most fearful oaths and imprecations, while groups of persons were hurrying to and fro, pushing and jostling one another. Jesus was stripped of all save his under garment, which was stained and soiled by the filth which had been flung upon it; a long chain was hanging round his neck, which struck his knees as he walked; his hands were pinioned as on the previous day, and the archers dragged him by the ropes which were fastened round his waist. He tottered rather than walked, and was almost unrecognisable from the effects of his sufferings during the night;—he was colourless, haggard, his face swollen and even bleeding, and his merciless persecutors continued to torment him each moment more and more. They had gathered together a large body of the dregs of the people, in order to make his present disgraceful entrance into the city a parody on his triumphal entrance on Palm Sunday. They mocked, and with derisive gestures called him king, and tossed in his path stones, bits of wood; and filthy rags; they made game of, and by a thousand taunting speeches mocked him, during this pretended triumphal entry.

In the corner of a building, not far from the house of Caiphas, the afflicted Mother of Jesus, with John and Magdalen, stood watching for him. Her soul was ever united to his; but propelled by her love, she left no means untried which could enable her really to approach him. She remained at the Cenacle for some time after her midnight visit to the tribunal of Caiphas, powerless and speechless from grief; but when Jesus was dragged forth from his prison, to be again brought before his judges, she arose, cast her veil and cloak about her, and said to Magdalen and John: 'Let us follow my Son to Pilate's court; I must again look upon him.' They went to a place through which the procession must pass, and waited for it. The Mother of Jesus knew that her Son was suffering dreadfully, but never could she have conceived the deplorable, the heartrending condition to which he was reduced by the brutality of his enemies. Her imagination had depicted him to her as suffering fearfully, but yet supported and illuminated by sanctity, love, and patience. Now, however, the sad reality burst upon her. First in the procession appeared the priests, those most bitter enemies of her Divine Son. They were decked in flowing robes; but at, terrible to say, instead of appearing resplendent in their character of priests of the Most High, they were transformed into priests of Satan, for no one could look upon their wicked countenances without beholding there, portrayed in vivid colours, the evil passions with which their souls were filled—deceit, infernal cunning, and a raging anxiety to carry out that most tremendous of crimes, the death of their Lord and Saviour, the only Son of God. Next followed the false witnesses, his perfidious accusers, surrounded by the vociferating populace; and last of all—himself—her Son—Jesus, the Son of God, the Son of Man, loaded with chains, scarcely able to support himself, but pitilessly dragged on by his infernal enemies, receiving blows from some, buffets from others, and from the whole assembled rabble curses, abuse, and the most scurrilous language. He would have been perfectly unrecognisable even to her maternal eyes, stripped as he was of all save a torn remnant of his garment, had she not instantly marked the contrast between his behaviour and that of his vile tormentors. He alone in the midst of persecution and suffering looked calm and resigned, and far from returning blow for blow, never raised his hands but in acts of supplication to his Eternal Father for the pardon of his enemies. As he approached, she was unable to restrain herself any longer, but exclaimed in thrilling accents: 'Alas! is that my Son? Ah, yes! I see that it is my beloved Son. O, Jesus, my Jesus!' When the procession was almost opposite, Jesus looked upon her with an expression of the greatest love and compassion; this look was too much for the heartbroken mother: she became for the moment totally unconscious, and John and Magdalen endeavoured to carry her home, but she quickly roused herself, and accompanied the beloved disciple to Pilate's house.

The inhabitants of the town of Ophel were all gathered together in an open space to meet Jesus, but far from administering comfort, they added a fresh ingredient to his cup of sorrow; they inflicted upon him that sharp pang which must ever be felt by those who see their friends abandon them in the hour of adversity. Jesus had done much for the inhabitants of Ophel, but no sooner did they see him reduced to such a state of misery and degradation, than their faith was shaken; they could no longer believe him to be a king, a prophet, the Messiah, and the Son of God. The Pharisees jeered and made game of them, on account of the admiration they had formerly expressed for Jesus. 'Look at your king now,' they exclaimed; 'do homage to him; have you no congratulations to offer him now that he is about to be crowned , and seated on his throne? All his boasted miracles are at an end; the High Priest has put an end to his tricks and witchcraft.'

Notwithstanding the remembrance which these poor people had of the miracles and wonderful cures which had been performed under their very eyes by Jesus; notwithstanding the great benefits he had bestowed upon them, their faith was shaken by beholding him thus derided and pointed out as an object of contempt by the High Priest and the members of the Sanhedrin, who were regarded in Jerusalem with the greatest veneration. Some went away doubting, while others remained and endeavoured to join the rabble, but they were prevented by the guards, who had been sent by the Pharisees, to prevent riots and confusion.

CHAPTER XVI.

Description of Pilate's Palace and the adjacent Buildings.

The palace of the Roman governor, Pilate, was built on the north-west side of the mountain on which the Temple stood, and to reach it persons were obliged to ascend a flight of marble steps. It overlooked a large square surrounded by a colonnade, under which the merchants sat to sell their various commodities. A parapet, and an entrance at the north, south, east, and west sides alone broke the uniformity of this part of the market-place, which was called the forum, and built on higher ground than the adjacent streets, which sloped down from it. The palace of Pilate was not quite close, but separated by a large court, the entrance to which at the eastern side was through a high arch facing a street leading to the door called the 'Probatica,' on the road to the Mount of Olives. The southern entrance was through another arch, which leads to Sion, in the neighbourhood of the fortress of Acre. From the top of the marble steps of Pilate's palace, a person could see across the court as far as the forum, at the entrance of which a few columns and stone seats were placed. It was at these seats that the Jewish priests stopped, in order not to defile themselves by entering the tribunal of Pilate, a line traced on the pavement of the court indicating the precise boundary beyond which they could not pass without incurring defilement. There was a large parapet near the western entrance, supported by the sides of Pilate's Praetorium, which formed a species of porch between it and the square. That part of Pilate's palace which he made use of when acting in the capacity of judge, was called the Praetorium. A number of columns surrounded the parapet of which we have just spoken, and in the centre was an uncovered portion, containing an underground part, where the two thieves condemned to be crucified with our Lord were confined, and this part was filled with Roman soldiers. The pillar upon which our Lord was scourged was placed on the forum itself, not far from this parapet and the colonnade. There were many other columns in this place; those nearest to the palace were made use of for the infliction of various corporal punishments, and the others served as posts to which were fastened the beasts brought for sale. Upon the forum itself, opposite this building, was a platform filled with seats made of stone; and from this platform, which was called Gabbatha, Pilate was accustomed to pronounce sentence on great criminals. The marble staircase ascended by persons going to the governor's palace led likewise to an uncovered terrace, and it was from this terrace that Pilate gave audience to the priests and Pharisees, when they brought forward their accusations against Jesus. They all stood before him in the forum, and refused to advance further than the stone seats before mentioned. A person speaking in a loud tone of voice from the terrace could be easily heard by those in the forum.

Behind Pilate's palace there were many other terraces, and likewise gardens, and a country house. The gardens were between the palace of the governor and the dwelling of his wife, Claudia Procles. A large moat separated these buildings from the mountain on which the Temple stood, and on this side might be seen the houses inhabited by those who served in the Temple. The palace of Herod the elder was placed on the eastern side of Pilate's palace; and it was in its inner court that numbers of the Innocents were massacred. At present the appearance of these two buildings is a little altered, as their entrances are changed. Four of the principal streets commenced at this part of the town, and ran in a southerly direction, three leading to the forum and Pilate's palace, and the fourth to the gate through which persons passed on their way to Bethsur. The beautiful house which belonged to Lazarus, and likewise that of Martha, were in a prominent part of this street.

One of these streets was very near to the Temple, and began at the gate which was called Probatica. The pool of Probatica was close to this gate on the right hand side, and in this pool the sheep were washed for the first time, before being taken to the Temple; while the second and more solemn washing took place in the pool of Bethsaida, which is near the south entrance to the Temple. The second of the above-mentioned streets contained a house belonging to St. Anna, the mother of the Blessed Virgin, which she usually inhabited when she came up to Jerusalem with her family to offer sacrifice in the Temple. I believe it was in this house that the espousals of St. Joseph and the Blessed Virgin were celebrated.

The forum, as I have already explained, was built on higher ground than the neighbouring streets, and the aqueducts which ran through these streets flowed into the Probatica pool. On Mount Sion, directly opposite to the old castle of King David, stood a building very similar to the forum, while to the south-east might be seen the Cenacle, and a little towards the north the tribunals of Annas and Caiphas. King David's castle was a deserted fortress, filled with courts, empty rooms, and stables, generally let to travellers. It had long been in this state of ruin, certainly before the time of our Lord's nativity. I saw the Magi with their numerous retinue enter it before going into Jerusalem.

When in meditation I behold the ruins of old castles and temples, see their neglected and forlorn state, and reflect on the uses to which they are now put, so different from the intentions of those who raised them, my mind always reverts to the events of our own days, when so many of the beautiful edifices erected by our pious and zealous ancestors are either destroyed, defaced, or used for worldly, if not wicked purposes. The little church of our convent, in which our Lord deigned to dwell, notwithstanding our unworthiness, and which was to me a paradise upon earth, is now without either roof or windows, and all the monuments are effaced or carried away. Our beloved convent, too, what will be done with it in a short time? That convent, where I was more happy in my little cell with my broken chair, than a king could be on his throne, for from its window I beheld that part of the church which contained the Blessed Sacrament. In a few years, perhaps, no one will know that it ever existed,—no one will know that it once contained hundreds of souls consecrated to God, who spent their days in imploring his mercy upon sinners. But God will know all, he never forgets,—the past and the future are equally present to him. He it is who reveals to me events which took place so long ago, and on the day of judgment, when all must be accounted for, and every debt paid, even to the farthing, he will remember both the good and the evil deeds performed in places long since forgotten. With God there is no exception of persons or places, his eyes see all, even the Vineyard of Naboth. It is a tradition among us that our convent was originally founded by two poor nuns, whose worldly possessions consisted in a jar of oil and a sack of beans. On the last day God will reward them for the manner in which they put out this small talent to interest, and for the large harvest which they reaped and presented to him. It is often said that poor souls remain in purgatory in punishment for what appears to us so small a crime as not having made restitution of a few coppers of which they had unlawful possession. May God therefore have mercy upon those who have seized the property of the poor, or of the Church.

CHAPTER XVII.

Jesus before Pilate.

It was about eight in the morning, according to our method of counting time, when the procession reached the palace of Pilate. Annas, Caiphas, and the chiefs of the Sanhedrin stopped at a part between the forum and the entrance to the Praetorium, where some stone seats were placed for them. The brutal guards dragged Jesus to the foot of the flight of stairs which led to the judgment-seat of Pilate. Pilate was reposing in a comfortable chair, on a terrace which overlooked the forum, and a small three-legged table stood by his side, on which was placed the insignia of his office, and a few other things. He was surrounded by officers and soldiers dressed with the magnificence usual in the Roman army. The Jews and the priests did not enter the Praetorium, for fear of defiling themselves, but remained outside.

When Pilate saw the tumultuous procession enter, and perceived how shamefully the cruel Jews had treated their prisoner, he arose, and addressed them in a tone as contemptuous as could have been assumed by a victorious general towards the vanquished chief of some insignificant village: 'What are you come about so early? Why have you illtreated this prisoner so shamefully? Is it not possible to refrain from thus tearing to pieces and beginning to execute your criminals even before they are judged?' They made no answer, but shouted out to the guards, 'Bring him on—bring him to be judged!' and then, turning to Pilate, they said, 'Listen to our accusations against this malefactor; for we cannot enter the tribunal lest we defile ourselves.' Scarcely had they finished these words; when a voice was heard to issue from the midst of the dense multitude; it proceeded from a venerable-looking old man, of imposing stature, who exclaimed, 'You are right in not entering the Praetorium, for it has been sanctified by the blood of Innocents; there is but one Person who has a right to enter, and who alone can enter, because he alone is pure as the Innocents who were massacred there.' The person who uttered these words in a loud voice, and then disappeared among the crowd, was a rich man of the name of Zadoc, first-cousin to Obed, the husband of Veronica; two of his children were among the Innocents whom Herod had caused to be butchered at the birth of our Saviour. Since that dreadful moment he had given up the world, and, together with his wife, followed the rules of the Essenians. He had once seen our Saviour at the house of Lazarus, and there heard him discourse, and the sight of the barbarous manner in which he was dragged before Pilate recalled to his mind all he himself had suffered when his babes were so cruelly murdered before his eyes, and he determined to give this public testimony of his belief in the innocence of Jesus. The persecutors of our Lord were far too provoked at the haughty manner which Pilate assumed towards them, and at the humble position they were obliged to occupy, to take any notice of the words of a stranger.

The brutal guards dragged our Lord up the marble staircase, and led him to the end of the terrace, from whence Pilate was conferring with the Jewish priests. The Roman governor had often heard of Jesus, although he had never seen him, and now he was perfectly astonished at the calm dignity of a man brought before him in so pitiable a condition. The inhuman behaviour of the priests and ancients both exasperated him and increased his contempt for them, and he informed them pretty quickly that the had not the slightest intention of condemning Jesus without satisfactory proofs of the truth of their accusation. 'What accusation do you bring against this man?' said he, addressing the priests in the most scornful tone possible. 'If he were not a malefactor we would not have delivered him up to thee,' replied the priests sullenly. 'Take him,' said Pilate, 'and judge you him according to your law.' 'Thou knowest well,' replied they, 'that it is not lawful for us to condemn any man to death.' The enemies of Jesus were furious—they wished to have the trial finished off, and their victim executed as quickly as possible, that they might be ready at the festival-day to sacrifice the Paschal lamb, not knowing, miserable wretches as they were, that he whom they had dragged before the tribunal of an idolatrous judge (into whose house they would not enter, for fear of defiling themselves before partaking of the figurative victim), that he, and he alone, was the true Paschal Lamb, of which the other was only the shadow.

Pilate, however, at last ordered them to produce their accusations. These accusations were three in number, and they brought forward ten witnesses to attest the truth of each. Their great aim was to make Pilate believe that Jesus was the leader of a conspiracy against the emperor, in order that he might condemn him to death as a rebel. They themselves were powerless in such matters, being allowed to judge none but religious offences. Their first endeavour was to convict him of seducing the people, exciting them to rebellion, and of being an enemy to public peace and tranquillity. To prove these charges they brought forward some false witnesses, and declared likewise that he violated the Sabbath, and even profaned it by curing the sick upon that day. At this accusation Pilate interrupted them, and said in a jeering tone, 'It is very evident you were none of you ill yourselves—had you been so you would not have complained of being cured on the Sabbath-day.' 'He seduces the people, and inculcates the most disgusting doctrines. He even says, that no person can attain eternal life unless they eat his flesh and drink his blood.' Pilate was quite provoked at the intense hatred which their words and countenances expressed and, turning from them with a look of scorn, exclaimed, 'You most certainly must wish to follow his doctrines and to attain eternal life, for you are thirsting for both his body and blood.'

The Jews then brought forward the second accusation against Jesus, which was that he forbad the people to pay tribute to the emperor. These words roused the indignation of Pilate, as it was his place to see that all the taxes were properly paid, and he exclaimed in an angry tone, 'That is a lie! I must know more about it than you.' This obliged the enemies of our Lord to proceed to the third accusation, which they did in words such as these: 'Although this man is of obscure birth, he is the chief of a large party. When at their head, he denounces curses upon Jerusalem, and relates parables of double meaning concerning a king who is preparing a wedding feast for his son. The multitude whom he had gathered together on a mountain endeavoured once to make him their king; but it was sooner than he intended: his plans were not matured; therefore he fled and hid himself. Latterly he has come forward much more: it was but the other day that he entered Jerusalem at the head of a tumultuous assembly, who by his orders made the people rend the air with acclamations of "Hosanna to the Son of David! Blessed be the empire of our Father David, which is now beginning." He obliges his partisans to pay him regal honours, and tells them that he is the Christ, the Anointed of the Lord, the Messiah, the king promised to the Jews, and he wishes to be addressed by these fine titles.' Then witnesses gave testimony concerning these things. The last accusation—that of Jesus causing himself to be called king—made some impression upon Pilate; he became a little thoughtful, left the terrace and, casting a scrutinising glance on Jesus, went into the adjoining apartment, and ordered the guards to bring him alone into his presence. Pilate was not only superstitious, but likewise extremely weak-minded and susceptible. He had often, during the course of his pagan education, heard mention made of sons of his gods who had dwelt for a time upon earth; he was likewise fully aware that the Jewish prophets had long foretold that one should appear in the midst of them who should be the Anointed of the Lord, their Saviour, and Deliverer from slavery; and that many among the people believed this firmly. He remembered likewise that kings from the east had come to Herod, the predecessor of the present monarch of that name, to pay homage to a newly-born king of the Jews, and that Herod had on this account given orders for the massacre of the Innocents. He had often heard of the traditions concerning the Messiah and the king of the Jews, and even examined them with some curiosity; although of course, being a pagan, without the slightest belief. Had he believed at all, he would probably have agreed with the Herodians, and with those Jews who expected a powerful and victorious king. With such impressions, the idea of the Jews accusing the poor miserable individual whom they had brought into his presence of setting himself up as the promised king and Messiah, of course appeared to him absurd; but as the enemies of Jesus brought forward these charges in proof of treason against the emperor, he thought it proper to interrogate him privately concerning them.

'Art thou the king of the Jews,' said Pilate, looking at our Lord, and unable to repress his astonishment at the divine expression of his countenance.

Jesus made answer, 'Sayest thou this thing of thyself, or have others told it thee of me?'

Pilate was offended that Jesus should think it possible for him to believe such a thing, and answered, 'Am I a Jew? Thy own nation and the chief priests have delivered thee up to me as deserving of death: what hast thou done?'

Jesus answered majestically, 'My kingdom is not of this world. If my kingdom were of this world, my servants would certainly strive that I should not be delivered to the Jews; but now my kingdom is not from hence.'

Pilate was somewhat moved by these solemn words, and said to him in a more serious tone, 'Art thou a king, then?'

Jesus answered, 'Thou sayest that I am a king. For this was I born, and for this I came into the world, that I should give testimony to the truth. Everyone that is of the truth heareth my voice.'

Pilate looked at him, and rising from his seat said, 'The truth! What is truth?'

They then exchanged a few more words, which I do not now remember, and Pilate returned to the terrace. The answers and deportment of Jesus were far beyond his comprehension; but he saw plainly that his assumption of royalty would not clash with that of the emperor, for that it was to no worldly kingdom that he laid claim; whereas the emperor cared for nothing beyond this world. He therefore again addressed the chief priests from the terrace, and said, 'I find no cause in him.' The enemies of Jesus became furious, and uttered a thousand different accusations against our Saviour. But he remained silent, solely occupied in praying for his base enemies, and replied not when Pilate addressed him in these words, 'Answerest thou nothing? Behold in how many things they accuse thee!' Pilate was filled with astonishment, and said, 'I see plainly that all they allege is false.' But his accusers, whose anger continued to increase, cried out, 'You find no cause in him? Is it no crime to incite the people to revolt in all parts of the kingdom?—to spread his false doctrines, not only here, but in Galilee likewise?'

The mention of Galilee made Pilate pause: he reflected for a moment, and then asked, 'Is this man a Galilean, and a subject of Herod's?' They made answer, 'He is; his parents lived at Nazareth, and his present dwelling is in Capharnaum.'

'Since that is the case,' replied Pilate, 'take him before Herod; he is here for the festival, and can judge him at once, as he is his subject.' Jesus was immediately led out of the tribunal, and Pilate dispatched an officer to Herod, to inform him that Jesus of Nazareth, who was his subject, was about to be brought to him to be judged. Pilate had two reasons for following this line of conduct; in the first place he was delighted to escape having to pass sentence himself, as he felt very uncomfortable about the whole affair; and in the second place he was glad of an opportunity of pleasing Herod, with whom he had had a disagreement, for he knew him to be very curious to see Jesus.

The enemies of our Lord were enraged at being thus dismissed by Pilate in the presence of the whole multitude, and gave vent to their anger by ill-treating him even more than before. They pinioned him afresh, and then ceased not overwhelming him with curses and blows as they led him hurriedly through the crowd, towards the palace of Herod, which was situated at no great distance from the forum. Some Roman soldiers had joined the procession.

During the time of the trial Claudia Procles, the wife of Pilate, had sent him frequent messages to intimate that she wished extremely to speak to him; and when Jesus was sent to Herod, she placed herself on a balcony and watched the cruel conduct of his enemies with mingled feelings of fear, grief, and horror.

CHAPTER XVIII.

The Origin of the Way of the Cross.

During the whole of the scene which we have just described, the Mother of Jesus, with Magdalen and John, had stood in a recess in the forum: they were overwhelmed with the most bitter sorrow, which was but increased by all they heard and saw. When Jesus was taken before Herod, John led the Blessed Virgin and Magdalen over the parts which had been sanctified by his footsteps. They again looked at the house of Caiphas, that of Annas, Ophel, Gethsemani, and the Garden of Olives; they stopped and contemplated each spot where he had fallen, or where he had suffered particularly; and they wept silently at the thought of all he had undergone. The Blessed Virgin knelt down frequently and kissed the ground where her Son had fallen, while Magdalen wrung her hands in bitter grief, and John, although he could not restrain his own tears, endeavoured to console his companions, supported and led them on. Thus was the holy devotion of the 'Way of the Cross' first practised; thus were the Mysteries of the Passion of Jesus first honoured, even before that Passion was accomplished, and the Blessed Virgin, that model of spotless purity, was the first to show forth the deep veneration felt by the Church for our dear Lord. How sweet and consoling to follow this Immaculate Mother, passing to and fro, and bedewing the sacred spots with her tears. But, ah! Who can describe the sharp, sharp sword of grief which then transfixed her tender soul? She who had once borne the Saviour of the world in her chaste womb, and suckled him for so long,—she who had truly conceived him who was the Word of God, in God from all eternity, and truly God,—she beneath whose heart, full of grace, he had deigned to dwell nine months, who had felt him living within her before he appeared among men to impart the blessing of salvation and teach them his heavenly doctrines; she suffered with Jesus, sharing with him not only the sufferings of his bitter Passion, but likewise that ardent desire of redeeming fallen man by an ignominious death, which consumed him.

In this touching manner did the most pure and holy Virgin lay the foundation of the devotion called the Way of the Cross; thus at each station, marked by the sufferings of her Son, did she lay up in her heart the inexhaustible merits of his Passion, and gather them up as precious stones or sweet-scented flowers to be presented as a choice offering to the Eternal Father in behalf of all true believers. The grief of Magdalen was so intense as to make her almost like an insane person. The holy and boundless love she felt for our Lord prompted her to cast herself at his feet, and there pour forth the feelings of her heart (as she once poured the precious ointment on his head as he sat at table); but when on the point of following this impulse, a dark gulf appeared to intervene between herself and him. The repentance she felt for her faults was immense, and not less intense was her gratitude for their pardon; but when she longed to offer acts of love and thanksgiving as precious incense at the feet of Jesus, she beheld him betrayed, suffering, and about to die for the expiation of her offences which he had taken upon himself, and this sight filled her with horror, and almost rent her soul asunder with feelings of love, repentance, and gratitude. The sight of the ingratitude of those for whom he was about to die increased the bitterness of these feelings tenfold, and every step, word, or movement demonstrated the agony of her soul. The heart of John was filled with love, and he suffered intensely, but he uttered not a word. He supported the Mother of his beloved Master in this her first pilgrimage through the stations of the Way of the Cross, and assisted her in giving the example of that devotion which has since been practised with so much fervour by the members of the Christian Church.

CHAPTER XIX.

Pilate and his Wife.

Whilst the Jews were leading Jesus to Herod, I saw Pilate go to his wife, Claudia Procles. She hastened to meet him, and they went together into a small garden-house which was on one of the terraces behind the palace. Claudia appeared to be much excited, and under the influence of fear. She was a tall, fine-looking woman, although extremely pale. Her hair was plaited and slightly ornamented, but partly covered by a long veil which fell gracefully over her shoulders. She wore earrings, a necklace, and her flowing dress was drawn together and held up by a species of clasp. She conversed with Pilate for a long time, and entreated him by all that he held sacred not to injure Jesus, that Prophet, that saint of saints; and she related the extraordinary dreams or visions which she had had on the previous night concerning him.

Whilst she was speaking I saw the greatest part of these visions: the following were the most striking. In the first place, the principal events in the life of our Lord—the annunciation, the nativity, the adoration of the shepherds and that of the kings, the prophecy of Simeon and that of Anna, the flight into Egypt, the massacre of the Innocents, and our Lord's temptation in the wilderness. She had likewise been shown in her sleep the most striking features of the public life of Jesus. He always appeared to her environed with a resplendent light, but his malicious and cruel enemies were under the most horrible and disgusting forms imaginable. She saw his intense sufferings, his patience, and his inexhaustible love, likewise the anguish of his Mother, and her perfect resignation. These visions filled the wife of Pilate with the greatest anxiety and terror, particularly as they were accompanied by symbols which made her comprehend their meaning, and her tender feelings were harrowed by the sight of such dreadful scenes. She had suffered from them during the whole of the night; they were sometimes obscure, but more often clear and distinct; and when morning dawned and she was roused by the noise of the tumultuous mob who were dragging Jesus to be judged, she glanced at the procession and instantly saw that the unresisting victim in the midst of the crows, bound, suffering, and so inhumanely treated as to be scarcely recognisable, was no other than that bright and glorious being who had been so often brought before her eyes in the visions of the past night. She was greatly affected by this sight, and immediately sent for Pilate, and gave him an account of all that had happened to her. She spoke with much vehemence and emotion; and although there was a great deal in what she had seen which she could not understand, much less express, yet she entreated and implored her husband in the most touching terms to grant her request.

Pilate was both astonished and troubled by the words of his wife. He compared the narration with all he had previously heard concerning Jesus; and reflected on the hatred of the Jews, the majestic silence of our Saviour, and the mysterious answers he had given to all his questions. He hesitated for some time, but was at last overcome by the entreaties of his wife, and told her that he had already declared his conviction of the innocence of Jesus, and that he would not condemn him, because he saw that the accusations were mere fabrications of his enemies. He spoke of the words of Jesus to himself, promised his wife that nothing should induce him to condemn this just man, and even gave her a ring before they parted as a pledge of his promise.

The character of Pilate was debauched and undecided, but his worst qualities were an extreme pride and meanness which made him never hesitate in the performance of an unjust action, provided it answered his ends. He was excessively superstitious, and when in any difficulty had recourse to charms and spells. He was much puzzled and alarmed about the trial of Jesus; and I saw him running backwards and forwards, offering incense first to one god and then to another, and imploring them to assist him; but Satan filled his imagination with still greater confusion; he first instilled one false idea and then another into his mind. He then had recourse to one of his favourite superstitious practices, that of watching the sacred chickens eat, but in vain,— his mind remained enveloped in darkness, and he became more and more undecided. He first thought that he would acquit our Saviour, whom he well knew to be innocent, but then he feared incurring the wrath of his false gods if he spared him, as he fancied he might be a species of demigod, and obnoxious to them. 'It is possible,' said he inwardly, 'that this man may really be that king of the Jews concerning whose coming there are so many prophecies. It was a king of the Jews whom the Magi came from the East to adore. Perhaps he is a secret enemy both of our gods and of the emperor; it might be most imprudent in me to spare his life. Who knows whether his death would not be a triumph to my gods?' Then he remembered the wonderful dreams described to him by his wife, who had never seen Jesus, and he again changed, and decided that it would be safer not to condemn him. He tried to persuade himself that he wished to pass a just sentence; but he deceived himself, for when he asked himself, 'What is the truth?' he did not wait for the answer. His mind was filled with confusion, and he was quite at a loss how to act, as his sole desire was to entail no risk upon himself.

CHAPTER XX.

Jesus before Herod.

The palace of the Tetrarch Herod was built on the north side of the forum, in the new town; not very far from that of Pilate. An escort of Roman soldiers, mostly from that part of the country which is situated between Switzerland and Italy, had joined the procession. The enemies of Jesus were perfectly furious at the trouble they were compelled to take in going backwards and forwards, and therefore vented their rage upon him. Pilate's messenger had preceded the procession, consequently Herod was expecting them. He was seated on a pile of cushions, heaped together so as to form a species of throne, in a spacious hall, and surrounded by courtiers and warriors. The Chief Priests entered and placed themselves by his side, leaving Jesus at the entrance. Herod was much elated and pleased at Pilate's having thus publicly acknowledged his right of judging the Galileans, and likewise rejoiced at seeing that Jesus who had never deigned to appear before him reduced to such a state of humiliation and degradation. His curiosity had been greatly excited by the high terms in which John the Baptist had announced the coming of Jesus, and he had likewise heard much about him from the Herodians, and through the many spies whom he had sent into different parts: he was therefore delighted at this opportunity of interrogating him in the presence of the courtiers and of the Jewish priests, hoping to make a grand display of this own knowledge and talents. Pilate having sent him word, 'that he could find no cause in the man,' he concluded that these words were intended as a hint that he (Pilate) wished the accusers to be treated with contempt and mistrust. He, therefore, addressed them in the most haughty distant manner possible, and thereby increased their rage and anger indescribably.

They all began at once to vociferate their accusations, to which Herod hardly listened, being intent solely on gratifying his curiosity by a close examination of Jesus, whom he had so often wished to see. But when he beheld him stripped of all clothing save the remnant of a mantel, scarcely able to stand, and his countenance totally disfigured from the blows he had received, and from the mud and missiles which the rabble had flung at his head, the luxurious and effeminate prince turned away in disgust, uttered the name of God, and said to the priests in a tone of mingled pity and contempt, 'Take him hence, and bring him not back into my presence in such a deplorable state.' The guards took Jesus into the outer court, and procured some water in a basin, with which they cleansed his soiled garments and disfigured countenance; but they could not restrain their brutality even while doing this, and paid no regard to the wounds with which he was covered.

Herod meantime accosted the priests in much the same strain as Pilate had done. 'Your behaviour vastly resembles that of butchers,' he said, 'and you commence your immolations pretty early in the morning.' The Chief Priests produced their accusations at once. Herod, when Jesus was again brought into his presence, pretended to feel some compassion, and offered him a glass of wine to recruit his strength; but Jesus turned his head away and refused this alleviation.

Herod then began to expatiate with great volubility on all he had heard concerning our Lord. He asked a thousand questions, and exhorted him to work a miracle in his presence; but Jesus answered not a word, and stood before him with his eyes cast down, which conduct both irritated and disconcerted Herod, although he endeavoured to conceal his anger, and continued his interrogations. He at first expressed surprise, and made use of persuasive words. 'Is it possible, Jesus of Nazareth,' he exclaimed, 'that it is thou thyself that appearest before me as a criminal? I have heard thy actions so much spoken of. Thou art not perhaps aware that thou didst offend me grievously by setting free the prisoners whom I had confined at Thirza, but possibly thy intentions were good. The Roman governor has now sent thee to me to be judged; what answer canst thou give to all these accusations? Thou art silent? I have heard much concerning thy wisdom, and the religion thou teachest, let me hear thee answer and confound thy enemies. Art thou the king of the Jews? Art thou the Son of God? Who art thou? Thou art said to have performed wonderful miracles; work one now in my presence. I have the power to release thee. Is it true that thou hast restored sight to the blind, raised up Lazarus from the dead, and fed two or three thousand persons with a few loaves? Why dost thou not answer? I recommend thee to work a miracle quickly before me; perhaps thou mayest rejoice afterwards at having complied with my wishes.'

Jesus still kept silence, and Herod continued to question him with even more volubility.

'Who art thou?' said he. 'From whence hast thou thy power? How is it that thou dost no longer possess it? Art thou he whose birth was foretold in such a wonderful manner? Kings from the East came to my father to see a newly-born king of the Jews: is it true that thou wast that child? Didst thou escape when so many children were massacred, and how was thy escape managed? Why hast thou been for so many years unknown? Answer my questions! Art thou a king? Thy appearance certainly is not regal. I have been told that thou wast conducted to the Temple in triumph a short time ago. What was the meaning of such an exhibition?—speak out at once!—Answer me!'

Herod continued to question Jesus in this rapid manner; but our Lord did not vouchsafe a reply. I was shown (as indeed I already knew) that Jesus was thus silent because Herod was in a state of excommunication, both on account of his adulterous marriage with Herodias, and of his having given orders for the execution of St. John the Baptist. Annas and Caiphas, seeing how indignant Herod was at the silence of Jesus, immediately endeavoured to take advantage of his feelings of wrath, and recommenced their accusations, saying that he had called Herod himself a fox; that his great aim for many years had been the overthrow of Herod's family; that he was endeavouring to establish a new religion, and had celebrated the Pasch on the previous day. Although Herod was extremely enraged at the conduct of Jesus, he did not lose sight of the political ends which he wished to forward. He was determined not to condemn our Lord, both because he experienced a secret and indefinable sensation of terror in his presence, and because he still felt remorse at the thought of having put John the Baptist to death, besides which he detested the High Priests for not having allowed him to take part in the sacrifices on account of his adulterous connection with Herodias.

But his principal reason for determining not to condemn Jesus was, that he wished to make some return to Pilate for his courtesy, and he thought the best return would be the compliment of showing deference to his decision and agreeing with him in opinion. But he spoke in the most contemptuous manner to Jesus, and turning to the guards and servants who surrounded him, and who were about two hundred in number, said: 'Take away this fool, and pay him that homage which is his due; he is mad, rather than guilty of any crime.'

Our Lord was immediately taken into a large court, where every possible insult and indignity was heaped upon him. This court was between the two wings of the palace, and Herod stood a spectator on a platform for some time. Annas and Caiphas were by his side, endeavouring to persuade him to condemn our Saviour. But their efforts were fruitless, and Herod answered in a tone loud enough to be heard by the Roman soldiers: 'No, I should act quite wrongly if I condemned him.' His meaning was, that it would be wrong to condemn as guilty one whom Pilate had pronounced innocent, although he had been so courteous as to defer the final judgment to him.

When the High Priests and the other enemies of Jesus perceived that Herod was determined no to give in to their wishes, they dispatched emissaries to that division of the city called Acre, which was chiefly inhabited by Pharisees, to let them know that they must assemble in the neighbourhood of Pilate's palace, gather together the rabble, and bribe them to make a tumult, and demand the condemnation of our Lord. They likewise sent forth secret agents to alarm the people by threats of the divine vengeance if they did not insist on the execution of Jesus, whom they termed a sacrilegious blasphemer. These agents were ordered likewise to alarm them by intimating that if Jesus were not put to death, he would go over to the Romans, assist in the extermination of the Jewish nation, for that it was to this he referred when he spoke of his future kingdom. They endeavoured to spread a report in other parts of the city, that Herod had condemned him, but still that it was necessary for the people likewise to express their wishes, as his partisans were to be feared; for that if he were released he would join the Romans, make a disturbance on the festival day, and take the most inhuman revenge. Some among them circulated contradictory and alarming reports, in order to excite the people and cause an insurrection; while others distributed money among the soldiers to bribe them to ill-treat Jesus, so as to cause his death, which they were most anxious should be brought about as quickly as possible, lest Pilate should acquit him.

Whilst the Pharisees were busying themselves in this manner, our Blessed Saviour was suffering the greatest outrages from the brutal soldiers to whom Herod had delivered him, that they might deride him as a fool. They dragged him into the court, and one of their number having procured a large white sack which had once been filled with cotton, they made a hole in its centre with a sword, and then tossed it over the head of Jesus, accompanying each action with bursts of the most contemptuous laughter. Another soldier brought the remnant of an old scarlet cloak, and passed it round his neck, while the rest bent their knee before him—shoved him—abused him—spat upon him—struck him on the check, because he had refused to answer their king, mocked him by pretending to pay homage—threw mud upon him—seized him by the waist, pretending to make him dance; then, having thrown him down, dragged him through a gutter which ran on the side of the court, thus causing his sacred head to strike against the columns and sides of the wall, and when at last they raised him up, it was only in order to recommence their insults. The soldiers and servants of Herod who were assembled in this court amounted to upwards of two hundred, and all thought to pay court to their monarch by torturing Jesus in some unheard-of way. Many were bribed by the enemies of our Lord to strike him on the head with their sticks, and they took advantage of the confusion and tumult to do so. Jesus looked upon them with compassion; excess of pain drew from him occasional moans and groans, but his enemies rejoiced in his sufferings, and mocked his moans, and not one among the whole assembly showed the slightest degree of compassion. I saw blood streaming from his head, and three times did the blows prostrate him, but angels were weeping at his side, and they anointed his head with heavenly balsam. It was revealed to me that had it not been for this miraculous assistance he must have died from those wounds. The Philistines at Gaza, who gave vent to their wrath by tormenting poor blind Samson; were far less barbarous than these cruel executioners of our Lord.

The priests were, however, impatient to return to the Temple; therefore, having made certain that their orders regarding Jesus would be obeyed, they returned to Herod, and endeavoured to persuade him to condemn our Lord. But he, being determined to do all in his power to please Pilate, refused to accede to their wishes, and sent Jesus back again clothed in the fool's garment.

CHAPTER XXI.

Jesus led back from the Court of Herod to that of Pilate.

The enemies of Jesus were perfectly infuriated at being obliged to take Jesus back, still uncondemned, to Pilate, who had so many times declared his innocence. They led him round by a much longer road, in order in the first place to let the persons of that part of the town see him in the state of ignominy to which he was reduced, and in the second place to give their emissaries more time to stir up the populace.

This road was extremely rough and uneven; and the soldiers, encouraged by the Pharisees, scarcely refrained a moment from tormenting Jesus. The long garment with which he was clothed impeded his steps, and caused him to fall heavily more than once; and his cruel guards, as also many among the brutal populace, instead of assisting him in his state of exhaustion, endeavoured by blows and kicks to force him to rise.

To all these outrages Jesus offered not the smallest resistance; he prayed constantly to his Father for grace and strength that he might not sink under them, but accomplish the work of his Passion for our redemption.

It was about eight o'clock when the procession reached the palace of Pilate. The crowd was dense, and the Pharisees might be seen walking to and fro, endeavouring to incite and infuriate them still more. Pilate, who remembered an insurrection which had taken place the year before at the Paschal time, had assembled upwards of a thousand soldiers, whom he posted around the Praetorium, the Forum, and his palace.

The Blessed Virgin, her elder sister Mary (the daughter of Heli), Mari (the daughter of Cleophas), Magdalen, and about twenty of the holy women, were standing in a room from whence they could see all which took place, and at first John was with them.

The Pharisees led Jesus, still clothed in the fool's garment, through the midst of the insolent mob, and had done all in their power to gather together the most vile and wicked of miscreants from among the dregs of the people. A servant sent by Herod had already reached Pilate, with a message to the effect that his master had fully appreciated his polite deference to his opinion, but that he looked upon the far famed Galilean as not better than a fool, that he had treated him as such, and now sent him back. Pilate was quite satisfied at finding that Herod had come to the same conclusion as himself, and therefore returned a polite message. From that hour they became friends, having been enemies many years; in fact, ever since the falling-in of the aqueduct.

[The cause of the quarrel between Pilate and Herod was, according to the account of Sister Emmerich, simply this: Pilate had undertaken to build an aqueduct on the south-east side of the mountain on which the Temple stood, at the edge of the torrent into which the waters of the pool of Bethsaida emptied themselves, and this aqueduct was to carry off the refuse of the Temple. Herod, through the medium of one of his confidants, who was a member of the Sanhedrin, agreed to furnish him with the necessary materials, as also with twenty-eight architects, who were also Herodians. His aim was to set the Jews still more against the Roman governor, by causing the undertaking to fail. He accordingly came to a private understanding with the architects, who agreed to construct the aqueduct in such a manner that it would be certain to fail. When the work was almost finished, and a number of bricklayers from Ophel were busily employed in removing the scaffolding, the twenty-eight builders went on to the top of the Tower of Siloe to contemplate the crash which they knew must take place. Not only did the whole of the building crumble to pieces, fall, and kill ninety-three workmen, but even the tower containing the twenty-eight architects came down, and not one escaped death. This accident occurred a short time previous to the 8th of January, two years after Jesus had commenced preaching; it took place on Herod's birthday, the same day that John the Baptist was beheaded in the Castle of Marcherunt. No Roman officer attended these festivities on account of the affair of the aqueduct, although Pilate had, with hypocritical politeness, been requested to take a part in them. Sister Emmerich saw some of the disciples of Jesus carry the news of this event into Samaria, where he was teaching, on the 8th of January. Jesus went from thence to Hebron, to comfort the family of John; and she saw him, on the 13th of January, cure many among the workmen of Ophel who had been injured by the fall of the aqueduct. We have seen by the relation previously given how little gratitude they showed him. The enmity of Herod towards Pilate was still farther increased by the manner in which the latter revenged himself on the followers of Herod. We will insert here a few details which were communicated at different times to Sister Emmerich. On the 25th of March, of the second year of our Lord's preaching, when Jesus and his disciples were in the neighbourhood of Bethania, they were warned by Lazarus that Judas of Gaulon intended to excite an insurrection against Pilate. On the 28th of March, Pilate issued a proclamation to the effect that he intended to impose a tax, the proceeds of which were partly to cover the expenses he had incurred in raising the building which had just fallen to the ground. This announcement was followed by a sedition headed by Judas of Gaulon, who always stood up for liberty, and who was (unknown to himself) a tool in the hands of the Herodians. The Herodians were rather like our Freemasons. On the 30th of March, at ten o'clock p.m., Jesus, dressed in a dark garment, was teaching in the Temple, with his Apostles and thirty disciples. The revolt of the Galileans against Pilate burst forth on this very day, and the rebels set free fifty of their number who had been imprisoned the day before; and many among the Romans were killed. On the 6th of April, Pilate caused the Galileans to be massacred at the moment of offering sacrifice, by disguised soldiers whom he had concealed in the Temple. Judas was killed with his companions. This massacre exasperated Herod still more against Pilate, and we have just seen by what means their reconciliation was effected.]

Jesus was again led to the house of Pilate. The archers dragged him up the stairs with their usual brutality; his feet became entangled in his long robe, and he fell upon the white marble steps, which were stained with blood from his sacred head. His enemies had again taken their seats at the entrance of the forum; the mob laughed at his fall, and the archers truck their innocent victim, instead of assisting him to rise. Pilate was reclining on a species of easy-chair, with a little table before him, and surrounded with officers and persons who held strips of parchment covered with writing in their hands. He came forward and said to the accusers of Jesus: 'You have presented unto me this man, as one that perverteth the people, and behold I, having examined him before you, find no cause in this man in those things wherein you accuse him. No, nor Herod neither. For I sent you to him, and behold, nothing worthy of death is done to him. I will chastise him, therefore, and release him.'

When the Pharisees heard these words, they became furious, and endeavoured to the utmost of their power to persuade the people to revolt, distributing money among them to effect this purpose. Pilate looked around with contempt, and addressed them in scornful words.

It happened to be the precise time when, according to an ancient custom, the people had the privilege of demanding the deliverance of one prisoner. The Pharisees had dispatched emissaries to persuade the people to demand the death, and not the life, of our Lord. Pilate hoped that they would ask for Jesus, and determined to give them to choose between him and a criminal called Barabbas, who had been convicted of a dreadful murder committed during a sedition, as also of many other crimes, and was, moreover, detested by the people.

There was considerable excitement among the crowd; a certain portion came forward, and their orators, addressing Pilate in a loud voice, said: 'Grant us the favour you have always granted on the festival day.' Pilate made answer: 'It is customary for me to deliver to you a criminal at the Paschal time; whom will you that I release to you, Barabbas, or Jesus that is called Christ?'

Although Pilate did not in his own mind feel at all certain that Jesus was the King of the Jews, yet he called him so, partly because his Roman pride made him take delight in humbling the Jews by calling such a despicable-looking person their king; and partly because he felt a kind of inward belief that Jesus might really be that miraculous king, that Messiah who had been promised. He saw plainly that the priests were incited by envy alone in their accusations against Jesus; this made him most anxious to disappoint them; and the desire was increased by that glimmering of the truth which partly enlightened his mind. There was some hesitation among the crowd when Pilate asked this question, and a few voices answered, 'Barabbas.' A servant sent by Pilate's wife asked for him at this moment; he left the platform, and the messenger presented the pledge which he had given her, saying at the same time: 'Claudia Procles begs you to remember your promise this morning.' The Pharisees and the priests walked anxiously and hastily about among the crowd, threatening some and ordering others, although, in fact, little was required to incite the already infuriated multitude.

Mary, with Magdalen, John, and the holy women, stood in a corner of the forum, trembling and weeping; for although the Mother of Jesus was fully aware that the redemption of man could not be brought about by any other means than the death of her Son, yet she was filled with the anguish of a mother, and with a longing desire to save him from those tortures and from that death which he was about to suffer. She prayed God not to allow such a fearful crime to be perpetrated; she repeated the words of Jesus in the Garden of Olives: 'If it is possible, let this chalice pass away.' She still felt a glimmering of hope, because there was a report current that Pilate wished to acquit Jesus. Groups of persons, mostly inhabitants of Capharnaum, where Jesus had taught, and among whom he had wrought so many miraculous cures, were congregated in her vicinity; they pretended not to remember either her or her weeping companions; they simply cast a glance now and then, as if by chance, at their closely-veiled figures. Many thought, as did her companions likewise, that these persons at least would reject Barabbas, and beg for the life of their Saviour and Benefactor; but these hopes were, alas, fallacious.

Pilate sent back the pledge to his wife, as an assurance of his intention to keep his promise. He again came forward on the platform, and seated himself at the little table. The Chief Priests took their seats likewise, and Pilate once more demanded: 'Which of the two am I to deliver up to you?' A general cry resounded through the hall: 'Not this man, but Barabbas!' 'But what am I to do with Jesus, who is called Christ?' replied Pilate. All exclaimed in a tumultuous manner: 'Let him be crucified! Let him be crucified!' 'But what evil has he done?' asked Pilate for the third time. 'I find no cause in him. I will scourge and then acquit him.' But the cry, 'Crucify him! Crucify him!' burst from the crowd, and the sounds echoed like an infernal tempest; the High Priests and the Pharisees vociferated and hurried backwards and forwards as if insane. Pilate at last yielded; his weak pusillanimous character could not withstand such violent demonstrations; he delivered up Barabbas to the people, and condemned Jesus to be scourged.

CHAPTER XXII.

The Scourging of Jesus.

That most weak and undecided of all judges, Pilate, had several times repeated these dastardly words: 'I find no crime in him: I will chastise him, therefore, and let him go;' to which the Jews had continued to respond, 'Crucify him! Crucify him!' but he determined to adhere to his resolution of not condemning our Lord to death, and ordered him to be scourged according to the manner of the Romans. The guards were therefore ordered to conduct him through the midst of the furious multitude to the forum, which they did with the utmost brutality, at the same time loading him with abuse, and striking him with their staffs. The pillar where criminals were scourged stood to the north of Pilate's palace, near the guard-house, and the executioners soon arrived, carrying whips, rods, and ropes, which they tossed down at its base. They were six in number, dark, swarthy men, somewhat shorter than Jesus; their chests were covered with a piece of leather, or with some dirty stuff; their loins were girded, and their hairy, sinewy arms bare. They were malefactors from the frontiers of Egypt, who had been condemned for their crimes to hard labour, and were employed principally in making canals, and in erecting public buildings, the most criminal being selected to act as executioners in the Praetorium.

These cruel men had many times scourged poor criminals to death at this pillar. They resembled wild beasts or demons, and appeared to be half drunk. They struck our Lord with their fists, and dragged him by the cords with which he was pinioned, although he followed them without offering the least resistance, and, finally, they barbarously knocked him down against the pillar. This pillar, placed in the centre of the court, stood alone, and did not serve to sustain any part of the building; it was not very high, for a tall man could touch the summit by stretching out his arm; there was a large iron ring at the top, and both rings and hooks a little lower down. It is quite impossible to describe the cruelty shown by these ruffians towards Jesus: they tore off the mantle with which he had been clothed in derision at the court of Herod, and almost threw prostrate again.

Jesus trembled and shuddered as he stood before the pillar, and took off his garments as quickly as he could, but his hands were bloody and swollen. The only return he made when his brutal executioners struck and abused him was, to pray for them in the most touching manner: he turned his face once towards his Mother, who was standing overcome with grief; this look quite unnerved her: she fainted, and would have fallen, had not the holy women who were there supported her. Jesus put his arms round the pillar, and when his hands were thus raised, the archers fastened them to the iron ring which was at the top of the pillar; they then dragged his arms to such a height that his feet, which were tightly bound to the base of the pillar, scarcely touched the ground. Thus was the Holy of Holies violently stretched, without a particle of clothing, on a pillar used for the punishment of the greatest criminals; and then did two furious ruffians who were thirsting for his blood begin in the most barbarous manner to scourge his sacred body from head to foot. The whips or scourges which they first made use of appeared to me to be made of a species of flexible white wood, but perhaps they were composed of the sinews of the ox, or of strips of leather.

Our loving Lord, the Son of God, true God and true Man, writhed as a worm under the blows of these barbarians; his mild but deep groans might be heard from afar; they resounded through the air, forming a kind of touching accompaniment to the hissing of the instruments of torture. These groans resembled rather a touching cry of prayer and supplication, than moans of anguish. The clamour of the Pharisees and the people formed another species of accompaniment, which at times as a deafening thunder-storm deadened and smothered these sacred and mournful cries, and in their place might be heard the words, 'Put him to death!' 'Crucify him!' Pilate continued parleying with the people, and when he demanded silence in order to be able to speak, he was obliged to proclaim his wishes to the clamorous assembly by the sound of a trumpet, and at such moments you might again hear the noise of the scourges, the moans of Jesus, the imprecations of the soldiers, and the bleating of the Paschal lambs which were being washed in the Probatica pool, at no great distance from the forum. There was something peculiarly touching in the plaintive bleating of these lambs: they alone appeared to unite their lamentations with the suffering moans of our Lord.

The Jewish mob was gathered together at some distance from the pillar at which the dreadful punishment was taking place, and Roman soldiers were stationed in different parts round about. Many persons were walking to and fro, some in silence, others speaking of Jesus in the most insulting terms possible, and a few appearing touched, and I thought I beheld rays of light issuing from our Lord and entering the hearts of the latter. I saw groups of infamous, bold-looking young men, who were for the most part busying themselves near the watch-house in preparing fresh scourges, while others went to seek branches of thorns. Several of the servants of the High Priests went up to the brutal executioners and gave them money; as also a large jug filled with a strong bright red liquid, which quite inebriated them, and increased their cruelty tenfold towards their innocent Victim. The two ruffians continued to strike our Lord with unremitting violence for a quarter of an hour, and were then succeeded by two others. His body was entirely covered with black, blue, and red marks; the blood was trickling down on the ground, and yet the furious cries which issued from among the assembled Jews showed that their cruelty was far from being satiated.

The night had been extremely cold, and the morning was dark and cloudy; a little hail had fallen, which surprised everyone, but towards twelve o'clock the day became brighter, and the sun shone forth.

The two fresh executioners commenced scourging Jesus with the greatest possible fury; they made use of a different kind of rod,—a species of thorny stick, covered with knots and splinters. The blows from these sticks tore his flesh to pieces; his blood spouted out so as to stain their arms, and he groaned, prayed, and shuddered. At this moment, some strangers mounted on camels passed through the forum; they stopped for a moment, and were quite overcome with pity and horror at the scene before them, upon which some of the bystanders explained the cause of what they witnessed. Some of these travellers had been baptised by John, and others had heard the sermon of Jesus on the mountain. The noise and the tumult of the mob was even more deafening near the house of Pilate.

Two fresh executioners took the places of the last mentioned, who were beginning to flag; their scourges were composed of small chains, or straps covered with iron hooks, which penetrated to the bone, and tore off large pieces of flesh at every blow. What word, alas! could describe this terrible— this heartrending scene!

The cruelty of these barbarians was nevertheless not yet satiated; they untied Jesus, and again fastened him up with his back turned towards the pillar. As he was totally unable to support himself in an upright position, they passed cords round his waist, under his arms, and above his knees, and having bound his hands tightly into the rings which were placed at the upper part of the pillar, they recommenced scourging him with even greater fury than before; and one among them struck him constantly on the face with a new rod. The body of our Lord was perfectly torn to shreds,—it was but one wound. He looked at his torturers with his eyes filled with blood; as if entreating mercy; but their brutality appeared to increase, and his moans each moment became more feeble.

The dreadful scourging had been continued without intermission for three quarters of an hour, when a stranger of lowly birth, a relation to Ctesiphon, the blind man whom Jesus had cured, rushed from amidst the crowd, and approached the pillar with a knife shaped like a cutlass in his hand. 'Cease!' he exclaimed, in an indignant tone; 'Cease! Scourge not this innocent man unto death!' The drunken miscreants, taken by surprise, stopped short, while he quickly severed the cords which bound Jesus to the pillar, and disappeared among the crowd. Jesus fell almost without consciousness on the ground, which was bathed with his blood. The executioners left him there, and rejoined their cruel companions, who were amusing themselves in the guardhouse with drinking, and plaiting the crown of thorns.

Our Lord remained for a short time on the ground, at the foot of the pillar, bathed in his own blood, and two or three bold-looking girls came up to gratify their curiosity away in disgust, but at the moment the pain of the wounds of Jesus was so intense that he raised his bleeding head and looked at them. They retired quickly, and the soldiers and guards laughed and made game of them.

During the time of the scourging of our Lord, I saw weeping angels approach him many times; I likewise heard the prayers he constantly addressed to his Father for the pardon of our sins—prayers which never ceased during the whole time of the infliction of this cruel punishment. Whilst he lay bathed in his blood I saw an angel present to him a vase containing a bright-looking beverage which appeared to reinvigorate him in a certain degree. The archers soon returned, and after giving him some blows with their sticks, bade him rise and follow them. He raised himself with the greatest difficulty, as his trembling limbs could scarcely support the weight of this body; they did not give him sufficient time to put on his clothes, but threw his upper garment over his naked shoulders and led him from the pillar to the guardhouse, where he wiped the blood which trickled down his face with a corner of his garment. When he passed before the benches on which the High Priests were seated, they cried out, 'Put him to death! Crucify him! Crucify him!' and then turned away disdainfully. The executioners led him into the interior of the guardhouse, which was filled with slaves, archers, hodmen, and the very dregs of the people, but there were no soldiers.

The great excitement among the populace alarmed Pilate so much, that he sent to the fortress of Antonia for a reinforcement of Roman soldiers, and posed these well-disciplined troops round the guard-house; they were permitted to talk and to deride Jesus in every possible way, but were forbidden to quit their ranks. These soldiers, whom Pilate had sent for to intimidate the mob, numbered about a thousand.

CHAPTER XXIII.

Mary during the Scourging of our Lord.

I saw the Blessed Virgin in a continual ecstasy during the time of the scourging of her Divine Son; she saw and suffered with inexpressible love and grief all the torments he was enduring. She groaned feebly, and her eyes were red with weeping. A large veil covered her person, and she leant upon Mary of Heli, her eldest sister, who was old and extremely like their mother, Anne.[3] Mary of Cleophas, the daughter of Mary of Heli, was there also. The friends of Jesus and Mary stood around the latter; they wore large veils, appeared overcome with grief and anxiety, an were weeping as if in the momentary expectation of death. The dress of Mary was blue; it was long, and partly covered by a cloak made of white wool, and her veil was of rather a yellow white. Magdalen was totally beside herself from grief, and her hair was floating loosely under her veil.

When Jesus fell down at the foot of the pillar, after the flagellation, I saw Claudia Procles, the wife of Pilate, sent some large pieces of linen to the Mother of God. I know not whether she thought that Jesus would be set free, and that his Mother would then require linen to dress his wounds, or whether this compassionate lady was aware of the use which would be made of her present. At the termination of the scourging, Mary came to herself for a time, and saw her Divine Son all torn and mangled, being led away by the archers after the scouring: he wiped his eyes, which were filled with blood, that he might look at his Mother, and she stretched out her hands towards him, and continued to look at the bloody traces of his footsteps. I soon after saw Mary and Magdalen approach the pillar where Jesus had been scourged; the mob were at a distance, and they were partly concealed by the other holy women, and by a few kind-hearted persons who had joined them; they knelt down on the ground near the pillar, and wiped up the sacred blood with the linen which Claudia Procles had sent. John was not at that time with the holy women, who were about twenty in number. The sons of Simeon and of Obed, and Veronica, as also the two nephews of Joseph of Arimathea—Aram and Themni—were in the Temple, and appeared to be overwhelmed with grief. It was not more than nine o'clock a.m. when the scourging terminated.

---

[3] Mary of Heli is often spoken of in this relation. According to Sister Emmerich, she was the daughter of St. Joachim and St. Anne, and was born nearly twenty years before the Blessed Virgin. She was not the child of promise, and is called Mary of Heli, by which she is distinguished from the other of the same name, because she was the daughter of Joachim, or Heliachim. Her husband bore the name of Cleophas, and her daughter that of Mary of Cleophas. This daughter was, however, older than her aunt, the Blessed Virgin, and had been married first to Alpheus, by whom she had three sons, afterwards the Apostles Simon, James the Less and Thaddeus. She had one son by her second husband, Sabat, and another called Simon, by her third husband, Jonas. Simon was afterwards Bishop of Jerusalem.

CHAPTER XXIV.

Interruption of the Visions of the Passion by the Appearance of St. Joseph under the form of a Child.

During the whole time of the visions which we have just narrated (that is to say, from the 18th of February until the 8th of March), Sister Emmerich continued to suffer all the mental and bodily tortures which were once endured by our Lord. Being totally immersed in these meditations, and, as it were, dead to exterior objects, she wept and groaned like a person in the hands of an executioner, trembled, shuddered, and writhed on her couch, while her face resembled that of a man about to expire under torture, and a bloody sweat often trickled over her chest and shoulders. She generally perspired so profusely that her bed and clothes were saturated. Her sufferings from thirst were likewise fearful, and she might truly be compared to a person perishing in a desert from the want of water. Generally speaking, her mouth was so parched in the morning, and her tongue so contracted and dried up, that she could not speak, but was obliged by signs and inarticulate sounds to beg for relief. Her constant state of fever was probably brought on by the great pains she endured, added to which she likewise often took upon herself the illnesses and temporal calamities merited by others. It was always necessary for her to rest for a time before relating the different scenes of the Passion, nor was it always that she could speak of what she had seen, and she was even often obliged to discontinue her narrations for the day. She was in this state of suffering on Saturday the 8th of March, and with the greatest difficulty and suffering described the scourging of our Lord which she had seen in the vision of the previous night, and which appeared to be present to her mind during the greatest part of the following day. Towards evening, however, a change took place, and there was an interruption in the course of meditations on the Passion which had latterly followed one another so regularly. We will describe this interruption, in order, in the first place, to give our readers a more full comprehension of the interior life of this most extraordinary person; and, in the second, to enable them to pause for a time to rest their minds, as I well know that meditations on the Passion of our Lord exhaust the weak, even when they remember that it was for their salvation that he suffered and died.

The life of Sister Emmerich, both as regarded her spiritual and intellectual existence, invariably harmonised with the spirit of the Church at different seasons of the year. It harmonised even more strongly than man's natural life does with season, or with the hours of the day, and this caused her to be (if we may thus express ourselves) a realisation of the existence and of the various intentions of the Church. Her union with its spirit was so complete, that no sooner did a festival day begin (that is to say, on the eve), than a perfect change took place within her, both intellectually and spiritually. As soon as the spiritual sun of these festival days of the Church was set, she directed all her thoughts towards that which would rise on the following day, and disposed all her prayers, good works, and sufferings for the attainment of the special graces attached to the feast about to commence, like a plant which absorbs the dew, and revels in the warmth and light of the first rays of the sun. These changes did not, as will readily be believed, always take place at the exact moment when the sound of the Angelus announced the commencement of a festival, and summoned the faithful to prayer; for this bell is often, either through ignorance or negligence, rung at the wrong time; but they commenced at the time when the feast really began.

If the Church commemorated a sorrowful mystery, she appeared depressed, faint, and almost powerless; but the instant the celebration of a joyful feast commenced, both body and soul revived to a new life, as if refreshed by the dew of new graces, and she continued in this calm, quiet, and happy state, quite released from every kind of suffering, until the evening. These things took place in her soul quite independently of her will; but as she had had from infancy the most ardent desire of being obedient to Jesus and to his Church, God had bestowed upon her those special graces which give a natural facility for practising obedience. Every faculty of her soul was directed towards the Church, in the same manner as a plant which, even if put into a dark cellar, naturally turns its leaves upwards, and appears to seek the light.

On Saturday, 8th of March 1823, after sunset, Sister Emmerich had, with the greatest difficulty, portrayed the different events of the scourging of our Lord, and the writer of these pages thought that her mind was occupied in the contemplation of the 'crowning with thorns,' when suddenly her countenance, which was preciously pale and haggard, like that of a person on the point of death, became bright and serene and she exclaimed in a coaxing tone, as if speaking to a child, 'O, that dear little boy! Who is he?—Stay, I will ask him. His name is Joseph. He has pushed his way through the crowd to come to me. Poor child, he is laughing: he knows nothing at all of what is going on. How light his clothing is! I fear he must be cold, the air is so sharp this morning. Wait, my child; let me put something more over you.' After saying these words in such a natural tone of voice that it was almost impossible for those present not to turn round and expect to see the child, she held up a dress which was near her, as would be done by a kind-hearted person wishing to clothe a poor frozen child. The friend who was standing by her bedside had not sufficient time to ask her to explain the words she had spoken, for a sudden change took place, both in her whole appearance and manner, when her attendant pronounced the word obedience,—one of the vows by which she had consecrated herself to our Lord. She instantly came to herself, and, like an obedient child awakening from a sound sleep and starting up at the voice of its mother, she stretched forth her hand, took the rosary and crucifix which were always at her side, arranged her dress, rubbed her eyes, and sat up. She was then carried from her bed to a chair, as she could neither stand nor walk; and it being the time for making her bed, her friend left the room in order to write out what he had heard during the day.

On Sunday, the 9th of March, the friend asked her attendant what Sister Emmerich meant the evening before when she spoke of a child called Joseph. The attendant answered, 'She spoke of him again many times yesterday evening; he is the son of a cousin of mine, and a great favourite of hers. I fear that her talking so much about him is a sign that he is going to have an illness, for she said so many times that the poor child was almost without clothing, and that he must be cold.'

The friend remembered having often seen this little Joseph playing on the bed of Sister Emmerich, and he supposed that she was dreaming about him on the previous day. When the friend went to see her later in the day to endeavour to obtain a continuation of the narrations of the Passion, he found her, contrary to his expectation, more calm, and apparently better in health than on the previous day. She told him that she had seen nothing more after the scourging of our Lord; and when he questioned her concerning what she had said about little Joseph, she could not remember having spoken of the child at all. He then asked the reason of her being so calm, serene, and apparently well in health; and she answered, 'I always feel thus when Mid-Lent comes, for then the Church sings with Isaias in the introit at Mass: "Rejoice, O, Jerusalem, and come together all you that love her; rejoice with joy, you that have been in sorrow, that you may exult and be filled from the breasts of your consolation." Mid-Lent Sunday is consequently a day of rejoicing; and you may likewise remember that, in the gospel of this day, the Church relates how our Lord fed five thousand men with five loaves and two fishes, of which twelve baskets of fragments remained, consequently we ought to rejoice.'

She likewise added, that our Lord had deigned to visit her on that day in the Holy Communion, and that she always felt especial spiritual consolation when she received him on that particular day of the year. The friend cast his eyes on the calendar of the diocese of Munster, and saw that on that day they not only kept Mid-Lent Sunday, but likewise the Feast of St. Joseph, the foster-father of our Lord; he was not aware of this before, because in other places the feast of St. Joseph is kept on the 19th, and he remarked this circumstance to Sister Emmerich, and asked her whether she did not think that was the cause of her speaking about Joseph. She answered that she was perfectly aware of its being the feast of the foster-father of Jesus, but that she had not been thinking of the child of that name. However, a moment after, she suddenly remembered what her thoughts had been the day before, and explained to her friend that the moment the feast of St. Joseph began, her vision of the sorrowful mysteries of the Passion ceased, and were superseded by totally different scenes, in which St. Joseph appeared under the form of a child, and that it was to him that the words we have mentioned above were addressed.

We found that when she received these communications the vision was often in the form of a child, especially in those cases when an artist would have made use of that simile to express his ideas. If, for instance, the accomplishment of some Scripture prophecy was being shown to her, she often saw by the side of the illustration a child, who clearly designated the characteristics of such or such a prophet, by his position, his dress, and the manner in which he held in his hand and waved to and fro the prophetic roll appended to a staff.

Sometimes, when she was in extreme suffering, a beautiful child, dressed in green, with a calm and serene countenance, would approach, and seat himself in a posture of resignation at the side of her bed, allowing himself to be moved from one side to the other, or even put down on to the ground, without the smallest opposition and constantly looking at her affectionately and consoling her. If, when quite prostrate from illness and the sufferings of others which she had taken upon herself, she entered into communication with a saint, either by participation in the celebration of his feast, or from his relics being brought to her, she sometimes saw passages of the childhood of martyrdom. In her greatest sufferings she was usually consoled, instructed, or reproved (whichever the occasion called for) by apparitions under the form of children. Sometimes, when totally overcome by trouble and distress, she would fall asleep, and be carried back in imagination to the scenes and perils of her childhood. She sometimes dreamed, as her exclamations and gestures demonstrated, that she was once more a little country girl of five years old, climbing over a hedge, caught in the briars, and weeping with fear.

These scenes of her childhood were always events which had really occurred, and the words which escaped her showed what was passing in her mind. She would exclaim (as if repeating the words of others): 'Why do you call out so?' 'I will not hold the hedge back until you are quiet and ask me gently to do so.' She had obeyed this injunction when she was a child and caught in the hedge, and she followed the same rule when grown up and suffering from the most terrible trials. She often spoke and joked about the thorn hedge, and the patience and prayer which had then been recommended to her, which admonition she, in after-life, had frequently neglected, but which had never failed her when she had recourse to it. This symbolical coincidence of the events of her childhood with those of her riper years shows that, in the individual no less than in humanity at large, prophetic types may be found. But, to the individual as well as to mankind in general, a Divine Type has been given in the person of our Redeemer, in order that both the one and the other, by walking in his footsteps and with his assistance, may surpass human nature and attain to perfect wisdom and grace with God and man. Thus it is that the will of God is done on earth as in heaven, and that this kingdom is attained by 'men of good will.'

She then gave a short account of the visions which had, on the previous night, interrupted her visions of the Passion at the commencement of the feast of St. Joseph.

CHAPTER XXV.

Description of the Personal Appearance of the Blessed Virgin.

While these sad events were taking place I was in Jerusalem, sometimes in one locality and sometimes in another; I was quite overcome, my sufferings were intense, and I felt as if about to expire. During the time of the scourging of my adorable Spouse I sat in the vicinity, in a part which no Jew dared approach, for fear of defiling himself; but I did not fear defilement, I was only anxious for a drop of our Lord's blood to fall upon me, to purify me. I felt so completely heartbroken that I thought I must die as I could not relieve Jesus, and each blow which he received drew from me such sobs and moans that I felt quite astonished at not being driven away. When the executioners took Jesus into the guardhouse, to crown him with thorns, I longed to follow that I might again contemplate him in his sufferings. Then it was that the Mother of Jesus, accompanied by the holy women, approached the pillar and wiped up the blood with which it and the ground around were saturated. The door of the guardhouse was open, and I heard the brutal laughter of the heartless men who were busily employed in finishing off the crown of thorns which they had prepared for our Lord. I was too much affected to weep, but I endeavoured to drag myself near to the place where our Lord was to be crowned with thorns.

I once more saw the Blessed Virgin; her countenance was wan and pale, her eyes red with weeping, but the simple dignity of her demeanour cannot be described. Notwithstanding her grief and anguish, notwithstanding the fatigue which she had endured (for she had been wandering ever since the previous evening through the streets of Jerusalem, and across the Valley of Josaphat), her appearance was placid and modest, and not a fold of her dress out of place. She looked majestically around, and her veil fell gracefully over her shoulders. She moved quietly, and although her heart was a prey to the most bitter grief, her countenance was calm and resigned. Her dress was moistened by the dew which had fallen upon it during the night, and by the tears which she had shed in such abundance; otherwise it was totally unsoiled. Her beauty was great, but indescribable, for it was super-human—a mixture of majesty, sanctity, simplicity, and purity.

The appearance of Mary Magdalen was totally different; she was taller and more robust, the expression of her countenance showed greater determination, but its beauty was almost destroyed by the strong passions which she had so long indulged, and by the violent repentance and grief she had since felt. It was painful to look upon her; she was the very picture of despair, her long dishevelled hair was partly covered by her torn and wet veil, and her appearance was that of one completely absorbed by woe and almost beside herself from sorrow. Many of the inhabitants of Magdalum were standing near, gazing at her with surprise and curiosity, for they had known her in former days, first in prosperity and afterwards in degradation and consequent misery. They pointed, they even cast mud upon her, but she saw nothing, knew nothing, and felt nothing, save her agonising grief.

CHAPTER XXVI.

The Crowning with Thorns.

No sooner did Sister Emmerich recommence the narrative of her visions on the Passion than she again became extremely ill, oppressed with fever, and so tormented by violent thirst that her tongue was perfectly parched and contracted; and on the Monday after Mid-Lent Sunday, she was so exhausted that it was not without great difficulty, and after many intervals of rest, that she narrated all which our Lord suffered in this crowning with thorns. She was scarcely able to speak, because she herself felt every sensation which she described in the following account:

Pilate harangued the populace many times during the time of the scourging of Jesus, but they interrupted him once, and vociferated, 'He shall be executed, even if we die for it.' When Jesus was led into the guardhouse, they all cried out again, 'Crucify him, crucify him!'

After this there was silence for a time. Pilate occupied himself in giving different orders to the soldiers, and the servants of the High Priests brought them some refreshments; after which Pilate, whose superstitious tendencies made him uneasy in mind, went into the inner part of his palace in order to consult his gods, and to offer them incense.

When the Blessed Virgin and the holy women had gathered up the blood of Jesus, with which the pillar and the adjacent parts were saturated, they left the forum and went into a neighbouring small house, the owner of which I do not know. John was not, I think, present at the scourging of Jesus.

A gallery encircled the inner court of the guardhouse where our Lord was crowned with thorns, and the doors were open. The cowardly ruffians, who were eagerly waiting to gratify their cruelty by torturing and insulting our Lord, were about fifty in number, and the greatest part slaves or servants of the jailers and soldiers. The mob gathered round the building, but were soon displaced by a thousand Roman soldiers, who were drawn up in good order and stationed there. Although forbidden to leave their ranks, these soldiers nevertheless did their utmost by laughter and applause to incite the cruel executioners to redouble their insults; and as public applause gives fresh energy to a comedian, so did their words of encouragement increase tenfold the cruelty of these men.

In the middle of the court there stood the fragment of a pillar, and on it was placed a very low stool which these cruel men maliciously covered with sharp flints and bits of broken potsherds. Then they tore off the garments of Jesus, thereby reopening all his wounds; threw over his shoulders an old scarlet mantle which barely reached his knees; dragged him to the seat prepared, and pushed him roughly down upon it, having first placed the crown of thorns upon his head. The crown of thorns was made of three branches plaited together, the greatest part of the thorns being purposely turned inwards so as to pierce our Lord's head. Having first placed these twisted branches on his forehead, they tied them tightly together at the back of his head, and no sooner was this accomplished to their satisfaction than they put a large reed into his hand, doing all with derisive gravity as if they were really crowning him king. They then seized the reed, and struck his head so violently that his eyes were filled with blood; they knelt before him, derided him, spat in his face, and buffeted him, saying at the same time, 'Hail, King of the Jews!' Then they threw down his stool, pulled him up again from the ground on which he had fallen, and reseated him with the greatest possible brutality.

It is quite impossible to describe the cruel outrages which were thought of and perpetrated by these monsters under human form. The sufferings of Jesus from thirst, caused by the fever which his wounds and sufferings had brought on, were intense.[4] He trembled all over, his flesh was torn piecemeal, his tongue contracted, and the only refreshment he received was the blood which trickled from his head on to his parched lips. This shameful scene was protracted a full half-hour, and the Roman soldiers continued during the whole time to applaud and encourage the perpetration of still greater outrages.

---

[4] These meditations on the sufferings of Jesus filled Sister Emmerich with such feelings of compassion that she begged of God to allow her to suffer as he had done. She instantly became feverish and parched with thirst, and, by morning, was speechless from the contraction of her tongue and of her lips. She was in this state when her friend came to her in the morning, and she looked like a victim which had just been sacrificed. Those around succeeded, with some difficulty, in moistening her mouth with a little water, but it was long before she could give any further details concerning her meditations on the Passion.

CHAPTER XXVII.

Ecce Homo.

The cruel executioners then reconducted our Lord to Pilate's palace, with the scarlet cloak still thrown over his shoulders, the crown of thorns on his head, and the reed in his fettered hands. He was perfectly unrecognisable, his eyes, mouth, and beard being covered with blood, his body but one wound, and his back bowed down as that of an aged man, while every limb trembled as he walked. When Pilate saw him standing at the entrance of his tribunal, even he (hart-hearted as he usually was) started, and shuddered with horror and compassion, whilst the barbarous priests and the populace, far from being moved to pity, continued their insults and mockery. When Jesus had ascended the stairs, Pilate came forward, the trumpet was sounded to announce that the governor was about to speak, and he addressed the Chief Priests and the bystanders in the following words: 'Behold, I bring him forth to you, that you may know that I find no cause in him.'

The archers then led Jesus up to Pilate, that the people might again feast their cruel eyes on him, in the state of degradation to which he was reduced. Terrible and heartrending, indeed, was the spectacle he presented, and an exclamation of horror burst from the multitude, followed by a dead silence, when he with difficulty raised his wounded head, crowned as it was with thorns, and cast his exhausted glance on the excited throng. Pilate exclaimed, as he pointed him out to the people; 'Ecce homo! Behold the man!' The hatred of the High Priests and their followers was, if possible, increased at the sight of Jesus, and they cried out, 'Put him to death; crucify him.' 'Are you not content?' said Pilate. 'The punishment he has received is, beyond question, sufficient to deprive him of all desire of making himself king.' But they cried out the more and the multitude joined in the cry, 'Crucify him, crucify him!' Pilate then sounded the trumpet to demand silence, and said: 'Take you him and crucify him, for I find no cause in him.' 'We have a law, and according to that law he ought to die,' replied the priests, 'because he made himself the Son of God.' These words, 'he made himself the Son of God,' revived the fears of Pilate; he took Jesus into another room, and asked him; 'Whence art thou?' But Jesus made no answer. 'Speakest thou not to me?' said Pilate; 'knowest thou not that I have power to crucify thee, and power to release thee?' 'Thou shouldst not have any power against me,' replied Jesus, 'unless it were given thee from above; therefore he that hath delivered me to thee hath the greater sin.'

The undecided, weak conduct of Pilate filled Claudia Procles with anxiety; she again sent him the pledge, to remind him of his promise, but he only returned a vague, superstitious answer, importing that he should leave the decision of the case to the gods. The enemies of Jesus, the High Priests and the Pharisees, having heard of the efforts which were being made by Claudia to save him, caused a report to be spread among the people, that the partisans of our Lord had seduced her, that he would be released, and then join the Romans and bring about the destruction of Jerusalem, and the extermination of the Jews.

Pilate was in such a state of indecision and uncertainty as to be perfectly beside himself; he did not know what step to take next, and again addressed himself to the enemies of Jesus, declaring that 'he found no crime in him,' but they demanded his death still more clamorously. He then remembered the contradictory accusations which had been brought against Jesus, the mysterious dreams of his wife, and the unaccountable impression which the words of Jesus had made on himself, and therefore determined to question him again in order thus to obtain some information which might enlighten him as to the course he ought to pursue; he therefore returned to the Praetorium, went alone into a room, and sent for our Saviour. He glanced at the mangled and bleeding Form before him, and exclaimed inwardly: 'Is it possible that he can be God?' Then he turned to Jesus, and adjured him to tell him if he was God, if he was that king who had been promised to the Jews, where his kingdom was, and to what class of gods he belonged. I can only give the sense of the words of Jesus, but they were solemn and severe. He told him 'that his kingdom was not of this world,' and likewise spoke strongly of the many hidden crimes with which the conscience of Pilate was defiled; warned him of the dreadful fate which would be his if he did not repent; and finally declared that he himself, the Son of Man, would come at the last day, to pronounce a just judgment upon him.

Pilate was half frightened and half angry at the words of Jesus; he returned to the balcony, and again declared that he would release Jesus; but they cried out: 'If thou release this man, thou art not Caesar's friend. For whosoever maketh himself a king speaketh against Caesar.' Others said that they would accuse him to the Emperor of having disturbed their festival; that he must make up his mind at once, because they were obliged to be in the Temple by ten o'clock at night. The cry, 'Crucify him! Crucify him!' resounded on all sides; it re-echoed even from the flat roofs of the houses near the forum, where many persons were assembled. Pilate saw that all his efforts were vain, that he could make no impression on the infuriated mob; their yells and imprecations were deafening, and he began to fear an insurrection. Therefore he took water, and washed his hands before the people, saying, 'I am innocent of the blood of this just man; look you to it.' A frightful and unanimous cry then came from the dense multitude, who were assembled from all parts of Palestine, 'His blood be upon us, and upon our children.'

CHAPTER XXVIII.

Reflections on the Visions.

Whenever, during my meditations on the Passion of our Lord, I imagine I hear that frightful cry of the Jews, 'His blood be upon us, and upon our children,' visions of a wonderful and terrible description display before my eyes at the same moment the effect of that solemn curse. I fancy I see a gloomy sky covered with clouds, of the colour of blood, from which issue fiery swords and darts, lowering over the vociferating multitude; and this curse, which they have entailed upon themselves, appears to me to penetrate even to the very marrow of their bones,—even to the unborn infants. They appear to me encompassed on all sides by darkness; the words they utter take, in my eyes, the form of black flames, which recoil upon them, penetrating the bodies of some, and only playing around others.

The last-mentioned were those who were converted after the death of Jesus, and who were in considerable numbers, for neither Jesus nor Mary ever ceased praying, in the midst of their sufferings, for the salvation of these miserable beings.

When, during visions of this kind, I turn my thoughts to the holy souls of Jesus and Mary, and to those of the enemies of Christ, all that takes place within them is shown me under various forms. I see numerous devils among the crowd, exciting and encouraging the Jews, whispering in their ears, entering their mouths, inciting them still more against Jesus, but nevertheless trembling at the sight of his ineffable love and heavenly patience. Innumerable angels surrounded Jesus, Mary, and the small number of saints who were there. The exterior of these angels denotes the office they fill; some represent consolation, others prayer, or some of the works of mercy.

I likewise often see consolatory, and at other times menacing voices, under the appearance of bright or coloured gleams of light, issuing from the mouths of these different apparitions; and I see the feelings of their souls, their interior sufferings, and in a word, their every thought, under the appearance of dark or bright rays. I then understand everything perfectly, but it is impossible for me to give an explanation to others; besides which, I am so ill, and so totally overcome by the grief which I feel for my own sins and for those of the world, I am so overpowered by the sight of the sufferings of our Lord, that I can hardly imagine how it is possible for me to relate events with the slightest coherency. Many of these things, but more especially the apparitions of devils and of angels, which are related by other persons who have had visions of the Passion of Jesus Christ, are fragments of symbolical interior perceptions of this species, which vary according to the state of the soul of the spectator. Hence the numerous contradictions, because many things are naturally forgotten or omitted.

Sister Emmerich sometimes spoke on these subjects, either during the time of her visions on the Passion, or before they commenced; but she more often refused to speak at all concerning them, for fear of causing confusion in the visions. It is easy to see how difficult it must have been for her, in the midst of such a variety of apparitions, to preserve any degree of connection in her narrations. Who can therefore be surprised at finding some omissions and confusion in her descriptions?

CHAPTER XXIX.

Jesus condemned to be crucified.

Pilate, who did not desire to know the truth, but was solely anxious to get out of the difficulty without harm to himself, became more undecided than ever; his conscience whispered—'Jesus is innocent;' his wife said, 'he is holy;' his superstitious feelings made him fear that Jesus was the enemy of his gods; and his cowardice filled him with dread lest Jesus, if he was a god, should wreak his vengeance upon his judge. He was both irritated and alarmed at the last words of Jesus, and he made another attempt for his release; but the Jews instantly threatened to lay an accusation against him before the Emperor. This menace terrified him, and he determined to accede to their wishes, although firmly convinced in his own mind of the innocence of Jesus, and perfectly conscious that by pronouncing sentence of death upon him he should violate every law of justice, besides breaking the promise he had made to his wife in the morning. Thus did he sacrifice Jesus to the enmity of the Jews, and endeavour to stifle remorse by washing his hands before the people, saying, 'I am innocent of the blood of this just man; look you to it.' Vainly dost thou pronounce these words, O Pilate! for his blood is on thy head likewise; thou canst not wash his blood from thy soul, as thou dost from thy hands.

Those fearful words, 'His blood be upon us and upon our children,' had scarcely ceased to resound, when Pilate commenced his preparations for passing sentence. He called for the dress which he wore on state occasions, put a species of diadem, set in precious stones, on his head, changed his mantle, and caused a staff to be carried before him. He was surrounded with soldiers, preceded by officers belonging to the tribunal, and followed by Scribes, who carried rolls of parchments and books used for inscribing names and dates. One man walked in front, who carried the trumpet. The procession marched in this order from Pilate's palace to the forum, where an elevated seat, used on these particular occasions, was placed opposite to the pillar where Jesus was scourged. This tribunal was called Gabbatha; it was a kind of round terrace, ascended by means of staircases; on the top was a seat for Pilate, and behind this seat a bench for those in minor offices, while a number of soldiers were stationed round the terrace and upon the staircases. Many of the Pharisees had left the palace and were gone to the Temple, so that Annas, Caiphas, and twenty-eight priests alone followed the Roman governor on to the forum, and the two thieves were taken there at the time that Pilate presented our Saviour to the people, saying: 'Ecce homo!'

Our Lord was still clothed in his purple garment, his crown of thorns upon his head, and his hands manacled, when the archers brought him up to the tribunal, and placed him between the two malefactors. As soon as Pilate was seated, he again addressed the enemies of Jesus, in these words, 'Behold your King!' But the cries of 'Crucify him! Crucify him!' resounded on all sides.

'Shall I crucify your King?' said Pilate.

'We have no King but Caesar!' responded the High Priests.

The Dolorous Passion of Our Lord Jesus Christ

Pilate found it was utterly hopeless to say anything more, and therefore commenced his preparations for passing sentence. The two thieves had received their sentence of crucifixion some time before; but the High Priests had obtained a respite for them, in order that our Lord might suffer the additional ignominy of being executed with two criminals of the most infamous description. The crosses of the two thieves were by their sides; that intended fro our Lord was not brought, because he was not as yet sentenced to death.

The Blessed Virgin, who had retired to some distance after the scourging of Jesus, again approached to hear the sentence of death pronounced upon her Son and her God. Jesus stood in the midst of the archers, at the foot of the staircase leading up to the tribunal. The trumpet was sounded to demand silence, and then the cowardly, the base judge, in a tremulous undecided voice, pronounced the sentence of death on the Just Man. The sight of the cowardice and duplicity of this despicable being, who was nevertheless puffed up with pride at his important position, almost overcame me, and the ferocious joy of the executioners—the triumphant countenances of the High Priests, added to the deplorable condition to which our loving Saviour was reduced, and the agonising grief of his beloved Mother—still further increased my pain. I looked up again, and saw the cruel Jews almost devouring their victim with their eyes, the soldiers standing coldly by, and multitudes of horrible demons passing to and fro and mixing in the crowd. I felt that I ought to have been in the place of Jesus, my beloved Spouse, for the sentence would not then have been unjust; but I was so overcome with anguish, and my sufferings were so intense, that I cannot exactly remember all that I did see. However, I will relate all as nearly as I can.

After a long preamble, which was composed principally of the most pompous and exaggerated eulogy of the Emperor Tiberias, Pilate spoke of the accusations which had been brought against Jesus by the High Priests. He said that they had condemned him to death for having disturbed the public peace, and broken their laws by calling himself the Son of God and King of the Jews; and that the people had unanimously demanded that their decree should be carried out. Notwithstanding his oft repeated conviction of the innocence of Jesus, this mean and worthless judge was not ashamed of saying that he likewise considered their decision a just one, and that he should therefore pronounce sentence—which he did in these words: 'I condemn Jesus of Nazareth, the King of the Jews, to be crucified;' and he ordered the executioners to bring the cross. I think I remember likewise that he took a long stick in his hands, broke it, and threw the fragments at the feet of Jesus.

On hearing these words of Pilate the Mother of Jesus became for a few moments totally unconscious, for she was now certain that her beloved Son must die the most ignominious and the most painful of all deaths. John and the holy women carried her away, to prevent the heartless beings who surrounded them from adding crime to crime by jeering at her grief; but no sooner did she revive a little than she begged to be taken again to each spot which had been sanctified by the sufferings of her Son, in order to bedew them with her tears;

and thus did the Mother of our Lord, in the name of the Church, take possession of those holy places.

Pilate then wrote down the sentence, and those who stood behind him copied it out three times. The words which he wrote were quite different from those he had pronounced; I could see plainly that his mind was dreadfully agitated—an angel of wrath appeared to guide his hand. The substance of the written sentence was this: 'I have been compelled, for fear of an insurrection, to yield to the wishes of the High Priests, the Sanhedrin, and the people, who tumultuously demanded the death of Jesus of Nazareth, whom they accused of having disturbed the public peace, and also of having blasphemed and broken their laws. I have given him up to them to be crucified, although their accusations appeared to be groundless. I have done so for fear of their alleging to the Emperor that I encourage insurrections, and cause dissatisfaction among the Jews by denying them the rights of justice.'

He then wrote the inscription for the cross, while his clerks copied out the sentence several times, that these copies might be sent to distant parts of the country.

The High Priests were extremely dissatisfied at the words of the sentence, which they said were not true; and they clamorously surrounded the tribunal to endeavour to persuade him to alter the inscription; and not to put King of the Jews, but that he said, I am the King of the Jews.

Pilate was vexed, and answered impatiently, 'What I have written I have written!' They were likewise anxious that the cross of our Lord should not be higher than those of the two thieves, but it was necessary for it to be so, because there would otherwise not have been sufficient place for Pilate's inscription; they therefore endeavoured to persuade him not to have this obnoxious inscription put up at all. But Pilate was determined, and their words made no impression upon him; the cross was therefore obliged to be lengthened by a fresh bit of wood. Consequently the form of the cross was peculiar—the two arms stood out like the branches of a tree growing from the stem, and the shape was very like that of the letter Y, with the lower part lengthened so as to rise between the arms, which had been put on separately, and were thinner than the body of the cross. A piece of wood was likewise nailed at the bottom of the cross for the feet to rest upon.

During the time that Pilate was pronouncing the iniquitous sentence, I saw his wife, Claudia Procles, send him back the pledge which he had given her, and in the evening she left his palace and joined the friends of our Lord, who concealed her in a subterraneous vault in the house of Lazarus at Jerusalem. Later in the same day, I likewise saw a friend of our Lord engrave the words, Judex injustus, and the name of Claudia Procles, on a greenlooking stone, which was behind the terrace called Gabbatha—this stone is still to be found in the foundations of a church or house at Jerusalem, which stands on the spot formerly called Gabbatha. Claudia Procles became a Christian, followed St. Paul, and became his particular friend.

No sooner had Pilate pronounced sentence than Jesus was given up into the hands of the archers, and the clothes which he had taken off in the court of

Caiphas were brought for him to put on again. I think some charitable persons had washed them, for they looked clean. The ruffians who surrounded Jesus untied his hands for his dress to be changed, and roughly dragged off the scarlet mantle with which they had clothed him in mockery, thereby reopening all his wounds; he put on his own linen under-garment with trembling hands, and they threw his scapular over his shoulders. As the crown of thorns was too large and prevented the seamless robe, which his Mother had made for him, from going over his head, they pulled it off violently, heedless of the pain thus inflicted upon him. His white woollen dress was next thrown over his shoulders, and then his wide belt and cloak. After this, they again tied round his waist a ring covered with sharp iron points, and to it they fastened the cords by which he was led, doing all with their usual brutal cruelty.

The two thieves were standing, one on the right and the other on the left of Jesus, with their hands tied and a chain round their necks; they were covered with black and lived marks, the effects of the scourging of the previous day. The demeanour of the one who was afterwards converted was quiet and peaceable, while that of the other, on the contrary, was rough and insolent, and he joined the archers in abusing and insulting Jesus, who looked upon his two companions with love and compassion, and offered up his sufferings for their salvation. The archers gathered together all the implements necessary for the crucifixions, and prepared everything for the terrible and painful journey to Calvary.

Annas and Caiphas at last left off disputing with Pilate, and angrily retired, taking with them the sheets of parchment on which the sentence was written; they went away in haste, fearing that they should get to the Temple too late for the Paschal sacrifice. Thus did the High Priests, unknowingly to themselves, leave the true Paschal Lamb. They went to a temple made of stone, to immolate and to sacrifice that lamb which was but a symbol, and they left the true Paschal Lamb, who was being led to the Altar of the Cross by the cruel executioners; they were most careful not to contract exterior defilement, while their souls were completely defiled by anger, hatred, and envy. They had said, 'His blood be upon us and upon our children!' And by these words they had performed the ceremony, and had placed the hand of the sacrificer upon the head of the Victim. Thus were the two paths formed—the one leading to the altar belonging to the Jewish law, the other leading to the Altar of Grace: Pilate, that proud and irresolute pagan, that slave of the world, who trembled in the presence of the true God, and yet adored his false gods, took a middle path, and returned to his palace.

The iniquitous sentence was given at about ten in the morning.

CHAPTER XXX.

The Carrying of the Cross.

When Pilate left the tribunal a portion of the soldiers followed him, and were drawn up in files before the palace; a few accompanying the criminals. Eight-and-twenty armed Pharisees came to the forum on horseback, in order to accompany Jesus to the place of execution, and among these were the six enemies of Jesus, who had assisted in arresting him in the Garden of Olives. The archers led Jesus into the middle of the court, the slaves threw down the cross at his feet, and the two arms were forthwith tied on to the centre piece. Jesus knelt down by its side, encircled it with his sacred arms, and kissed it three times, addressing, at the same time, a most touching prayer of thanksgiving to his Heavenly Father for that work of redemption which he had begun. It was the custom among pagans for the priest to embrace a new altar, and Jesus in like manner embraced his cross, that august altar on which the bloody and expiatory sacrifice was about to be offered. The archers soon made him rise, and then kneel down again, and almost without any assistance, place the heavy cross on his right shoulder, supporting its great weight with his right hand. I saw angels come to his assistance, otherwise he would have been unable even to raise it from the ground. Whilst he was on his knees, and still praying, the executioners put the arms of the crosses, which were a little curbed and not as yet fastened to the centre pieces, on the backs of the two thieves, and tied their hands tightly to them. The middle parts of the crosses were carried by slaves, as the transverse pieces were not to be fastened to them until just before the time of execution. The trumpet sounded to announce the departure of Pilate's horsemen, and one of the Pharisees belonging to the escort came up to Jesus, who was still kneeling, and said, 'Rise, we have had a sufficiency of thy fine speeches; rise and set off.' They pulled him roughly up, for he was totally unable to rise without assistance, and he then felt upon his shoulders the weight of that cross which we must carry after him, according to his true and holy command to follow him. Thus began that triumphant march of the King of Kings, a march so ignominious on earth, and so glorious in heaven.

By means of ropes, which the executioners had fastened to the foot of the cross, two archers supported it to prevent its getting entangled in anything, and four other soldiers took hold of the ropes, which they had fastened to Jesus underneath his clothes. The sight of our dear Lord trembling beneath his burden, reminded me forcibly of Isaac, when he carried the wood destined for his own sacrifice up the mountains. The trumpet of Pilate was sounded as the signal for departure, for he himself intended to go to Calvary at the head of a detachment of soldiers, to prevent the possibility of an insurrection. He was on horseback, in armour, surrounded by officers and a body of cavalry, and followed by about three hundred of the infantry, who came from the frontiers of Italy and Switzerland. The procession was headed by a trumpeter, who sounded his trumpet at every corner and proclaimed the sentence. A number of women and children walked behind the procession with ropes, nails, wedges, and baskets filled with different articles, in their hands; others, who were stronger, carried poles, ladders, and the centre pieces of the crosses of the two thieves, and some of the Pharisees followed on horseback. A boy who had charge of the inscription which Pilate had written for the cross, likewise carried the crown of thorns (which had been taken off the head of Jesus) at the end of a long stick, but he did not appear to be wicked and hard-hearted like the rest. Next I beheld our Blessed Saviour and Redeemer—his bare feet swollen and bleeding—his back bent as though he were about to sink under the heavy weight of the cross, and his whole body covered with wounds and blood. He appeared to be half fainting from exhaustion (having had neither refreshment or sleep since the supper of the previous night), weak from loss of blood, and parched with thirst produced by fever and pain. He supported the cross on his right shoulder with his right hand, the left hung almost powerless at his side, but he endeavoured now and then to hold up his long garment to prevent his bleeding feet from getting entangled in it. The four archers who held the cords which were fastened round his waist, walked at some distance from him, the two in front pulled him on, and the two behind dragged him back, so that he could not get on at all without the greatest difficulty. His hands were cut by the cords with which they had been bound; his face bloody and disfigured; his hair and beard saturated with blood; the weight of the cross and of his chains combined to press and make the woollen dress cleave to his wounds, and reopen them: derisive and heartless words alone were addressed to him, but he continued to pray for his persecutors, and his countenance bore an expression of combined love and resignation. Many soldiers under arms walked by the side of the procession, and after Jesus came the two thieves, who were likewise led, the arms of their crosses, separate from the middle, being placed upon their backs, and their hands tied tightly to the two ends. They were clothed in large aprons, with a sort of sleeveless scapular which covered the upper part of their bodies, and they had straw caps upon their heads. The good thief was calm, but the other was, on the contrary furious, and never ceased cursing and swearing. The rear of the procession was brought up by the remainder of the Pharisees on horseback, who rode to and fro to keep order. Pilate and his courtiers were at a certain distance behind; he was in the midst of his officers clad in armour, preceded by a squadron of cavalry, and followed by three hundred foot soldiers; he crossed the forum, and then entered one of the principal streets, for he was marching through the town in order to prevent any insurrection among the people.

Jesus was conducted by a narrow back street, that the procession might not inconvenience the persons who were going to the Temple, and likewise in order that Pilate and his band might have the whole principal street entirely to themselves. The crowd had dispersed and started in different directions almost immediately after the reading of the sentence, and the greatest part of the Jews either returned to their own houses, or to the Temple, to hasten their preparations for sacrificing the Paschal lamb; but a certain number were still hurrying on in disorder to see the melancholy procession pass; the Roman soldiers prevented all persons from joining the procession, therefore the most curious were obliged to go round by back streets, or to quicken their steps so as to reach Calvary before Jesus. The street through which they led Jesus was both narrow and dirty; he suffered much in passing through it, because the archers were close and harassed him. Persons stood on the roofs of the houses, and at the windows, and insulted him with opprobrious language; the slaves who were working in the streets threw filth and mud at him; even the children, incited by his enemies, had filled their pinafores with sharp stones, which they throw down before their doors as he passed, that he might be obliged to walk over them.

CHAPTER XXXI.

The First Fall of Jesus.

The street of which we have just spoken, after turning a little to the left, became rather steep, as also wider, a subterranean aqueduct proceeding from Mount Sion passed under it, and in its vicinity was a hollow which was often filled with water and mud after rain, and a large stone was placed in its centre to enable persons to pass over more easily. When Jesus reached this spot, his strength was perfectly exhausted; he was quite unable to move; and as the archers dragged and pushed him without showing the slightest compassion, he fell quite down against this stone, and the cross fell by his side. The cruel executioners were obliged to stop, they abused and struck him unmercifully, but the whole procession came to a standstill, which caused a degree of confusion. Vainly did he hold out his hand for someone to assist him to rise: 'Ah!' he exclaimed, 'all will soon be over;' and he prayed for his enemies. Lift him up,' said the Pharisees, 'otherwise he will die in our hands.' There were many women and children following the procession; the former wept, and the latter were frightened. Jesus, however, received support from above, and raised his head; but these cruel men, far from endeavouring to alleviate his sufferings, put the crown of thorns again on his head before they pulled him out of the mud, and no sooner was he once more on his feet than they replaced the cross on his back. The crown of thorns which encircled his head increased his pain inexpressibly, and obliged him to bend on one side to give room for the cross, which lay heavily on his shoulders.

CHAPTER XXXII.

The Second Fall of Jesus.

The afflicted Mother of Jesus had left the forum, accompanied by John and some other women, immediately after the unjust sentence was pronounced. She had employed herself in walking to many of the spots sanctified by our Lord and watering them with her tears; but when the sound of the trumpet, the rush of people, and the clang of the horsemen announced that the procession was about to start for Calvary, she could not resist her longing desire to behold her beloved Son once more, and she begged John to take her to some place through which he must pass. John conducted her to a palace, which had an entrance in that street which Jesus traversed after his first fall; it was, I believe, the residence of the high priest Caiphas, whose tribunal was in the division called Sion. John asked and obtained leave from a kind-hearted servant to stand at the entrance mentioned above, with Mary and her companions. The Mother of God was pale, her eyes were red with weeping, and she was closely wrapped in a cloak of a bluish-grey colour. The clamour and insulting speeches of the enraged multitude might be plainly heard; and a herald at that moment proclaimed in a loud voice, that three criminals were about to be crucified. The servant opened the door; the dreadful sounds became more distinct every moment; and Mary threw herself on her knees. After praying fervently, she turned to John and said, 'Shall I remain? Ought I to go away? Shall I have strength to support such a sight?' John made answer, 'If you do not remain to see him pass, you will grieve afterwards.' They remained therefore near the door, with their eyes fixed on the procession, which was still distant, but advancing by slow degrees. When those who were carrying the instruments for the execution approached, and the Mother of Jesus saw their insolent and triumphant looks, she could not control her feelings, but joined her hands as if to implore the help of heaven; upon which one among them said to his companions: 'What woman is that who is uttering such lamentations?' Another answered: 'She is the Mother of the Galilean.' When the cruel men heard this, far from being moved to compassion, they began to make game of the grief of this most afflicted Mother: they pointed at her, and one of them took the nails which were to be used for fastening Jesus to the cross, and presented them to her in an insulting manner; but she turned away, fixed her eyes upon Jesus, who was drawing near, and leant against the pillar for support, lest she should again faint from grief, for her cheeks were as pale as death, and her lips almost blue. The Pharisees on horseback passed by first, followed by the boy who carried the inscription. Then came her beloved Son. He was almost sinking under the heavy weight of his cross, and his head, still crowned with thorns, was drooping in agony on his shoulder. He cast a look of compassion and sorrow upon his Mother, staggered, and fell for the second time upon his hands and knees. Mary was perfectly agonised at this sight; she forgot all else; she saw neither soldiers nor executioners; she saw nothing but her dearly-loved Son; and, springing from the doorway into the midst of the group who were insulting and abusing him, she threw herself on her knees by his side and embraced him. The only words I heard were, 'Beloved Son!' and 'Mother!' but I do not know whether these words were really uttered, or whether they were only in my own mind.

A momentary confusion ensued. John and the holy women endeavoured to raise Mary from the ground, and the archers reproached her, one of them saying, 'What hast thou to do her, woman? He would not have been in our hands if he had been better brought up.'

A few of the soldiers looked touched; and, although they obliged the Blessed Virgin to retire to the doorway, not one laid hands upon her. John and the women surrounded her as she fell half fainting against a stone, which was near the doorway, and upon which the impression of her hands remained. This stone was very hard, and was afterwards removed to the first Catholic church built in Jerusalem, near the Pool of Bethsaida, during the time that St. James the Less was Bishop of that city. The two disciples who were with the Mother of Jesus carried her into the house, and the door was shut. In the mean time the archers had raised Jesus, and obliged him to carry the cross in a different manner. Its arm being unfastened from the centre, and entangled in the ropes with which he was bound, he supported them on his arm, and by this means the weight of the body of the cross was a little taken off, as it dragged more on the ground. I saw numbers of persons standing about in groups, the greatest part amusing themselves by insulting our Lord in different ways, but a few veiled females were weeping.

CHAPTER XXXIII.

Simon of Cyrene. Third Fall of Jesus.

The procession had reached an arch formed in an old wall belonging to the town, opposite to a square, in which three streets terminated, when Jesus stumbled against a large stone which was placed in the middle of the archway, the cross slipped from his shoulder, he fell upon the stone, and was totally unable to rise. Many respectable-looking persons who were on their way to the Temple stopped, and exclaimed compassionately: 'Look at that poor man, he is certainly dying!' but his enemies showed no compassion. This fall caused a fresh delay, as our Lord could not stand up again, and the Pharisees said to the soldiers: 'We shall never get him to the place of execution alive, if you do not find someone to carry his cross.' At this moment Simon of Cyrene, a pagan, happened to pass by, accompanied by his three children. He was a gardener, just returning home after working in a garden near the eastern wall of the city, and carrying a bundle of lopped branches. The soldiers perceiving by his dress that he was a pagan, seized him, and ordered him to assist Jesus in carrying his cross. He refused at first, but was soon compelled to obey, although his children, being frightened, cried and made a great noise, upon which some women quieted and took charge of them. Simon was much annoyed, and expressed the greatest vexation at being obliged to walk with a man in so deplorable a condition of dirt and misery; but Jesus wept, and cast such a mild and heavenly look upon him that he was touched, and instead of continuing to show reluctance, helped him to rise, while the executioners fastened one arm of the cross on his shoulders, and he walked behind our Lord, thus relieving him in a great measure from its weight; and when all was arranged, the procession moved forward. Simon was a stout-looking man, apparently about forty years of age. His children were dressed in tunics made of a variegated material; the two eldest, named Rufus and Alexander, afterwards joined the disciples; the third was much younger, but a few years later went to live with St. Stephen. Simon had not carried the cross after Jesus any length of time before he felt his heart deeply touched by grace.

CHAPTER XXXIV.

The Veil of Veronica.

While the procession was passing through a long street, an incident took place which made a strong impression upon Simon. Numbers of respectable persons were hurrying towards the Temple, of whom many got out of the way when they saw Jesus, from a Pharisaical fear of defilement, while others, on the contrary, stopped and expressed pity for his sufferings. But when the procession had advanced about two hundred steps from the spot where Simon began to assist our Lord in carrying his cross, the door of a beautiful house on the left opened, and a woman of majestic appearance, holding a young girl by the hand, came out, and walked up to the very head of the procession. Seraphia was the name of the brave woman who thus dared to confront the enraged multitude; she was the wife of Sirach, one of the councillors belonging to the Temple, and was afterwards known by the name of Veronica, which name was given from the words vera icon (true portrait), to commemorate her brave conduct on this day.

Seraphia had prepared some excellent aromatic wine, which she piously intended to present to our Lord to refresh him on his dolorous way to Calvary. She had been standing in the street for some time, and at last went back into the house to wait. She was, when I first saw her, enveloped in a long veil, and holding a little girl of nine years of age, whom she had adopted, by the hand; a large veil was likewise hanging on her arm, and the little girl endeavoured to hide the jar of wine when the procession approached. Those who were marching at the head of the procession tried to push her back; but she made her way through the mob, the soldiers, and the archers, reached Jesus, fell on her knees before him, and presented the veil, saying at the same time, 'Permit me to wipe the face of my Lord.' Jesus took the veil in his left hand, wiped his bleeding face, and returned it with thanks. Seraphia kissed it, and put it under her cloak. The girl then timidly offered the wine, but the brutal soldiers would not allow Jesus to drink it. The suddenness of this courageous act of Seraphia had surprised the guards, and caused a momentary although unintentional halt, of which she had taken advantage to present the veil to her Divine Master. Both the Pharisees and the guards were greatly exasperated, not only by the sudden halt, but much more by the public testimony of veneration which was thus paid to Jesus, and they revenged themselves by striking and abusing him, while Seraphia returned in haste to her house.

No sooner did she reach her room than she placed the woollen veil on a table, and fell almost senseless on her knees. A friend who entered the room a short time after, found her thus kneeling, with the child weeping by her side, and saw, to his astonishment, the bloody countenance of our Lord imprinted upon the veil, a perfect likeness, although heartrending and painful to look upon. He roused Seraphia, and pointed to the veil. She again knelt down before it, and exclaimed through her tears, 'Now I shall indeed leave all with a happy heart, for my Lord has given me a remembrance of himself.' The texture of this veil was a species of very fine wool; it was three times the length of its width, and was generally worn on the shoulders. It was customary to present these veil to persons who were in affliction, or overfatigued, or ill, that they might wipe their faces with them, and it was done in order to express sympathy or compassion. Veronica kept this veil until her death, and hung it at the head of her bed; it was then given to the Blessed Virgin, who left it to the Apostles and they afterwards passed it on to the Church.

Seraphis and John the Baptist were cousins, her father and Zacharias being brothers. When Joachim and Anna brought the Blessed Virgin, who was then only four years old, up to Jerusalem, to place her among the virgins in the Temple, they lodged in the house of Zacharias, which was situated near the fish-market. Seraphia was at least five years older than the Blessed Virgin, was present at her marriage with St. Joseph, and was likewise related to the aged Simeon, who prophesied when the Child Jesus was put into his arms. She was brought up with his sons, both of whom, as well as Seraphia, he imbued with his ardent desire of seeing our Lord. When Jesus was twelve years old, and remained teaching in the Temple, Seraphia, who was not then married, sent food for him every day to a little inn, a quarter of a mile from Jerusalem, where he dwelt when he was not in the Temple. Mary wet there for two days, when on her way from Bethlehem to Jerusalem to offer her Child in the Temple. The two old men who kept this inn were Essenians, and well acquainted with the Holy Family; it contained a kind of foundation for the poor, and Jesus and his disciples often went there for a night's lodging.

Seraphia married rather late in life; her husband, Sirach, was descended from the chaste Susannah, and was a member of the Sanhedrin. He was at first greatly opposed to our Lord, and his wife suffered much on account of her attachment to Jesus, and to the holy women, but Joseph of Arimathea and Nicodemus brought him to a better state of feeling, and he allowed Seraphia to follow our Lord. When Jesus was unjustly accused in the court of Caiphas, the husband of Seraphia joined with Joseph and Nicodemus in attempts to obtain the liberation of our Lord, and all three resigned their seats in the Council.

Seraphia was about fifty at the time of the triumphant procession of our Lord when he entered into Jerusalem on Palm Sunday, and I then saw her take off her veil and spread it on the ground for him to walk upon. It was this same veil, which she presented to Jesus, at this his second procession, a procession which outwardly appeared to be far less glorious, but was in fact much more so. This veil obtained for her the name of Veronica, and it is still shown for the veneration of the faithful.

CHAPTER XXXV.

The Fourth and Fifth Falls of Jesus.

The Daughters of Jerusalem.

The procession was still at some distance from the south-west gate, which was large, and attached to the fortifications, and the street was rough and steep; it had first to pass under a vaulted arch, then over a bridge, and finally under a second arch. The wall on the left side of the gate runs first in southerly direction, then deviates a little to the west, and finally runs to the south behind Mount Sion. When the procession was near this gate, the brutal archers shoved Jesus into a stagnant pool, which was close to it; Simon of Cyrene, in his endeavours to avoid the pool, gave the cross a twist, which caused Jesus to fall down for the fourth time in the midst of the dirty mud, and Simon had the greatest difficulty in lifting up the cross again. Jesus then exclaimed in a tone which, although clear, was moving and sad: 'Jerusalem, Jerusalem, how often would I have gathered together thy children as the hen doth gather her chickens under her wings, and thou wouldst not!' When the Pharisees heard these words, they became still more angry, and recommencing their insults and blows endeavoured to force him to get up out of the mud. Their cruelty to Jesus so exasperated Simon of Cyrene that he at last exclaimed, 'If you continue this brutal conduct, I will throw down the cross and carry it no farther. I will do so if you kill me for it.'

A narrow and stony path was visible as soon as the gate was passed, and this path ran in a northerly direction, and led to Calvary. The high road from which it deviates divided shortly after into three branches, one to the south-west, which led to Bethlehem, through the vale of Gihon; a second to the south towards Emmaus and Joppa; a third, likewise to the south-west, wound round Calvary, and terminated at the gate which led to Bethsur. A person standing at the gate through which Jesus was led might easily see the gate of Bethlehem. The officers had fastened an inscription upon a post which stood at the commencement of the road to Calvary, to inform those who passed by that Jesus and the two thieves were condemned to death. A group of women had gathered together near this spot, and were weeping and lamenting; many carried young children in their arms; the greatest part were young maidens and women from Jerusalem, who had preceded the procession, but a few came from Bethlehem, from Hebron, and from other neighbouring places, in order to celebrate the Pasch.

Jesus was on the point of again falling, but Simon, who was behind, perceiving that he could not stand, hastened to support him; he leant upon Simon, and was thus saved from falling to the ground. When the women and children of whom we have spoken above, saw the deplorable condition to which our Lord was reduced, they uttered loud cries, wept, and, according to the Jewish custom, presented him cloths to wipe his face. Jesus turned towards them and said: 'Daughters of Jerusalem, weep not over me, but weep for yourselves and for your children. For behold the days shall come wherein they will say: Blessed are the barren, and the wombs that have not borne, and the papas that have not given suck. Then shall they begin to say to the mountains: Fall upon us, and to the hills: Cover us. For if in the green wood they do these things, what shall be done in the dry?' He then addressed a few words of consolation to hem, which I do not exactly remember.

The procession made a momentary halt. The executioners, who set of first, had reached Calvary with the instruments for the execution, and were followed by a hundred of the Roman soldiers who had started with Pilate; he only accompanied the procession as far as the gateway, and returned to the town.

CHAPTER XXXVI.

Jesus on Mount Golgotha.

Sixth and Seventh Falls of Jesus.

The procession again moved on; the road was very steep and rough between the walls of the town and Calvary, and Jesus had the greatest difficulty in walking with his heavy burden on his shoulders; but his cruel enemies, far from feeling the slightest compassion, or giving the least assistance, continued to urge him on by the infliction of hard blows, and the utterance of dreadful curses. At last they reached a spot where the pathway turned suddenly to the south; here he stumbled and fell for the sixth time. The fall was a dreadful one, but the guards only struck him the harder to force him to get up, and no sooner did he reach Calvary that he sank down again for the seventh time.

Simon of Cyrene was filled with indignation and pity; notwithstanding his fatigue, he wished to remain that he might assist Jesus, but the archers first reviled, and then drove him away, and he soon after joined the body of disciples. The executioners then ordered the workmen and the boys who had carried the instruments of the execution to depart, and the Pharisees soon arrived, for they were on horseback, and had taken the smooth and easy road which ran to the east of Calvary. There was a fine view of the whole town of Jerusalem from the top of Calvary. This top was circular, and about the size of an ordinary ridingschool, surrounded by a low wall, and with five separate entrances. This appeared to be the usual number in those parts, for there were five roads at the baths, at the place where they baptised, at the pool of Bethsaida, and there were likewise many towns with five gates. In this, as in many other peculiarities of the Holy Land, there was a deep prophetic signification; that number five, which so often occurred, was a type of those five sacred wound of our Blessed Saviour, which were to open to us the gates of Heaven.

The horsemen stopped on the west side of the mount, where the declivity was not so steep; for the side up which the criminals were brought was both rough and steep. About a hundred soldiers were stationed on different parts of the mountain, and as space was required, the thieves were not brought to the top, but ordered to halt before they reached it, and to lie on the ground with their arms fastened to their crosses. Soldiers stood around and guarded them, while crowds of persons who did not fear defiling themselves, stood near the platform or on the neighbouring heights; these were mostly of the lower classes—strangers, slaves, and pagans, and a number of them were women.

It wanted about a quarter to twelve when Jesus, loaded with his cross, sank down at the precise spot where he was to be crucified. The barbarous executioners dragged him up by the cords which they had fastened round his waist, and then untied the arms of the cross, and threw them on the ground. The sight of our Blessed Lord at this moment was, indeed, calculated to move the hardest heart to compassion; he stood or rather bent over the cross, being scarcely able to support himself; his heavenly countenance was pale and was as that of a person on the verge of death, although wounds and blood disfigured it to a frightful degree; but the hearts of these cruel men were, alas! harder than iron itself, and far from showing the slightest commiseration, they threw him brutally down, exclaiming in a jeering tone, 'Most powerful king, we are about to prepare thy throne.' Jesus immediately placed himself upon the cross, and they measured him and marked the places for his feet and hands; whilst the Pharisees continued to insult their unresisting Victim. When the measurement was finished, they led him to a cave cut in the rock, which had been used formerly as a cellar, opened the door, and pushed him in so roughly that had it not been for the support of angels, his legs must have been broken by so hard a fall on the rough stone floor. I most distinctly heard his groans of pain, but they closed the door quickly, and placed guards before it, and the archers continued their preparations for the crucifixion. The centre of the platform mentioned above was the most elevated part of Calvary,—it was a round eminence, about two feet high, and persons were obliged to ascend two of three steps to reach its top. The executioners dug the holes for the three crosses at the top of this eminence, and placed those intended for the thieves one on the right and the other on the left of our Lord's; both were lower and more roughly made than his. They then carried the cross of our Saviour to the spot where they intended to crucify him, and placed it in such a position that it would easily fall into the hole prepared for it. They fastened the two arms strongly on to the body of the cross, nailed the board at the bottom which was to support the feet, bored the holes for the nails, and cut different hollows in the wood in the parts which would receive the head and back of our Lord, in order that his body might rest against the cross, instead of being suspended from it. Their aim in this was the prolongation of his tortures, for if the whole weight of this body was allowed to fall upon the hands the holes might be quite torn open, and death ensue more speedily than they desired. The executioners then drove into the ground the pieces of wood which were intended to keep the cross upright, and made a few other similar preparations.

CHAPTER XXXVII.

The Departure of Mary and the holy Women of Calvary.

Although the Blessed Virgin was carried away fainting after the sad meeting with her Son loaded with his cross, yet she soon recovered consciousness; for love, and the ardent desire of seeing him once more, imparted to her a supernatural feeling of strength. Accompanied by her companions she went to the house of Lazarus, which was at the bottom of the town, and where Martha, Magdalen, and many holy women were already assembled. All were sad and depressed, but Magdalen could not restrain her tears and lamentations. They started from this house, about seventeen in number, to make the way of the cross, that is to say, to follow every step Jesus had taken in this most painful journey. Mary counted each footstep, and being interiorly enlightened, pointed out to her companions those places which had been consecrated by peculiar sufferings. Then did the sharp sword predicted by aged Simeon impress for the first time in the heart of Mary that touching devotion which has since been so constantly practised in the Church. Mary imparted it to her companions, and they in their turn left it to future generations,—a most precious gift indeed, bestowed by our Lord on his beloved Mother, and which passed from her heart to the hearts of her children through the revered voice of tradition.

When these holy women reached the house of Veronica they entered it, because Pilate and his officers were at that moment passing through the street, on their way home. They burst forth into unrestrained tears when they beheld the countenance of Jesus imprinted on the veil, and they returned thanks to God for the favour he had bestowed on his faithful servant. They took the jar of aromatic wine which the Jews had prevented Jesus from drinking, and set off together towards Golgotha. Their number was considerably increased, for many pious men and women whom the sufferings of our Lord had filled with pity had joined them, and they ascended the west side of Calvary, as the declivity there was not so great. The Mother of Jesus, accompanied by her niece, Mary (the daughter of Cleophas), John, and Salome went quite up to the round platform; but Martha, Mary of Heli, Veronica, Johanna Chusa, Susanna, and Mary, the mother of Mark, remained below with Magdalen, who could hardly support herself. Lower down on the mountain there was a third group of holy women, and there were a few scattered individuals between the three groups, who carried messages from one to the other. The Pharisees on horseback rode to and fro among the people, and the five entrances were guarded by Roman soldiers. Mary kept her eyes fixed on the fatal spot, and stood as if entranced,—it was indeed a sight calculated to appal and rend the heart of a mother. There lay the terrible cross, the hammers, the ropes, the nails, and alongside of these frightful instruments to torture stood the brutal executioners, half drunk, and almost without clothing, swearing and blaspheming, whilst making their preparations. The sufferings of the Blessed Virgin were greatly increased by her not being able to see her Son; she knew that he was still alive, and she felt the most ardent desire once more to behold him, while the thought of the torments he still had to endure made her heart ready to burst with grief.

A little hail had been falling at times during the morning, but the sun came out again after ten o'clock, and a thick red fog began to obscure it towards twelve.

CHAPTER XXXVIII.

The Nailing of Jesus to the Cross.

The preparations for the crucifixion being finished four archers went to the cave where they had confined our Lord and dragged him out with their usual brutality, while the mob looked on and made use of insulting language, and the Roman soldiers regarded all with indifference, and thought of nothing but maintaining order. When Jesus was again brought forth, the holy women gave a man some money, and begged him to pay the archer anything they might demand if they would allow Jesus to drink the wine which Veronica had prepared; but the cruel executioners, instead of giving it to Jesus, drank it themselves. They had brought two vases with them, one of which contained vinegar and gall, and the other a mixture which looked like wine mixed with myrrh and absinthe; they offered a glass of the latter to our Lord, which he tasted, but would not drink.

There were eighteen archers on the platform; the six who had scourged Jesus, the four who had conducted him to Calvary, the two who held the ropes which supported the cross, and six others who came for the purpose of crucifying him. They were strangers in the pay of either the Jews or the Romans, and were short thick-set men, with most ferocious countenances, rather resembling wild beasts than human beings, and employing themselves alternately in drinking and in making preparations for the crucifixion.

This scene was rendered the more frightful to me by the sight of demons, who were invisible to others, and I saw large bodies of evil spirits under the forms of toads, serpents, sharp-clawed dragons, and venomous insects, urging these wicked men to still greater cruelty, and perfectly darkening the air. They crept into the mouths and into the hearts of the assistants, sat upon their shoulders, filled their minds with wicked images, and incited them to revile and insult our Lord with still greater brutality. Weeping angels, however, stood around Jesus, and the sight of their tears consoled me not a little, and they were accompanied by little angels of glory, whose heads alone I saw. There were likewise angels of pity and angels of consolation among them; the latter frequently approached the Blessed Virgin and the rest of the pious persons who were assembled there, and whispered words of comfort which enabled them to bear up with firmness.

The executioners soon pulled off our Lord's cloak, the belt to which the ropes were fastened, and his own belt, when they found it was impossible to drag the woollen garment which his Mother had woven for him over his head, on account of the crown of thorns; they tore off this most painful crown, thus reopening every wound, and seizing the garment, tore it mercilessly over his bleeding and wounded head. Our dear Lord and Saviour then stood before his cruel enemies, stripped of all save the short scapular which was on his shoulders, and the linen which girded his loins. His scapular was of wool; the wool had stuck to the wounds, and indescribable was the agony of pain he suffered when they pulled it roughly off. He shook like the aspen as he stood before them, for he was so weakened from suffering and loss of blood that he could not support himself for more than a few moments; he was covered with open wounds, and his shoulders and back were torn to the bone by the dreadful scourging he had endured. He was about to fall when the executioners, fearing that he might die, and thus deprive them of the barbarous pleasure of crucifying him, led him to a large stone and placed him roughly down upon it, but no sooner was he seated than they aggravated his sufferings by putting the crown of thorns again upon his head. They then offered him some vinegar and gall, from which, however, he turned away in silence. The executioners did not allow him to rest long, but bade him rise and place himself on the cross that they might nail him to it. Then seizing his right arm they dragged it to the hole prepared for the nail, and having tied it tightly down with a cord, one of them knelt upon his sacred chest, a second held his hand flat, and a third taking a long thick nail, pressed it on the open palm of that adorable hand, which had ever been open to bestow blessings and favours on the ungrateful Jews, and with a great iron hammer drove it through the flesh, and far into the wood of the cross. Our Lord uttered one deep but suppressed groan, and his blood gushed forth and sprinkled the arms of the archers. I counted the blows of the hammer, but my extreme grief made me forget their number. The nails were very large, the heads about the size of a crown piece, and the thickness that of a man's thumb, while the points came through at the back of the cross. The Blessed Virgin stood motionless; from time to time you might distinguish her plaintive moans; she appeared as if almost fainting from grief, and Magdalen was quite beside herself. When the executioners had nailed the right hand of our Lord, they perceived that his left hand did not reach the hole they had bored to receive the nail, therefore they tied ropes to his left arm, and having steadied their feet against the cross, pulled the left hand violently until it reached the place prepared for it. This dreadful process caused our Lord indescribable agony, his breast heaved, and his legs were quite contracted. They again knelt upon him, tied down his arms, and drove the second nail into his left hand; his blood flowed afresh, and his feeble groans were once more heard between the blows of the hammer, but nothing could move the hard-hearted executioners to the slightest pity. The arms of Jesus, thus unnaturally stretched out, no longer covered the arms of the cross, which were sloped; there was a wide space between them and his armpits. Each additional torture and insult inflicted on our Lord caused a fresh pang in the heart of his Blessed Mother; she became white as a corpse, but as the Pharisees endeavoured to increase her pain by insulting words and gestures, the disciples led her to a group of pious women who were standing a little farther off.

The executioners had fastened a piece of wood at the lower part of the cross under where the feet of Jesus would be nailed, that thus the weight of his body might not rest upon the wounds of his hands, as also to prevent the bones of his feet from being broken when nailed to the cross. A hole had been pierced in this wood to receive the nail when driven through his feet, and there was likewise a little hollow place for his heels. These precautions were taken lest his wounds should be torn open by the weight of this body, and death ensue before he had suffered all the tortures which they hoped to see him endure. The whole body of our Lord had been dragged upward, and contracted by the violent manner with which the executioners had stretched out his arms, and his knees were bent up; they therefore flattened and tied them down tightly with cords; but soon perceiving that his feet did not reach the bit of wood which was placed for them to rest upon, they became infuriated. Some of their number proposed making fresh holes for the nails which pierced his hands, as there would be considerable difficulty in removing the bit of wood, but the others would do nothing of the sort, and continued to vociferate, 'He will not stretch himself out, but we will help him;' they accompanied these words with the most fearful oaths and imprecations, and having fastened a rope to his right leg, dragged it violently until it reached the wood, and then tied it down as tightly as possible. The agony which Jesus suffered from this violent tension was indescribable; the words 'My God, my God,' escaped his lips, and the executioners increased his pain by tying his chest and arms to the cross, lest the hands should be torn from the nails. They then fastened his left foot on to his right foot, having first bored a hole through them with a species of piercer, because they could not be placed in such a position as to be nailed together at once. Next they took a very long nail and drove it completely through both feet into the cross below, which operation was more than usually painful, on account of his body being so unnaturally stretched out; I counted at least six and thirty blows of the hammer. During the whole time of the crucifixion our Lord never ceased praying, and repeating those passages in the Psalms which he was then accompanying, although from time to time a feeble moan caused by excess of suffering might be heard. In this manner he had prayed when carrying his cross, and thus he continued to pray until his death. I heard him repeat all these prophecies; I repeated them after him, and I have often since noted the different passages when reading the Psalms, but I now feel so exhausted with grief that I cannot at all connect them.

When the crucifixion of Jesus was finished, the commander of the Roman soldiers ordered Pilate's inscription to be nailed on the top of the cross. The Pharisees were much incensed at this, and their anger was increased by the jeers of the Roman soldiers, who pointed at their crucified king; they therefore hastened back to Jerusalem, determined to use their best endeavours to persuade the governor to allow them to substitute another inscription.

It was about a quarter past twelve when Jesus was crucified, and at the moment the cross was lifted up, the Temple resounded with the blast of trumpets, which were always blown to announce the sacrifice of the Paschal Lamb.

CHAPTER XXXIX.

Raising of the Cross.

When the executioners had finished the crucifixion of our Lord, they tied ropes to the trunk of the cross, and fastened the ends of these ropes round a long beam which was fixed firmly in the ground at a little distance, and by means of these ropes they raised the cross. Some of their number supported it while others shoved its foot towards the hole prepared for its reception—the heavy cross fell into this hole with a frightful shock—Jesus uttered a faint cry, and his wounds were torn open in the most fearful manner, his blood again burst forth, and his half dislocated bones knocked one against the other. The archers pushed the cross to get it thoroughly into the hole, and caused it to vibrate still more by planting five stakes around to support it.

A terrible, but at the same time a touching sight it was to behold the cross raised up in the midst of the vast concourse of persons who were assembled all around; not only insulting soldiers, proud Pharisees, and the brutal Jewish mob were there, but likewise strangers from all parts. The air resounded with acclamations and derisive cries when they beheld it towering on high, and after vibrating for a moment in the air, fall with a heavy crash into the hole cut for it in the rock. But words of love and compassion resounded through the air at the same moment; and need we say that these words, these sounds, were emitted by the most saintly of human beings—Mary—John—the holy women, and all who were pure of heart? They bowed down and adored the 'Word made flesh,' nailed to the cross; they stretched forth their hands as if desirous of giving assistance to the Holy of Holies, whom they beheld nailed to a cross and in the power of his furious enemies. But when the solemn sound of the fall of the cross into the hole prepared for it in the rock was heard, a dead silence ensued, every heart was filled with an indefinable feeling of awe—a feeling never before experienced, and for which no one could account, even to himself; all the inmates of hell shook with terror, and vented their rage by endeavouring to stimulate the enemies of Jesus to still greater fury and brutality; the souls in Limbo were filled with joy and hope, for the sound was to them a harbinger of happiness, the prelude to the appearance of their Deliverer. Thus was the blessed cross of our Lord planted for the first time on the earth; and well might it be compared to the tree of life in Paradise, for the wounds of Jesus were as sacred fountains, from which flowed four rivers destined both to purify the world from the curse of sin, and to give it fertility, so as to produce fruit unto salvation.

The eminence on which the cross was planted was about two feet higher than the surrounding parts; the feet of Jesus were sufficiently near the ground for his friends to be able to reach to kiss them, and his face was turned to the north-west.

CHAPTER XL.

Crucifixion of the Thieves.

During the time of the crucifixion of Jesus, the two thieves were left lying on the ground at some distance off; their arms were fastened to the crosses on which they were to be executed, and a few soldiers stood near on guard. The accusation which had been proved against them was that of having assassinated a Jewish woman who, with her children, was travelling from Jerusalem to Joppa. They were arrested, under the disguise of rich merchants, at a castle in which Pilate resided occasionally, when employed in exercising his troops, and they had been imprisoned for a long time before being brought to trial. The thief placed on the left-hand side was much older than the other; a regular miscreant, who had corrupted the younger. They were commonly called Dismas and Gesmas, and as I forget their real names I shall distinguish them by these terms, calling the good one Dismas, and the wicked one Gesmas. Both the one and the other belonged to a band of robbers who infested the frontiers of Egypt; and it was in a cave inhabited by these robbers that the Holy Family took refuge when flying into Egypt, at the time of the massacre of the Innocents. The poor leprous child, who was instantly cleansed by being dipped in the water which had been used for washing the infant Jesus, was no other than this Dismas, and the charity of his mother, in receiving and granting hospitality to the Holy Family, had been rewarded by the cure of her child; while this outward purification was an emblem of the inward purification which was afterwards accomplished in the soul of Dismas on Mount Calvary, through that Sacred Blood which was then shed on the cross for our redemption. Dismas knew nothing at all about Jesus, but as his heart was not hardened, the sight of the extreme patience of our Lord moved him much. When the executioners had finished putting up the cross of Jesus, they ordered the thieves to rise without delay, and they loosened their fetters in order to crucify them at once, as the sky was becoming very cloudy and bore every appearance of an approaching storm. After giving them some myrrh and vinegar, they stripped off their ragged clothing, tied ropes round their arms, and by the help of small ladders dragged them up to their places on the cross. The executioners then bound the arms of the thieves to the cross, with cords made of the bark of trees, and fastened their wrists, elbows, knees, and feet in like manner, drawing the cords so tight that their joints cracked, and the blood burst out. They uttered piercing cries, and the good thief exclaimed as they were drawing him up, 'This torture is dreadful, but if they had treated us as they treated the poor Galilean, we should have been dead long ago.'

The executioners had divided the garments of Jesus, in order to draw lots for them; his mantle, which was narrow at the top, was very wide at the bottom, and lined over the chest, thus forming a pocket between the lining and the material itself; the lining they pulled out, tore into bands, and divided. They did the same with his long white robe, belt, scapular, and under-garment, which was completely saturated with his Sacred Blood. Not being able to agree as to who was to be the possessor of the seamless robe woven by his Mother, which could not be cut up and divided, they brought out a species of chessboard marked with figures, and were about to decide the point by lots, when a messenger, sent by Nicodemus and Joseph of Arimathea, informed them that there were persons ready to purchase all the clothes of Jesus; they therefore gathered them together and sold them in a bundle. Thus did the Christians get possession of these precious relics.

CHAPTER XLI.

Jesus hanging on the Cross between two Thieves.

The tremendous concussion caused by the fall of the cross into the hole prepared for it drove the sharp points of the crown of thorns, which was still upon the head of our dear Saviour, still deeper into his sacred flesh, and blood ran down again in streams, both from it and from his hands and feet. The archers then placed ladders against the sides of the cross, mounted them and unfastened the ropes with which they had bound our Lord to the cross, previous to lifting it up, fearing that the shock might tear open the wounds in his hands and feet, and that then the nails would no longer support his body. His blood had become, in a certain degree, stagnated by his horizontal position and the pressure of the cords, but when these were withdrawn, it resumed its usual course, and caused such agonising sensations throughout his countless wounds, that he bowed his head, and remained as if dead for more than seven minutes. A pause ensued; the executioners were occupied with the division of his garments; the trumpets in the Temple no longer resounded; and all the actors in this fearful tragedy appeared to be exhausted, some by grief, and others by the efforts they had made to compass their wicked ends, and by the joy which they felt now at having at last succeeded in bringing about the death of him whom they had so long envied. With mixed feelings of fear and compassion I cast my eyes upon Jesus,—Jesus my Redeemer,—the Redeemer of the world. I beheld him motionless, and almost lifeless. I felt as if I myself must expire; my heart was overwhelmed between grief, love, and horror; my mind was half wandering, my hands and feet burning with a feverish heat; each vein, nerve, and limb was racked with inexpressible pain; I saw nothing distinctly, excepting my beloved Spouse hanging on the cross. I contemplated his disfigured countenance, his head encircled with that terrible crown of thorns, which prevented his raising it even for a moment without the most intense suffering, his mouth parched and half open from exhaustion, and his hair and beard clotted with blood. His chest was torn with stripes and wounds, and his elbows, wrists, and shoulders so violently distended as to be almost dislocated; blood constantly trickled down from the gaping wounds in his hands, and the flesh was so torn from his ribs that you might almost count them. His legs and thighs, as also his arms, were stretched out almost to dislocation, the flesh and muscles so completely laid bare that every bone was visible, and his whole body covered with black, green, and reeking wounds. The blood which flowed from his wounds was at first red, but it became by degrees light and watery, and the whole appearance of his body was that of a corpse ready for interment. And yet, notwithstanding the horrible wounds with which he was covered, notwithstanding the state of ignominy to which he was reduced, there still remained that inexpressible look of dignity and goodness which had ever filled all beholders with awe.

The complexion of our Lord was fair, like that of Mary, and slightly tinted with red; but his exposure to the weather during the last three years had tanned him considerably. His chest was wide, but not hairy like that of St. John Baptist; his shoulders broad, and his arms and thighs sinewy; his knees were strong and hardened, as is usually the case with those who have either walked or knelt much, and his legs long, with very strong muscles; his feet were well formed, and his hands beautiful, the fingers being long and tapering, and although not delicate like those of a woman, still not resembling those of a man who had laboured hard. His neck was rather long, with a well-set and finely proportioned head; his forehead large and high; his face oval; his hair, which was far from thick, was of a golden brown colour, parted in the middle and falling over his shoulders; his beard was not any great length, but pointed and divided under the chin. When I contemplated him on the cross, his hair was almost all torn off, and what remained was matted and clotted with blood; his body was one wound, and every limb seemed as if dislocated.

The crosses of the two thieves were placed, the one to the right and the other to the left of Jesus; there was sufficient space left for a horseman to ride between them. Nothing can be imagined more distressing than the appearance of the thieves on their crosses; they suffered terribly, and the one on the left-hand side never ceased cursing and swearing. The cords with which they were tied were very tight, and caused great pain; their countenances were livid, and their eyes enflamed and ready to start from the sockets. The height of the crosses of the two thieves was much less than that of our Lord.

CHAPTER XLII.

First Word of Jesus on the Cross.

As soon as the executioners had crucified the two thieves and divided the garment of Jesus between them, they gathered up their tools, addressed a few more insulting words to our Lord, and went away. The Pharisees, likewise, rode up to Jesus, looked at him scornfully, made use of some opprobrious expression, and then left the place. The Roman soldiers, of whom a hundred had been posted round Calvary, were marched away, and their places filled by fifty others, the command of whom was given to Abenadar, an Arab by birth, who afterwards took the name of Ctesiphon in baptism; and the second in command was Cassius, who, when he became a Christian, was known by the name of Longinus: Pilate frequently made use of him as a messenger. Twelve Pharisees, twelve Sadducees, as many scribes, and a few ancients, accompanied by those Jews who had been endeavouring to persuade Pilate to change the inscription on the Cross of Jesus, then came up: they were furious, as the Roman governor had given them a direct refusal. They rode round the platform, and drove away the Blessed Virgin, whom St. John led to the holy women. When they passed the Cross of Jesus, they shook their heads disdainfully at him, exclaiming at the same time, 'Vah! thou that destroyest the temple of God, and in three days buildest it up again, save thyself, coming down from the Cross. Let Christ, the King of Israel, come down now from the Cross, that we may see and believe.' The soldiers, likewise, made use of deriding language.

The countenance and whole body of Jesus became even more colourless: he appeared to be on the point of fainting, and Gesmas (the wicked thief) exclaimed, 'The demon by whom he is possessed is about to leave him.' A soldier then took a sponge, filled it with vinegar, put it on a reed, and presented it to Jesus, who appeared to drink. 'If thou art the King of the Jews,' said the soldier, 'save thyself, coming down from the Cross.' These things took place during the time that the first band of soldiers was being relieved by that of Abenadar. Jesus raised his head a little, and said, 'Father, forgive them, for they know not what they do.' And Gesmas cried out, 'If thou art the Christ, save thyself and us.' Dismas (the good thief) was silent, but he was deeply moved at the prayer of Jesus for his enemies. When Mary heard the voice of her Son, unable to restrain herself, she rushed forward, followed by John, Salome, and Mary of Cleophas, and approached the Cross, which the kind-hearted centurion did not prevent. The prayers of Jesus obtained for the good thief a moist powerful grace; he suddenly remembered that it was Jesus and Mary who had cured him of leprosy in his childhood, and he exclaimed in a loud and clear voice, 'How can you insult him when he prays for you? He has been silent, and suffered all your outrages with patience; he is truly a Prophet—he is our King—he is the Son of God.' This unexpected reproof from the lips of a miserable malefactor who was dying on a cross caused a tremendous commotion among the spectators; they gathered up stones, and wished to throw them at him; but the centurion Abenadar would not allow it.

The Blessed Virgin was much comforted and strengthened by the prayer of Jesus, and Dismas said to Gesmas, who was still blaspheming Jesus, 'Neither dost thou fear God, seeing thou art under the same condemnation. And we indeed justly, for we receive the due reward of our deeds; but this man hath done no evil. Remember thou art now at the point of death, and repent.' He was enlightened and touched: he confessed his sins to Jesus, and said: 'Lord, if thou condemnest me it will be with justice.' And Jesus replied, 'Thou shalt experience my mercy.' Dismas, filled with the most perfect contrition, began instantly to thank God for the great graces he had received, and to reflect over the manifold sins of his past life. All these events took place between twelve and the half-hour shortly after the crucifixion; but such a surprising change had taken place in the appearance of nature during that time as to astonish the beholders and fill their minds with awe and terror.

CHAPTER XLIII.

Eclipse of the Sun.

Second and Third Word of Jesus on the Cross.

A little hail had fallen at about ten o'clock,—when Pilate was passing sentence,—and after that the weather cleared up, until towards twelve, when the thick red-looking fog began to obscure the sun. Towards the sixth hour, according to the manner of counting of the Jews, the sun was suddenly darkened. I was shown the exact cause of this wonderful phenomenon; but I have unfortunately partly forgotten it, and what I have not forgotten I cannot find words to express; but I was lifted up from the earth, and beheld the stars and the planets moving about out of their proper spheres. I saw the moon like an immense ball of fire rolling along as if flying from the earth. I was then suddenly taken back to Jerusalem, and I beheld the moon reappear behind the Mountain of Olives, looking pale and full, and advancing rapidly towards the sun, which was dim and over-shrouded by a fog. I saw to the east of the sun a large dark body which had the appearance of a mountain, and which soon entirely hid the sun. The centre of this body was dark yellow, and a red circle like a ring of fire was round it. The sky grew darker and the stars appeared to cast a red and lurid light. Both men and beasts were struck with terror; the enemies of Jesus ceased reviling him, while the Pharisees endeavoured to give philosophical reasons for what was taking place, but they failed in their attempt, and were reduced to silence. Many were seized with remorse, struck their breasts, and cried out, 'May his blood fall upon his murderers!' Numbers of others, whether near the Cross or at a distance, fell on their knees and entreated forgiveness of Jesus, who turned his eyes compassionately upon them in the midst of his sufferings. However, the darkness continued to increase, and everyone excepting Mary and the most faithful among the friends of Jesus left the Cross. Dismas then raised his head, and in a tone of humility and hope said to Jesus, 'Lord, remember me when thou shalt come into thy kingdom.' And Jesus made answer, 'Amen, I say to thee, This day thou shalt be with me in Paradise.' Magdalen, Mary of Cleophas, and John stood near the Cross of our Lord and looked at him, while the Blessed Virgin, filled with intense feelings of motherly love, entreated her Son to permit her to die with him; but he, casting a look of ineffable tenderness upon her, turned to John and said, 'Woman, behold thy son;' then he said to John, 'Behold thy mother.' John looked at his dying Redeemer, and saluted this beloved mother (whom he henceforth considered as his own) in the most respectful manner. The Blessed Virgin was so overcome by grief at these words of Jesus that she almost fainted, and was carried to a short distance from the Cross by the holy women.

I do not know whether Jesus really pronounced these words, but I felt interiorly that he gave Mary to John as a mother, and John to Mary as a son. In similar visions a person is often conscious of things which are not written, and words can only express a portion of them, although to the individual to whom they are shown they are so clear as not to require explanation. For this reason it did not appear to me in the least surprising that Jesus should call the Blessed Virgin 'Woman,' instead of 'Mother.' I felt that he intended to demonstrate that she was that woman spoken of in Scripture who was to crush the head of the serpent, and that then was the moment in which that promise was accomplished in the death of her Son. I knew that Jesus, by giving her as a mother to John, gave her also as a mother to all who believe in him, who become children of God, and are not born of flesh and blood, or of the will of man, but of God. Neither did it appear to me surprising that the most pure, the most humble, and the most obedient among women, who, when saluted by the angel as 'full of grace,' immediately replied, 'Behold the handmaid of the Lord, be it done to me according to thy word,' and in whose sacred womb the Word was instantly made flesh,—that she, when informed by her dying Son that she was to become the spiritual mother of another son, should repeat the same words with humble obedience, and immediately adopt as her children all the children of God, the brothers of Jesus Christ. These things are much easier to feel by the grace of God than to be expressed in words. I remember my celestial Spouse once saying to me, 'Everything is imprinted in the hearts of those children of the Church who believe, hope, and love.'

CHAPTER XLIV.

The Fear felt by the Inhabitants of Jerusalem.

Fourth Word of Jesus on the Cross.

It was about half-past one o'clock when I was taken into Jerusalem to see what was going on there. The inhabitants were perfectly overcome with terror and anxiety; the streets dark and gloomy, and some persons were feeling their way about, while others, seated on the ground with their heads veiled, struck their breasts, or went up to the roofs of their houses, looked at the sky, and burst forth in bitter lamentations. Even the animals uttered mournful cries, and hid themselves; the birds flew low, and fell to the ground. I saw Pilate conferring with Herod on the alarming state of things: they were both extremely agitated, and contemplated the appearance of the sky from that terrace upon which Herod was standing when he delivered up Jesus to be insulted by the infuriated rabble. 'These events are not in the common course of nature,' they both exclaimed: 'they must be caused by the anger of the gods, who are displeased at the cruelty which has been exercised towards Jesus of Nazareth.' Pilate and Herod, surrounded by guards, then directed their hasty trembling steps through the forum to Herod's palace. Pilate turned away his head when he passed Gabbatha, from whence he had condemned Jesus to be crucified. The square was almost empty; a few persons might be seen re-entering their houses as quickly as possible, and a few others running about and weeping, while two or three small groups might be distinguished in the distance. Pilate sent for some of the ancients and asked them what they thought the astounding darkness could possible portend, and said that he himself considered it a terrific proof of the anger of their God at the crucifixion of the Galilean, who was most certainly their prophet and their king: he added that he had nothing to reproach himself with on that head, for he had washed his hands of the whole affair, and was, therefore, quite innocent. The ancients were as hardened as ever, and replied, in a sullen tone, that there was nothing unnatural in the course of events, that they might be easily accounted for by philosophers, and that they did not repent of anything they had done. However, many persons were converted, and among others those soldiers who fell to the ground at the words of our Lord when they were sent to arrest him in the Garden of Olives.

The rabble assembled before Pilate's house, and instead of the cry of 'Crucify him, crucify him!' which had resounded in the morning, you might have heard vociferations of 'Down with the iniquitous judge!' 'May the blood of the just man fall upon his murderers!' Pilate was much alarmed; he sent for additional guards, and endeavoured to cast all the blame upon the Jews. He again declared that the crime was not his; that he was no subject of this Jesus, whom they had put to death unjustly, and who was their king, their prophet, their Holy One; that they alone were guilty, as it must be evident to all that he condemned Jesus solely from compulsion.

The Dolorous Passion of Our Lord Jesus Christ

The Temple was thronged with Jews, who were intent on the immolation of the Paschal lamb; but when the darkness increased to such a degree that it was impossible to distinguish the countenance of one from that of the other, they were seized with fear, horror, and dread, which they expressed by mournful cries and lamentations. The High Priests endeavoured to maintain order and quiet. All the lamps were lighted; but the confusion became greater every moment, and Annas appeared perfectly paralysed with terror. I saw him endeavouring to hide first in one place, and then in another. When I left the Temple, and walked through the streets, I remarked that, although not a breath of wind was stirring, yet both the doors and windows of the houses were shaking as if in a storm, and the darkness was becoming every moment more dense.

The consternation produced by the sudden darkness at Mount Calvary was indescribable. When it first commenced, the confusion of the noise of the hammers, the vociferations of the rabble, the cries of the two thieves on being fastened to their crosses, the insulting speeches of the Pharisees, the evolutions of the soldiers, and the drunken shouts of the executioners, had so completely engrossed the attention of everyone, that the change which was gradually coming over the face of nature was not remarked; but as the darkness increased, every sound ceased, each voice was hushed, and remorse and terror took possession of every heart, while the bystanders retired one by one to a distance from the Cross. Then it was that Jesus gave his Mother to St. John, and that she, overcome by grief, was carried away to a short distance. As the darkness continued to grow more and more dense, the silence became perfectly astounding; everyone appeared terror struck; some looked at the sky, while others, filled with remorse, turned towards the Cross, smote their breasts, and were converted. Although the Pharisees were in reality quite as much alarmed as other persons, yet they endeavoured at first to put a bold face on the matter, and declared that they could see nothing unaccountable in these events; but at last even they lost assurance, and were reduced to silence. The disc of the sun was of a dark-yellow tint, rather resembling a mountain when viewed by moonlight, and it was surrounded by a bright fiery ring; the stars appeared, but the light they cast was red and lurid; the birds were so terrified as to drop to the ground; the beasts trembled and moaned; the horses and the asses of the Pharisees crept as close as possible to one another, and put their heads between their legs. The thick fog penetrated everything.

Stillness reigned around the Cross. Jesus hung upon it alone; forsaken by all,—disciples, followers, friends, his Mother even was removed from his side; not one person of the thousands upon whom he had lavished benefits was near to offer him the slightest alleviation in his bitter agony,—his soul was overspread with an indescribable feeling of bitterness and grief,—all within him was dark, gloomy, and wretched. The darkness which reigned around was but symbolical of that which overspread his interior; he turned, nevertheless, to his Heavenly Father, he prayed for his enemies, he offered the chalice of his sufferings for their redemption, he continued to pray as he had done during the whole of his Passion, and repeated portions of those Psalms the prophecies of which were then receiving their accomplishment in him. I saw angels standing around. Again I looked at Jesus—my beloved Spouse—on his Cross, agonising and dying, yet still in dreary solitude. He at that moment endured anguish which no mortal pen can describe,—he felt that suffering which would overwhelm a poor weak mortal if deprived at once of all consolation, both divine and human, and then compelled, without refreshment, assistance, or light, to traverse the stormy desert of tribulation upheld by faith, hope, and charity alone.

His sufferings were inexpressible; but it was by them that he merited for us the grace necessary to resist those temptations to despair which will assail us at the hour of death,—that tremendous hour when we shall feel that we are about to leave all that is dear to us here below. When our minds, weakened by disease, have lost the power of reasoning, and even our hopes of mercy and forgiveness are become, as it were, enveloped in mist and uncertainty,—then it is that we must fly to Jesus, unite our feelings of desolation with that indescribable dereliction which he endured upon the Cross, and be certain of obtaining a glorious victory over our infernal enemies. Jesus then offered to his Eternal Father his poverty, his dereliction, his labours, and, above all, the bitter sufferings which our ingratitude had caused him to endure in expiation for our sins and weakness; no one, therefore, who is united to Jesus in the bosom of his Church must despair at the awful moment preceding his exit from this life, even if he be deprived of all sensible light and comfort; for he must then remember that the Christian is no longer obliged to enter this dark desert alone and unprotected, as Jesus has cast his own interior and exterior dereliction on the Cross into this gulf of desolation, consequently he will not be left to cope alone with death, or be suffered to leave this world in desolation of spirit, deprived of heavenly consolation. All fear of loneliness and despair in death must therefore be cast away; for Jesus, who is our true light, the Way, the Truth, and the Life, has preceded us on that dreary road, has overspread it with blessings, and raised his Cross upon it, one glance at which will calm our every fear. Jesus then (if we may so express ourselves) made his last testament in the presence of his Father, and bequeathed the merits of his Death and Passion to the Church and to sinners. Not one erring soul was forgotten; he thought of each and everyone; praying, likewise, even for those heretics who have endeavoured to prove that, being God, he did not suffer as a man would have suffered in his place. The cry which he allowed to pass his lips in the height of his agony was intended not only to show the excess of the sufferings he was then enduring, but likewise to encourage all afflicted souls who acknowledge God as their Father to lay their sorrows with filial confidence at his feet. It was towards three o'clock when he cried out in a loud voice, 'Eloi, Eloi, lamma sabacthani?' 'My God, my God, why hast thou forsaken me?' These words of our Lord interrupted the dead silence which had continued so long; the Pharisees turned towards him, and one of them said, 'Behold, he calleth Elias;' and another, 'Let us see whether Elias will come to deliver him.' When Mary heard the voice of her divine Son, she was unable to restrain herself any longer, but rushed forwards, and returned to the foot of the Cross, followed by John, Mary the daughter of Cleophas, Mary Magdalen, and Salome. A troop of about thirty horsemen from Judea and the environs of Joppa, who were on their way to Jerusalem for the festival, passed by just at the time when all was silent round the Cross, both assistants and spectators being transfixed with terror and apprehensions. When they beheld Jesus hanging on the Cross, saw the cruelty with which he had been treated, and remarked the extraordinary signs of God's wrath which overspread the face of nature, they were filled with horror, and exclaimed, 'If the Temple of God were not in Jerusalem, the city should be burned to the ground for having taken upon itself so fearful a crime.' These words from the lips of strangers—strangers too who bore the appearance of persons of rank—made a great impression on the bystanders, and loud murmurs and exclamations of grief were heard on all sides; some individuals gathered together in groups, more freely to indulge their sorrow, although a certain portion of the crowd continued to blaspheme and revile all around them. The Pharisees were compelled to assume a more humble tone, for they feared great existing excitement among the inhabitants of Jerusalem. They therefore held a consultation with Abenadar, the centurion, and agreed with him that the gate of the city, which was in the vicinity, should be closed, in order to prevent farther communication, and that they should send to Pilate and Herod for 500 men to guard against the chance of an insurrection, the centurion, in the mean time, doing all in his power to maintain order, and preventing the Pharisees from insulting Jesus, lest it should exasperate the people still more.

Shortly after three o'clock the light reappeared in a degree, the moon began to pass away from the disc of the sun, while the sun again shone forth, although its appearance was dim, being surrounded by a species of red mist; by degrees it became more bright, and the stars vanished, but the sky was still gloomy. The enemies of Jesus soon recovered their arrogant spirit when they saw the light returning; and it was then that they exclaimed, 'Behold, he calleth Elias.'

CHAPTER XLV.

Fifth, Sixth, and Seventh Words of Jesus on the Cross.

His Death.

The light continued to return by degrees, and the livid exhausted countenance of our Lord again became visible. His body was become much more white from the quantity of blood he had lost; and I heard him exclaim, 'I am pressed as the grape, which is trodden in the winepress. My blood shall be poured out until water cometh, but wine shall here be made no more.' I cannot be sure whether he really pronounced these words, so as to be heard by others, or whether they were only an answer given to my interior prayer. I afterwards had a vision relating to these words, and in it I saw Japhet making wine in this place.

Jesus was almost fainting; his tongue was parched, and he said: 'I thirst.' The disciples who were standing round the Cross looked at him with the deepest expression of sorrow, and he added, 'Could you not have given me a little water?' By these words he gave them to understand that no one would have prevented them from doing so during the darkness. John was filled with remorse, and replied: 'We did not think of doing so, O Lord.' Jesus pronounced a few more words, the import of which was: 'My friends and my neighbours were also to forget me, and not give me to drink, that so what was written concerning me might be fulfilled.' This omission had afflicted him very much. The disciples then offered money to the soldiers to obtain permission to give him a little water: they refused to give it, but dipped a sponge in vinegar and gall, and were about to offer it to Jesus, when the centurion Abenadar, whose heart was touched with compassion, took it from them, squeezed out the gal, poured some fresh vinegar upon it, and fastening it to a reed, put the reed at the end of a lance, and presented it for Jesus to drink. I heard our Lord say several other things, but I only remember these words: 'When my voice shall be silent, the mouths of the dead shall be opened.' Some of the bystanders cried out: 'He blasphemeth again.' But Abenadar compelled them to be silent.

The hour of our Lord was at last come; his death-struggle had commenced; a cold sweat overspread every limb. John stood at the foot of the Cross, and wiped the feet of Jesus with his scapular. Magdalen was crouched to the ground in a perfect frenzy of grief behind the Cross. The Blessed Virgin stood between Jesus and the good thief, supported by Salome and Mary of Cleophas, with her eyes rivetted on the countenance of her dying Son. Jesus then said: 'It is consummated;' and, raising his head, cried out in a loud voice, 'Father, into thy hands I commend my spirit.' These words, which he uttered in a clear and thrilling tone, resounded through heaven and earth; and a moment after, he bowed down his head and gave up the ghost. I saw his soul, under the appearance of a bright meteor, penetrate the earth at the foot of the Cross. John and the holy women fell prostrate on the ground. The centurion Abenadar had kept his eyes steadfastly fixed on the disfigured countenance of our Lord, and was perfectly overwhelmed by all that had taken place. When our Lord pronounced his last words, before expiring, in a loud tone, the earth trembled, and the rock of Calvary burst asunder, forming a deep chasm between the Cross of our Lord and that of Gesmas. The voice of God—that solemn and terrible voice—had re-echoed through the whole universe; it had broken the solemn silence which then pervaded all nature. All was accomplished. The soul of our Lord had left his body: his last cry had filled every breast with terror. The convulsed earth had paid homage to its Creator: the sword of grief had pierced the hearts of those who loved him. This moment was the moment of grace for Abenadar: his horse trembled under him; his heart was touched; it was rent like the hard rock; he threw his lance to a distance, struck his breast, and cried out: 'Blessed be the Most High God, the God of Abraham, of Isaac, and of Jacob; indeed this Man was the Son of God!' His words convinced many among the soldiers, who followed his example, and were likewise converted.

Abenadar became from this moment a new man; he adored the true God, and would no longer serve his enemies. He gave both his horse and his lance to a subaltern of the name of Longinus, who, having addressed a few words to the soldiers, mounted his horse, and took the command upon himself. Abenadar then left Calvary, and went through the Valley of Gihon to the caves in the Valley of Hinnom, where the disciples were hidden, announced the death of our Lord to them, and then went to the town, in order to see Pilate. No sooner had Abenadar rendered public testimony of his belief in the divinity of Jesus, than a large number of soldiers followed his example, as did also some of the bystanders, and even a few Pharisees. Many struck their breasts, wept, and returned home, while others rent their garments, and cast dust on their heads, and all were filled with horror and fear. John arose; and some of the holy women who were at a short distance came up to the Blessed Virgin, and led her away from the foot of the Cross.

When Jesus, the Lord of life and death, gave up his soul into the hands of his Father, and allowed death to take possession of his body, this sacred body trembled and turned lividly white; the countless wounds which were covered with congealed blood appeared like dark marks; his cheeks became more sunken, his nose more pointed, and his eyes, which were obscured with blood, remained but half open. He raised his weary head, which was still crowned with thorns, for a moment, and then dropped it again in agony of pain; while his parched and torn lips, only partially closed, showed his bloody and swollen tongue. At the moment of death his hands, which were at one time contracted round the nails, opened and returned to their natural size, as did also his arms; his body became stiff, and the whole weight was thrown upon the feet, his knees bent, and his feet twisted a little on one side.

What words can, alas, express the deep grief of the Blessed Virgin? Her eyes closed, a death-like tint overspread her countenance; unable to stand, she fell to the ground, but was soon lifted up, and supported by John, Magdalen, and the others. She looked once more upon her beloved Son—that Son whom she had conceived by the Holy Ghost, the flesh of her flesh, the bone of her bone, the heart of her heart—hanging on a cross between two thieves;

crucified, dishonoured, contemned by those whom he came on earth to save; and well might she at this moment be termed 'the queen of martyrs.'

The sun still looked dim and suffused with mist; and during the time of the earthquake the air was close and oppressive, but by degrees it became more clear and fresh.

It was about three o'clock when Jesus expired. The Pharisees were at first much alarmed at the earthquake; but when the first shock was over they recovered themselves, began to throw stones into the chasm, and tried to measure its depth with ropes. Finding, however, that they could not fathom its bottom, they became thoughtful, listened anxiously to the groans of the penitents, who were lamenting and striking their breasts, and then left Calvary. Many among the spectators were really converted, and the greatest part returned to Jerusalem perfectly overcome with fear. Roman soldiers were placed at the gates, and in other principal parts of the city, to prevent the possibility of an insurrection. Cassius remained on Calvary with about fifty soldiers. The friends of Jesus stood round the Cross, contemplated our Lord, and wept; many among the holy women had returned to their homes, and all were silent and overcome with grief.

CHAPTER XLVI.

The Earthquake.

Apparitions of the Dead in Jerusalem.

I saw the soul of Jesus, at the moment he expired, appear under the form of a bright orb, and accompanied by angels, among whom I distinguished the angel Gabriel penetrate the earth at the foot of the Cross. I likewise saw these angels cast a number of evil spirits into the great abyss, and I heard Jesus order several of the souls in Limbo to re-enter the bodies in which they once dwelt, in order that the sight might fill sinners with a salutary terror, and that these souls might render a solemn testimony to his divinity.

The earthquake which produced the deep chasm at Calvary did much damage in different parts of Palestine, but ifs effects were even more fatal in Jerusalem. Its inhabitants were just beginning to be a little reassured by the return of light, when their terror was reawakened with double force by the shocks of the earthquake, and the terrible noise and confusion caused by the downfall of houses and walls on all sides, which panic was still farther increased by the sudden appearance of dead persons, confronting the trembling miscreants who were flying to hide themselves, and addressing them in the most severe and reproachful language.

The High Priests had recommenced the sacrifice of the Paschal lamb (which had been stopped by the unexpected darkness), and they were triumphing at the return of light, when suddenly the ground beneath them trembled, the neighbouring buildings fell down, and the veil of the Temple was rent in two from the top to the bottom. Excess of terror at first rendered those on the outside speechless, but after a time they burst forth into cries and lamentations. The confusion in the interior of the Temple was not, however, as great as would naturally have been expected, because the strictest order and decorum were always enforced there, particularly with regard to the regulation to be followed by those who entered to make their sacrifice, and those who left after having offered it. The crowd was great, but the ceremonies were so solemnly carried out by the priests, that they totally engrossed the minds of the assistants. First came the immolation of the lamb, then the sprinkling of its blood, accompanied by the chanting of canticles and the sounding of trumpets. The priests were endeavouring to continue the sacrifices, when suddenly an unexpected and most appalling pause ensued; terror and astonishment were depicted on each countenance; all was thrown into confusion; not a sound was heard; the sacrifices ceased; there was a general rush to the gates of the Temple; everyone endeavoured to fly as quickly as possible. And well might they fly, well might they fear and tremble; for in the midst of the multitude there suddenly appeared persons who had been dead and buried for many years! These persons looked at them sternly, and reproved them most severely for the crime they had committed that day, in bringing about the death of 'the just man,' and calling down his blood upon their heads. Even in the midst of this confusion, some attempts were, however, made by the priests to preserve order; they prevented those who were in the inner part of the Temple from rushing forward, pushing their way through the crowds who were in advance of them, and descending the steps which led out of the Temple: they even continued the sacrifices in some parts, and endeavoured to calm the fears of the people.

The appearance of the Temple at this moment can only be described by comparing it to an ant-hill on which persons have thrown stones, or which has been disturbed by a sick being driven into its centre. The ants in those parts on which the stones have fallen, or which the stick had disturbed, are filled with confusion and terror; they run to and fro and do nothing; while the ants in those parts which have not been disturbed continue to labour quietly, and even begin to repair the damaged parts.

The High Priest Caiphas and his retinue did not lose their presence of mind, and by the outward tranquillity which their diabolical hardness of heart enabled them to preserve, they calmed the confusion in a great degree, and then did their utmost to prevent the people from looking upon these stupendous events as testimonies of the innocence of Jesus. The Roman garrison belonging to the fortress of Antonia likewise made great efforts to maintain order; consequently, the disturbance of the festival was not followed by an insurrection, although every heart was fixed with fear and anxiety, which anxiety the Pharisees endeavoured (and in some instances with success) to calm.

I remember a few other striking incidents: in the first place, the two columns which were placed at the entrance of their Holy of Holies, and to which a magnificent curtain was appended, were shaken to the very foundations; the column on the left side fell down in a southerly, and that on the right side in a northerly direction, thus rending the veil in two from the top to the bottom with a fearful sound, and exposing the Holy of Holies uncovered to the public gaze. A large stone was loosened and fell from the wall at the entrance of the sanctuary, near where the aged Simeon used to kneel, and the arch was broken. The ground was heaved up, and many other columns were thrown down in other parts of the Temple.

An apparition of the High Priest Zacharias, who was slain between the porch and the altar, was seen in the sanctuary. He uttered fearful menaces, spoke of the death of the second Zacharias, and of that of St. John Baptist, as also of the violent deaths of the other prophets.[5] The two sons of the High Priest Simon, surnamed the Just (ancestors of the aged Simeon who prophesied when Jesus was presented in the Temple), made their appearance in the part usually occupied by the doctors of the law; they also spoke in terrific terms of the deaths of the prophets, of the sacrifice of the old law which was now about to cease, and they exhorted all present to be converted, and to embrace the doctrines which had been preached by him whom they had crucified. The prophet Jeremiah likewise appeared; he stood near the altar, and

---

[5] The Zacharias here referred to was the father of John the Baptist, who was tortured and afterwards put to death by Herod, because he would not betray John into the hands of the tyrant. He was buried by his friends within the precincts of the Temple.

proclaimed, in a menacing tone, that the ancient sacrifice was at an end, and that a new one had commenced. As these apparitions took place in parts where none but priests were allowed to enter, Caiphas and a few others were alone cognisant of them, and they endeavoured, as far as possible, either to deny their reality, or to conceal them. These prodigies were followed by others still more extraordinary. The doors of the sanctuary flew open of themselves, and a voice was heard to utter these words: 'Let us leave this place;' and I saw all the angels of the Lord instantly leave the Temple. The thirty-two Pharisees who went to Calvary a short time before our Lord expired were almost all converted at the foot of the Cross. They returned to the Temple in the midst of the confusion, and were perfectly thunderstruck at all which had taken place there. They spoke most sternly, both to Annas and to Caiphas, and left the Temple. Annas had always been the most bitter of the enemies of Jesus, and had headed every proceeding against him; but the supernatural events which had taken place had completely unnerved him that he knew not where to hide himself. Caiphas was, in realty excessively alarmed, and filled with anxiety, but his pride was so great that he concealed his feelings as far as possible, and endeavoured to reassure Annas. He succeeded for a time; but the sudden appearance of a person who had been dead many years marred the effect of his words, and Annas became again a prey to the most fearful terror and remorse.

Whilst these things were going on in the Temple, the confusion and panic were not less in Jerusalem. Dead persons were walking about, and many walls and buildings had been shaken by the earthquake, and parts of them fallen down. The superstition of Pilate rendered him even more accessible to fear; he was perfectly paralysed and speechless with terror; his palace was shaken to the very foundation, and the earth quaked beneath his feet. He ran wildly from room to room, and the dead constantly stood before him, reproaching him with the unjust sentence he had passed upon Jesus. He thought that they were the gods of the Galilean, and took refuge in an inner room, where he offered incense, and made vows to his idols to invoke their assistance in his distress. Herod was usually alarmed; but he shut himself up in his palace, out of the sight of everyone.

More than a hundred persons who had died at different epochs re-entered the bodies they had occupied when on earth, made their appearance in different parts of Jerusalem, and filled the inhabitants with inexpressible consternation. Those souls which had been released by Jesus from Limbo uncovered their faces and wandered to and fro in the streets, and although their bodies were the same as those which they had animated when on earth, yet these bodies did not appear to touch the ground as they walked. They entered the houses of their descendants, proclaimed the innocence of Jesus, and reproved those who had taken part in his death most severely. I saw them passing through the principal streets; they were generally in couples, and appeared to me to glide through the airs without moving their feet. The countenances of some were pale; others of a yellow tint; their beards were long, and their voices sounded strange and sepulchral. Their grave-clothes were such as it was customary to use at the period of their decease. When they reached the place where sentence of death was proclaimed on Jesus before the procession started for Calvary, they paused for a moment, and exclaimed in a loud voice: 'Glory be to Jesus for ever and ever, and destruction to his enemies!' Towards four o'clock all the dead returned to their graves. The sacrifices in the Temple had been so interrupted, and the confusion caused by the different prodigies was so great, that very few persons ate the Paschal lamb on that evening.

CHAPTER XLVII.

The Request of Joseph of Arimathea to be allowed to have the Body of Jesus.

Scarcely had the commotion which the town had been thrown into begun to subside in a degree, when the Jews belonging to the Council sent to Pilate to request that the legs of the criminals might be broken, in order to put an end to their lives before the Sabbath-day dawned. Pilate immediately dispatched executioners to Calvary to carry out their wishes.

Joseph of Arimathea then demanded an audience; he had heard of the death of Jesus, and he and Nicodemus had determined to bury him in a new sepulchre which he had made at the end of his garden, not far from Calvary. Pilate was still filled with anxiety and solicitude, and was much astonished at seeing a person holding a high position like Joseph so anxious for leave to give honourable burial to a criminal whom he had sentenced to be ignominiously crucified. He sent for the centurion Abenadar, who returned to Jerusalem after he had conferred with the disciples who were hidden in the caverns, and asked him whether the King of the Jews was really dead. Abenadar gave Pilate a full account of the death of our Lord, of his last words, and of the loud cry he uttered immediately before death, and of the earthquake which had rent the great chasm in the rock. The only thing at which Pilate expressed surprise was that the death of Jesus should have taken place so quickly, as those who were crucified usually lived much longer; but although he said so little, every word uttered by Joseph increased his dismay and remorse. He instantly gave Joseph an order, by which he was authorised to take down the body of the King of the Jews from the Cross, and to perform the rites of sepulture at once. Pilate appeared to endeavour, by his readiness in granting this request, to wish to make up, in a degree, for his previous cruel and unjust conduct, and he was likewise very glad to do what he was certain would annoy the priests extremely, as he knew their wish was to have Jesus buried ignominiously between the two thieves. He dispatched a messenger to Calvary to see his orders executed. I believe the messenger was Abenadar, for I saw him assisting in taking Jesus down from the Cross.

When Joseph of Arimathea left Pilate's palace, he instantly rejoined Nicodemus, who was waiting for him at the house of a pious woman, which stood opposite to a large street, and was not far from that alley where Jesus was so shamefully ill-treated when he first commenced carrying his Cross. The woman was a vendor of aromatic herbs, and Nicodemus had purchased many perfumes which were necessary for embalming the body of Jesus from her. She procured the more precious kinds from other places, and Joseph went away to procure a fine winding-sheet. His servants then fetched ladders, hammers, pegs, jars of water, and sponges, from a neighbouring shed, and placed them in a hand-barrow similar to that on which the disciples of John the Baptist put his body when they carried it off from the castle of Macherus.

CHAPTER XLVIII.

The Opening of the Side of Jesus.

Death of the two thieves.

Whilst these events were taking place in Jerusalem, silence reigned around Calvary. The crowd which had been for a time so noisy and tumultuous, was dispersed; all were panicstricken; in some that panic had produced sincere repentance, but on others it had had no beneficial effects. Mary, John, Magdalen, Mary of Cleophas, and Salome had remained, either standing or sitting before the Cross, closely veiled and weeping silently. A few soldiers were leaning over the terrace which enclosed the platform; Cassius rode up and down; the sky was lowering, and all nature wore a garb of mourning. Six archers soon after made their appearance, bringing with them ladders, spades, ropes, and large iron staves for the purpose of breaking the legs of the criminals, in order to hasten their deaths. When they approached our Lord's Cross, his friends retired a few paces back, and the Blessed Virgin was seized with fear lest they should indulge their hatred of Jesus by insulting even his dead body. Her fears were not quite unfounded, for when they first placed their ladders against the Cross they declared that he was only pretending to be dead; in a few moments, however, seeing that he was cold and stiff, they left him, and removed their ladders to the crosses on which the two thieves were still hanging alive. They took up their iron staves and broke the arms of the thieves above and below the elbow; while another archer at the same moment broke their legs, both above and below the knee. Gesmas uttered frightful cries, therefore the executioner finished him off by three heavy blows of a cudgel on his chest. Dismas gave a deep groan, and expired: he was the first among mortals who had the happiness of rejoining his Redeemer. The cords were then loosened, the two bodies fell to the ground, and the executioners dragged them to a deep morass, which was between Calvary and the walls of the town, and buried them there.

The archers still appeared doubtful whether Jesus was really dead, and the brutality they had shown in breaking the legs of the thieves made the holy women tremble as to what outrage they might next perpetrate on the body of our Lord. But Cassius, the subaltern officer, a young man of about five-and-twenty, whose weak squinting eyes and nervous manner had often excited the derision of his companions, was suddenly illuminated by grace, and being quite overcome at the sight of the cruel conduct of the soldiers, and the deep sorrow of the holy women, determined to relieve their anxiety by proving beyond dispute that Jesus was really dead. The kindness of his heart prompted him, but unconsciously to himself he fulfilled a prophecy. He seized his lance and rode quickly up to the mound on which the Cross was planted, stopped just between the cross of the good thief and that of our Lord, and taking his lance in both hands, thrust it so completely into the right side of Jesus that the point went through the heart, and appeared on the left side. When Cassius drew his lance out of the wound a quantity of blood and water rushed from it, and flowed over his face and body. This species of washing produced effects somewhat similar to the vivifying waters of Baptism: grace and salvation at once entered his soul. He leaped from his horse, threw himself upon his knees, struck his breast, and confessed loudly before all his firm belief in the divinity of Jesus.

The Blessed Virgin and her companions were still standing near, with their eyes fixed upon the Cross, but when Cassius thrust his lance into the side of Jesus they were much startled, and rushed with one accord up to it. Mary looked as if the lance had transfixed her heart instead of that of her Divine Son, and could scarcely support herself. Cassius meantime remained kneeling and thanking God, not only for the grace he had received but likewise for the cure of the complaint in his eyes, which had caused the weakness and the squint. This cure had been effected at the same moment that the darkness with which his soul was previously filled was removed. Every heart was overcome at the sight of the blood of our Lord, which ran into a hollow in the rock at the foot of the Cross. Mary, John, the holy women, and Cassius, gathered up the blood and water in flasks, and wiped up the remainder with pieces of linen.[6]

Cassius, whose sight was perfectly restored at the same moment that the eyes of his soul were opened, was deeply moved, and continued his humble prayer of thanksgiving. The soldiers were truck with astonishment at the miracle which had taken place, and cast themselves on their knees by his side, at the same time striking their breasts and confessing Jesus. The water and blood continued to flow from the large wound in the side of our Lord; it ran into the hollow in the rock, and the holy women put it in vases, while Mary and Magdalen mingled their tears. The archers, who had received a message from Pilate, ordering them not to touch the body of Jesus, did not return at all.

All these events took place near the Cross, at a little before four o'clock, during the time that Joseph of Arimathea and Nicodemus were gathering together the articles necessary for the burial of Jesus. But the servants of Joseph having been sent to clean out the tomb, informed the friends of our Lord that their master intended to take the body of Jesus and place it in his new sepulchre. John immediately returned to the town with the holy women; in the first place, that Mary might recruit her strength a little, and in the second, to purchase a few things which would be required for the burial. The Blessed Virgin had a small lodging among the buildings near the Cenaculum. They did not re-enter the town through the gate which was the nearest to Calvary, because it was closed, and guarded by soldiers placed there by the Pharisees; but they went through that gate which leads to Bethlehem.

---

[6] Sister Emmerich added: 'Cassius was baptised by the name of Longinus; and was ordained deacon, and preached the faith. He always kept some of the blood of Christ,—it dried up, but was found in his coffin in Italy. He was buried in a town at no great distance from the locality where St. Clare passed her life. There is a lake with an island upon it near this town, and the body of Longinus must have been taken there.' Sister Emmerich appears to designate Mantua by this description, and there is a tradition preserved in that town to the effect. I do not know which St. Clare lived in the neighbourhood.

CHAPTER XLIX.

A Description of some Parts of ancient Jerusalem.

This chapter will contain some descriptions of places given by Sister Emmerich on various occasions. They will be followed by a description of the tomb and garden of Joseph of Arimathea, that so we may have no need to interrupt the account of the burial of our Lord.

The first gate which stood on the eastern side of Jerusalem, to the south of the south-east angle of the Temple, was the one leading to the suburb of Ophel. The gate of the sheep was to the north of the north-east angle of the Temple. Between these two gates there was a third, leading to some streets situated to the east of the Temple, and inhabited for the most part by stonemasons and other workmen. The houses in these streets were supported by the foundations of the Temple; and almost all belonged to Nicodemus, who had caused them to be built, and who employed nearly all the workmen living there. Nicodemus had not long before built a beautiful gate as an entrance to these streets, called the Gate of Moriah. It was but just finished, and through it Jesus had entered the town on Palm Sunday. Thus he entered by the new gate of Nicodemus, through which no one had yet passed, and was buried in the new monument of Joseph of Arimathea, in which no one had yet been laid. This gate was afterwards walled up, and there was a tradition that the Christians were once again to enter the town through it. Even in the present day, a walled-up gate, called by the Turks the Golden Gate, stands on this spot.

The road leading to the west from the gate of the sheep passed almost exactly between the north-western side of Mount Sion and Calvary. From this gate to Golgotha the distance was about two miles and a quarter; and from Pilate's palace to Golgotha about two miles. The fortress Antonia was situated to the north-west of the mountain of the Temple, on a detached rock. A person going towards the west, on leaving Pilate's palace, would have had this fortress to his left. On one of its walls there was a platform commanding the forum, and from which Pilate was accustomed to make proclamations to the people: he did this, for instance, when he promulgated new laws. When our Divine Lord was carrying his Cross, in the interior of the town, Mount Calvary was frequently on his right hand. This road, which partly ran in a south-westerly direction, led to a gate made in an inner wall of the town, towards Sion. Beyond this wall, to the left, there was a sort of suburb, containing more gardens than houses; and towards the outer wall of the city stood some magnificent sepulchres with stone entrances. On this side was a house belonging to Lazarus, with beautiful gardens, extending towards that part where the outer western wall of Jerusalem turned to the south. I believe that a little private door, made in the city wall, and through which Jesus and his disciples often passed by permission of Lazarus, led to these gardens. The gate standing at the north-western angle of the town led to Bethsur, which was situated more towards the north than Emmaus and Joppa. The western part of Jerusalem was lower than any other: the land on which it was built first sloped in the direction of the surrounding wall, and then rose again when close to it; and on this declivity there stood gardens and vineyards, behind which wound a wide road, with paths leading to the walls and towers. On the other side, without the wall, the land descended towards the valley, so that the walls surrounding the lower part of the town looked as if built on a raised terrace. There are gardens and vineyards even in the present day on the outer hill. When Jesus arrived at the end of the Way of the Cross, he had on his left hand that part of the town where there were so many gardens; and it was from thence that Simon of Cyrene was coming when he met the procession. The gate by which Jesus left the town was not entirely facing the west, but rather the south-west. The city wall on the left-hand side, after passing through the gate, ran somewhat in a southerly direction, then turned towards the west, and then again to the south, round Mount Sion. On this side there stood a large tower, like a fortress. The gate by which Jesus left the town was at no great distance from another gate more towards the south, leading down to the valley, and where a road, turning to the left in the direction of Bethlehem, commenced. The road turned to the north towards Mount Calvary shortly after that gate by which Jesus left Jerusalem when bearing his Cross. Mount Calvary was very steep on its eastern side, facing the town, and a gradual descent on the western; and on this side, from which the road to Emmaus was to be seen, there was a field, in which I saw Luke gather several plants when he and Cleophas were going to Emmaus, and met Jesus on the way. Near the walls, to the east and south of Calvary, there were also gardens, sepulchres, and vineyards. The Cross was buried on the north-east side, at the foot of Mount Calvary.

The garden of Joseph of Arimathea was situated near the gate of Bethlehem, at about a seven minutes' walk from Calvary: it was a very fine garden, with tall trees, banks, and thickets in it, which gave much shade, and was situated on a rising ground extending to the walls of the city.[7] A person coming from the northern side of the valley, and entering the garden, had on his left hand a slight ascent extending as far as the city wall; and on his right, at the end of the garden, a detached rock, where the cave of the sepulchre was situated. The grotto in which it was made looked to the east; and on the south-western and north-western sides of the same rock were two other smaller sepulchres, which were also new, and with depressed fronts. A pathway, beginning on the western side of this rock, ran all round it. The ground in front of the sepulchre was higher than that of the entrance, and a person wishing to

---

[7] We must here remark that, in the four years during which Sister Emmerich had her visions, she described everything that had happened to the holy places from the earliest times down to our own. More than once she beheld them profaned and laid waste, but always venerated, either publicly or privately. She saw many stones and pieces of rock, which had been silent witnesses of the Passion and Resurrection of our Lord, placed by St. Helena in the Church of the Holy Sepulchre upon occasion of the foundation of that sacred building. When Sister Emmerich visited it in spirit she was accustomed to venerate the spots where the Cross had stood and the Holy Sepulchre been situated. It must be observed, however, that she used sometimes to see a greater distance between the actual position of the Tomb and the spot where the Cross stood than there is between the chapels which bear their names in the church at Jerusalem.

enter the cavern had to descend several steps. The cave was sufficiently large for four men to be able to stand close up to the wall on either side without impeding the movements of the bearers of the body. Opposite the door was a cavity in the rock, in which the tomb was made; it was about two feet above the level of the ground, and fastened to the rock by one side only, like an altar: two persons could stand, one at the head and one at the foot; and there was a place also for a third in front, even if the door of the cavity was closed. This door was made of some metal, perhaps of brass, and had two folding doors. These doors could be closed by a stone being rolled against them; and the stone used for this purpose was kept outside the cavern. Immediately after our Lord was placed in the sepulchre it was rolled in front of the door. It was very large, and could not be removed without the united effort of several men. Opposite the entrance of the cavern there stood a stone bench, and by mounting on this a person could climb on to the rock, which was covered with grass, and from whence the city walls, the highest parts of Mount Sion, and some towers could be seen, as well as the gate of Bethlehem and the fountain of Gihon. The rock inside was of a white colour, intersected with red and blue veins.

CHAPTER L.

The Descent from the Cross.

At the time when everyone had left the neighbourhood of the Cross, and a few guards alone stood around it, I saw five persons, who I think were disciples, and who had come by the valley from Bethania, draw nigh to Calvary, gaze for a few moments upon the Cross, and then steal away. Three times I met in the vicinity two men who were making examinations and anxiously consulting together. These men were Joseph of Arimathea and Nicodemus. The first time was during the Crucifixion (perhaps when they caused the clothes of Jesus to be brought back from the soldiers), and they were then at no great distance from Calvary. The second was when, after standing to look whether the crowd was dispersing, they went to the town to make some preparations. The third was on their return from the tomb to the Cross, when they were looking around in every direction, as if waiting for a favourable moment, and then concerted together as to the manner in which they should take the body of our Lord down from the Cross, after which they returned to the town.

Their next care was to make arrangements for carrying with them the necessary articles for embalming the body, and their servants took some tools with which to detach it from the Cross, as well as two ladders which they found in a barn close to Nicodemus's house. Each of these ladders consisted of a single pole, crossed at regular intervals by pieces of wood, which formed the steps. There were hooks which could be fastened on any part of the pole, and by means of which the ladder could be steadied, or on which, perhaps, anything required for the work could also be hung.

The woman from whom they had bought their spices had packed the whole neatly together. Nicodemus had bought a hundred pounds' weight of roots, which quantity is equal to about thirty-seven pounds of our measure, as has been explained to me. They carried these spices in little barrels make of bark, which were hung round their necks, and rested on their breasts. One of these barrels contained some sort of powder. They had also some bundles of herbs in bags made of parchment or leather, and Joseph carried a box of ointment; but I do not know what this box was made of. The servants were to carry vases, leathern bottles, sponges, and tools, on a species of litter, and they likewise took fire with them in a closed lantern. They left the town before their master, and by a different gate (perhaps that of Bethania), and then turned their steps towards Mount Calvary. As they walked through the town they passed by the house where the Blessed Virgin; St. John, and the holy women had gone to seek different things required for embalming the body of Jesus, and John and the holy women followed the servants at a certain distance. The women were about five in number, and some of them carried large bundles of linen under their mantles. It was the custom for women, when they went out in the evening, or if intending to perform some work of piety secretly, to wrap their persons carefully in a long sheet at least a yard wide. They began by one arm, and then wound the linen so closely round their body that they could not walk without difficulty. I have seen them wrapped up in this manner, and the sheet not only extended to both arms, but likewise veiled the head. On the present occasion, the appearance of this dress was most striking in my eyes, for it was a real mourning garment. Joseph and Nicodemus were also in mourning attire, and wore black sleeves and wide sashes. Their cloaks, which they had drawn over their heads, were both wide and long, of a common grey colour, and served to conceal everything that they were carrying. They turned their steps in the direction of the gate leading to Mount Calvary. The streets were deserted and quiet, for terror kept everyone at home. The greatest number were beginning to repent, and but few were keeping the festival. When Joseph and Nicodemus reached the gate they found it closed, and the road, streets, and every corner lined with soldiers. These were the soldiers whom the Pharisees had asked for at about two o'clock, and whom they had kept under arms and on guard, as they still feared a tumult among the people. Joseph showed an order, signed by Pilate, to let them pass freely, and the soldiers were most willing that they should do so, but explained to him that they had endeavoured several times to open the gate, without being able to move it; that apparently the gate had received a shock, and been strained in some part; and that on this account the archers sent to break the legs of the thieves had been obliged to return to the city by another gate. But when Joseph and Nicodemus seized hold of the bolt, the gate opened as if of itself, to the great astonishment of all the bystanders.

It was still dark and the sky cloudy when they reached Mount Calvary, where they found the servants who had been sent on already arrived, and the holy women sitting weeping in front of the Cross. Cassius and several soldiers who were converted remained at a certain distance, and their demeanour was respectful and reserved. Joseph and Nicodemus described to the Blessed Virgin and John all they had done to save Jesus from an ignominious death, and learned from them how they had succeeded in preventing the bones of our Lord from being broken, and how the prophecy had been fulfilled. They spoke also of the wound which Cassius had made with his lance. No sooner was the centurion Abenadar arrived than they began, with the deepest recollection of spirit, their mournful and sacred labour of taking down from the Cross and embalming the adorable body of our Lord.

The Blessed Virgin and Magdalen were seated at the foot of the Cross; while, on the right-hand side, between the cross of Dismas and that of Jesus, the other women were engaged in preparing the linen, spices, water, sponges, and vases. Cassius also came forward, and related to Abenadar the miraculous cure of his eyes. All were deeply affected, and their hearts overflowing with sorrow and love; but, at the same time, they preserved a solemn silence, and their every movement was full of gravity and reverence. Nothing broke the stillness save an occasional smothered word of lamentation, or a stifled groan, which escaped from one or other of these holy personages, in spite of their earnest eagerness and deep attention to their pious labour. Magdalen gave way unrestrainedly to her sorrow, and neither the presence of so many different persons, nor any other consideration, appeared to distract her from it.

Nicodemus and Joseph placed the ladders behind the Cross, and mounted them, holding in their hands a large sheet, to which three long straps were fastened. They tied the body of Jesus, below the arms and knees, to the tree of the Cross, and secured the arms by pieces of linen placed underneath the hands. Then they drew out the nails, by pushing them from behind with strong pins pressed upon the points. The sacred hands of Jesus were thus not much shaken, and the nails fell easily out of the wounds; for the latter had been made wider by the weight of the body, which, being now supported by the cloths, no longer hung on the nails. The lower part of the body, which since our Lord's death had sunk down on the knees, now rested in a natural position, supported by a sheet fastened above to the arms of the Cross. Whilst Joseph was taking out the nail from the left hand, and then allowing the left arm, supported by its cloth, to fall gently down upon the body, Nicodemus was fastening the right arm of Jesus to that of the Cross, as also the sacred crowned head, which had sunk on the right shoulder. Then he took out the right nail, and having surrounded the arm with its supporting sheet, let it fall gently on to the body. At the same time, the centurion Abenadar, with great difficulty, drew out the large nail which transfixed the feet. Cassius devoutly received the nails, and laid them at the feet of the Blessed Virgin.

Then Joseph and Nicodemus, having placed ladders against the front of the Cross, in a very upright position, and close to the body, untied the upper strap, and fastened it to one of the hooks on the ladder; they did the same with the two other straps, and passing them all on from hook to hook, caused the sacred body to descend gently towards the centurion, who having mounted upon a stool received it in his arms, holding it below the knees; while Joseph and Nicodemus, supporting the upper part of the body, came gently down the ladder, stopping at every step, and taking every imaginable precaution, as would be done by men bearing the body of some beloved friend who had been grievously wounded. Thus did the bruised body of our Divine Saviour reach the ground.

It was a most touching sight. They all took the same precautions, the same care, as if they had feared to cause Jesus some suffering. They seemed to have concentrated on the sacred body all the love and veneration which they had felt for their Saviour during his life. The eyes of each were fixed upon the adorable body, and followed all its movements; and they were continually uplifting their hands towards Heaven, shedding tears, and expressing in every possible way the excess of their grief and anguish. Yet they all remained perfectly calm, and even those who were so busily occupied about the sacred body broke silence but seldom, and, when obliged to make some necessary remark, did so in a low voice. During the time that the nails were being forcible removed by blows of the hammer, the Blessed Virgin, Magdalen; and all those who had been present at the Crucifixion, felt each blow transfix their hearts. The sound recalled to their minds all the sufferings of Jesus, and they could not control their trembling fear, lest they should again hear his piercing cry of suffering; although, at the same time they grieved at the silence of his blessed lips, which proved, alas too surely, that he was really dead. When the body was taken down it was wrapped in linen from the knees to the waist, and then placed in the arms of the Blessed Virgin, who, overwhelmed with sorrow and love, stretched them forth to receive their precious burden.

CHAPTER LI.

The Embalming of the Body of Jesus.

The Blessed Virgin seated herself upon a large cloth spread on the ground, with her right knee, which was slightly raised, and her back resting against some mantles, rolled together so as to from a species of cushion. No precaution had been neglected which could in any way facilitate to her—the Mother of Sorrows—in her deep affliction of soul, the mournful but most sacred duty which she was about to fulfil in regard to the body of her beloved Son. The adorable head of Jesus rested upon Mary's knee, and his body was stretched upon a sheet. The Blessed Virgin was overwhelmed with sorrow and love. Once more, and for the last time, did she hold in her arms the body of her most beloved Son, to whom she had been unable to give any testimony of love during the long hours of his martyrdom. And she gazed upon his wounds and fondly embraced his blood-stained cheeks, while Magdalen pressed her face upon his feet.

The men withdrew into a little cave, situated on the south-west side of Calvary, there to prepare the different things needful for the embalming; but Cassius, with a few other soldiers who had been converted, remained at a respectful distance. All ill-disposed persons were gone back to the city, and the soldiers who were present served merely to form a guard to prevent any interruption in the last honours which were being rendered to the body of Jesus. Some of these soldiers even gave assistance when desired. The holy women held the vases, sponges, linen, unction, and spices, according as required; but when not thus employed, they remained at a respectful distance, attentively gazing upon the Blessed Virgin as she proceeded in her mournful task. Magdalen did not leave the body of Jesus; but John gave continual assistance to the Blessed Virgin, and went to and fro from the men to the women, lending aid to both parties. The women had with them some large leathern bottles and a vase filled with water standing upon a coal fire. They gave the Blessed Virgin and Magdalen, according as they required, vases filled with clear water, and sponges, which they afterwards squeezed in the leathern bottles.

The courage and firmness of Mary remained unshaken even in the midst of her inexpressible anguish.[8] It was absolutely impossible for her to leave the body of her Son in the awful state to which it had been reduced by his

---

[8] On Good Friday, March 30th, 1820, as Sister Emmerich was contemplating the descent from the Cross she suddenly fainted, in the presence of the writer of these lines, and appeared to be really dead. But after a time she recovered her senses and gave the following explanation, although still in a state of great suffering: 'As I was contemplating the body of Jesus lying on the knees of the Blessed Virgin I said to myself: "How great is her strength! She has not fainted even once!" My guide reproached me for this thought—in which there was more astonishment than compassion—and said to me, "Suffer then what she has suffered!" And at the same moment a sensation of the sharpest anguish transfixed me like a sword, so that I believed I must have died from it.' She had had an illness which reduced her almost to the brink of the grave.

sufferings, and therefore she began with indefatigable earnestness to wash and purify it from the traces of the outrages to which it had been exposed. With the utmost care she drew off the crown of thorns, opening it behind, and then cutting off one by one the thorns which had sunk deep into the head of Jesus, in order that she might not widen the wounds. The crown was placed by the side of the nails, and then Mary drew out the thorns which had remained in the skin with a species of rounded pincers, and sorrowfully showed them to her friends.[9] These thorns were placed with the crown, but still some of them must have been preserved separately.

The divine face of our Saviour was scarcely recognisable, so disfigured was it by the wounds with which it was covered. The beard and hair were matted together with blood. Mary washed the head and face, and passed damp sponges over the hair to remove the congealed blood. As she proceeded in her pious office, the extent of the awful cruelty which had been exercised upon Jesus became more and more apparent, and caused in her soul emotions of compassion and tenderness which increased as she passed from one wound to another. She washed the wounds of the head, the eyes filled with blood, the nostrils, and the ears, with a sponge and a small piece of linen spread over the fingers of her right hand; and then she purified, in the same manner, the half-opened mouth, the tongue, the teeth, and the lips. She divided what remained of our Lord's hair into three parts, a part falling over each temple, and the third over the back of his head; and when she had disentangled the front hair and smoothed it, she passed it behind his ears.[10]

When the head was thoroughly cleansed and purified, the Blessed Virgin covered it with a veil, after having kissed the sacred cheeks of her dear Son. She then turned her attention to the neck, shoulders, chest, back, arms, and pierced hands. All the bones of the breast and the joints were dislocated, and could not be bent. There was a frightful wound on the shoulders which had borne the weight of the Cross, and all the upper part of the body was covered with bruises and deeply marked with blows of the scourges. On the left breast there was a small wound where the point of Cassius's lance had come out, and

---

[9] Sister Emmerich said that the shape of these pincers reminded her of the scissors with which Samson's hair was cut off. In her visions of the third year of the public life of Jesus she had seen our Lord keep the Sabbathday at Misael—a town belonging to the Levites, of the tribe of Aser— and as a portion of the Book of Judges was read in the synagogue, Sister Emmerich beheld upon that occasion the life of Samson.

[10] Sister Emmerich was accustomed, when speaking of persons of historical importance, to explain how they divided their hair. 'Eve,' she said, 'divided her hair in two parts, but Mary into three.' And she appeared to attach importance to these words. No opportunity presented itself for her to give any explanation upon the subject, which probably would have shown what was done with the hair in sacrifices, funerals, consecrations, or vows, etc. She once said of Samson: 'His fair hair, which was long and thick, was gathered up on his head in seven tresses, like a helmet, and the ends of these tresses were fastened upon his forehead and temples. His hair was not in itself the source of his strength, but only as the witness to the vow which he had made to let it grow in God's honour. The powers which depended upon these seven tresses were the seven gifts of the Holy Ghost. He must have already broken his vows and lost many graces, when he allowed this sign of being a Nazarene to be cut off. I did not see Dalila cut off all his hair, and I think one lock remained on his forehead. He retained the grace to do penance and of that repentance by which he recovered strength sufficient to destroy his enemies. The life of Samson is figurative and prophetic.'

on the right side was the large wound made by the same lance, and which had pierced the heart through and through. Mary washed all these wounds, and Magdalen, on her knees, helped her from time to time; but without leaving the sacred feet of Jesus, which she bathed with tears and wiped with her hair.

The head, bosom, and feet of our Lord were now washed, and the sacred body, which was covered with brown stains and red marks in those places where the skin had been torn off, and of a bluish-white colour, like flesh that has been drained of blood, was resting on the knees of Mary, who covered the parts which she had washed with a veil, and then proceeded to embalm all the wounds. The holy women knelt by her side, and in turn presented to her a box, out of which she took some precious ointment, and with it filled and covered the wounds. She also anointed the hair, and then, taking the sacred hands of Jesus in her left hand, respectfully kissed them, and filled the large wounds made by the nails with this ointment or sweet spice. She likewise filled the ears, nostrils, and wound in the side with the same precious mixture. Meanwhile Magdalen wiped and embalmed our Lord's feet, and then again washed them with her tears, and often pressed her face upon them.

The water which had been used was not thrown away, but poured into the leathern bottles in which the sponges had been squeezed. I saw Cassius or some other soldier go several times to fetch fresh water from the fountain of Gihon, which was at no great distance off. When the Blessed Virgin had filled all the wounds with ointment, she wrapped the head up in linen cloths, but she did not as yet cover the face. She closed the half-open eyes of Jesus, and kept her hand upon them for some time. She also closed the mouth, and then embraced the sacred body of her beloved Son, pressing her face fondly and reverently upon his. Joseph and Nicodemus had been waiting for some time, when John drew near to the Blessed Virgin, and besought her to permit the body of her Son to be taken from her, that the embalming might be completed, because the Sabbath was close at hand. Once more did Mary embrace the sacred body of Jesus, and utter her farewells in the most touching language, and then the men lifted it from her arms on the sheet, and carried it to some distance. The deep sorrow of Mary had been for the time assuaged by the feelings of love and reverence with which she had accomplished her sacred task; but now it once more overwhelmed her, and she fell, her head covered with her veil, into the arms of the holy women. Magdalen felt almost as though her Beloved were being forcibly carried away from her, and hastily ran forward a few steps, with her arms stretched forth; but then, after a moment, returned to the Blessed Virgin.

The sacred body was carried to a spot beneath the level of the top of Golgotha, where the smooth surface of a rock afforded a convenient platform on which to embalm the body. I first saw a piece of open-worked linen, looking very much like lace, and which made me think of the large embroidered curtain hung between the choir and nave during Lent.[11] It was

---

[11] This refers to a custom of the Diocese of Munster. During Lent there was hung up in the churches a curtain, embroidered in open work, representing the Five Wounds, the instruments of the Passion, etc.

probably worked in that open stitch for the water to run through. I also saw another large sheet unfolded. The body of our Saviour was placed on the open-worked piece of linen, and some of the other men held the other sheet spread above it. Nicodemus and Joseph then knelt down, and underneath this covering took off the linen which they had fastened round the loins of our Saviour, when they took his body down from the Cross. They then passed sponges under this sheet, and washed the lower parts of the body; after which they lifted it up by the help of pieces of linen crossed beneath the loins and knees, and washed the back without turning it over. They continued washing until nothing but clear water came from the sponges when pressed. Next they poured water of myrrh over the whole body, and then, handling it with respect, stretched it out full length, for it was still in the position in which our Divine Lord had died—the loins and knees bent. They then placed beneath his hips a sheet which was a yard in width and three in length, laid upon his lap bundles of sweet-scented herbs, and shook over the whole body a powder which Nicodemus had brought. Next they wrapped up the lower part of the body, and fastened the cloth which they had placed underneath round it strongly. After this they anointed the wounds of the thighs, placed bundles of herbs between the legs, which were stretched out to their full length, and wrapped them up entirely in these sweet spices.

Then John conducted the Blessed Virgin and the other holy women once more to the side of the body. Mary knelt down by the head of Jesus, and placed beneath it a piece of very fine linen which had been given her by Pilate's wife, and which she had worn round her neck under her cloak; next, assisted by the holy women, she placed from the shoulders to the cheeks bundles of herbs, spices, and sweet-scented powder, and then strongly bound this piece of linen round the head and shoulders. Magdalen poured besides a small bottle of balm into the wound of the side, and the holy women placed some more herbs into those of the hands and feet. Then the men put sweet spices around all the remainder of the body, crossed the sacred stiffened arms on the chest, and bound the large white sheet round the body as high as the chest, in the same manner as if they had been swaddling a child. Then, having fastened the end of a large band beneath the armpits, they rolled it round the head and the whole body. Finally, they placed our Divine Lord on the large sheet, six yards in length, which Joseph of Arimathea had bought, and wrapped him in it. He was lying diagonally upon it, and one corner of the sheet was raised from the feet to the chest, the other drawn over the head and shoulders, while the remaining two ends were doubled round the body.

The Blessed Virgin, the holy women, the men—all were kneeling round the body of Jesus to take their farewell of it, when a most touching miracle took place before them. The sacred body of Jesus, with all its wounds, appeared imprinted upon the cloth which covered it, as though he had been pleased to reward their care and their love, and leave them a portrait of himself through all the veils with which he was enwrapped. With tears they embraced the adorable body, and then reverently kissed the wonderful impression which it had left. Their astonishment increased when, on lifting up the sheet, they saw that all the bands which surrounded the body had remained white as before, and that the upper cloth alone had been marked in this wonderful manner. It was not a mark made by the bleeding wounds, since the whole body was wrapped up and covered with sweet spices, but it was a supernatural portrait, bearing testimony to the divine creative power ever abiding in the body of Jesus. I have seen many things relative to the subsequent history of this piece of linen, but I could not describe them coherently. After the resurrection it remained in the possession of the friends of Jesus, but fell twice into the hands of the Jews, and later was honoured in several different places. I have seen it in a city of Asia, in the possession of some Christians, who were not Catholics. I have forgotten the name of the town, which is situated in a province near the country of the Three Kings.

CHAPTER LII.

The Body of our Lord placed in the Sepulchre.

The men placed the sacred body on a species of leathern hand-barrow, which they covered wit a brown-coloured cloth, and to which they fastened two long stakes. This forcibly reminded me of the Ark of the Covenant. Nicodemus and Joseph bore on their shoulders the front shafts, while Abenadar and John supported those behind. After them came the Blessed Virgin, Mary of Heli, her eldest sister, Magdalen and Mary of Cleophas, and then the group of women who had been sitting at some distance—Veronica, Johanna Chusa, Mary Salome, Salome of Jerusalem, Susanna, and Anne the niece of St. Joseph. Cassius and the soldiers closed the procession. The other women, such as Marone of Naim, Dina the Samaritaness, and Mara the Suphanitess, were at Bethania, with Martha and Lazarus. Two soldiers, bearing torches in their hands, walked on first, that there might be some light in the grotto of the sepulchre; and the procession continued to advance in this order for about seven minutes, the holy men and women singing psalms in sweet but melancholy tones. I saw James the Greater, the brother of John, standing upon a hill the other side of the valley, to look at them as they passed, and he returned immediately afterwards, to tell the other disciples what he had seen.

The procession stopped at the entrance of Joseph's garden, which was opened by the removal of some stakes, afterwards used as levers to roll the stone to the door of the sepulchre. When opposite the rock, they placed the Sacred Body on a long board covered with a sheet. The grotto, which had been newly excavated, had been latterly cleaned by the servants of Nicodemus, so that the interior was neat and pleasing to the eye. The holy women sat down in front of the grotto, while the four men carried in the body of our Lord, partially filled the hollow couch destined for its reception with aromatic spices, and spread over them a cloth, upon which they reverently deposited the sacred body. After having once more given expression to their love by tears and fond embraces, they left the grotto. Then the Blessed Virgin entered, seated herself close to the head of her dear Son, and bent over his body with many tears. When she left the grotto, Magdalen hastily and eagerly came forward, and flung on the body some flowers and branches which she had gathered in the garden. Then she clasped her hands together, and with sobs kissed the feet of Jesus; but the men having informed her that they must close the sepulchre, she returned to the other women. They covered the sacred body with the extremities of the sheet on which it was lying, placed on the top of all the brown coverlet, and closed the folding-doors, which were made of a bronze-coloured metal, and had on their front two sticks, one straight down and the other across, so as to form a perfect cross.

The large stone with which they intended to close the sepulchre, and which was still lying in front of the grotto, was in shape very like a chest or tomb;[12]

its length was such that a man might have laid himself down upon it, and it was so heavy that it was only by means of levers that the men could roll it before the door of the sepulchre. The entrance of the grotto was closed by a gate made of branches twined together. Everything that was done within the grotto had to be accomplished by torchlight, for daylight never penetrated there.

---

[12] Apparently Sister Emmerich here spoke of the ancient cases in which her poor countrymen keep their clothes. The lower part of these cases is smaller than the upper, and this gives them some likeness to a tomb. She had one of these cases, which she called her chest. She often described the stone by this comparison, but her descriptions have not, nevertheless, given us a very clear idea of its shape.

CHAPTER LIII.

The Return from the Sepulchre.

Joseph of Arimathea is put in Prison.

The Sabbath was close at hand, and Nicodemus and Joseph returned to Jerusalem by a small door not far from the garden, and which Joseph had been allowed by special favour to have made in the city wall. They told the Blessed Virgin, Magdalen, John, and some of the women, who were returning to Calvary to pray there, that this door, as well as that of the super-room, would be opened to them whenever they knocked. The elder sister of the Blessed Virgin, Mary of Heli, returned to the town with Mary the mother of Mark, and some other women. The servants of Nicodemus and Joseph went to Calvary to fetch several things which had been left there.

The soldiers joined those who were guarding the city gate near Calvary; and Cassius went to Pilate with the lance, related all that he had seen, and promised to give him an exact account of everything that should happen, if he would put under his command the guards whom the Jews would not fail to ask to have put round the tomb. Pilate listened to his words with secret terror, but only told him in reply that his superstition amounted to madness.

Joseph and Nicodemus met Peter and the two Jameses in the town. They all shed many tears, but Peter was perfectly overwhelmed by the violence of this grief. He embraced them, reproached himself for not having been present at the death of our Saviour, and thanked them for having bestowed the rites of sepulture upon his sacred body. It was agreed that the door of the supper-room should be opened to them whenever they knocked, and then they went away to seek some other disciples who were dispersed in various directions. Later I saw the Blessed Virgin and her companions enter the upper-room; Abenadar next came and was admitted; and by degrees the greatest part of the Apostles and disciples assembled there. The holy women retired to that part of the building where the Blessed Virgin was living. They took some food, and spent a few minutes more in tears, and in relating to one another what each had seen. Then men changed their dresses, and I saw them standing under the lamp, and keeping the Sabbath. They ate some lambs in the supper-room, but without observing any ceremony, for they had eaten the Paschal lamb the evening before. They were all perturbed in spirit, and filled with grief. The holy women also passed their time in praying with the Blessed Virgin under the lamp. Later, when night had quite fallen, Lazarus, the widow of Naim, Dina the Samaritan woman, and Mara of Suphan, came from Bethania, and then, once more, descriptions were given of all that had taken place, and many tears shed.

[According to the visions of Sister Emmerich, the three women named in the text had been living for some time at Bethania, in a sort of community established by Martha for the purpose of providing for the maintenance of the disciples when our Lord was moving about, and for the division and distribution of the alms which were collected. The widow of Naim, whose son

Martial was raised from the dead by Jesus, according to Sister Emmerich, on the 28th Marcheswan (the 18th of November), was named Maroni. She was the daughter of an uncle, on the father's side, of St. Peter. Her first husband was the son of a sister of Elizabeth, who herself was the daughter of a sister of the mother of St. Anne. Maroni's first husband having died without children, she had married Elind, a relation of St. Anne, and had left Chasaluth, near Tabor, to take up her abode at Naim, which was not far off, and where she soon lost her second husband.

Dina, the Samaritan woman, was the same who conversed with Jesus by Jacob's well. She was born near Damascus, of parents who were half Jewish and half Pagan. They died while she was yet very young, and she being brought up by a woman of bad character, the seeds of the most evil passions were early sown in her heart. She had had several husbands, who supplanted one another in turn, and the last lived at Sichar, whither she had followed him and changed her name from Dina to Salome. She had three grown-up daughters and two sons, who afterwards joined the disciples. Sister Emmerich used to say that the life of this Samaritan woman was prophetic—that Jesus had spoken to the entire sect of Samaritans in her person, and that they were attached to their errors by as many ties as she had committed adulteries.

Mara of Suphan was a Moabitess, came from the neighbourhood of Suphan, and was a descendant of Orpha, the widow of Chelion, Noemi's son. Orpha had married again in Moab. By Orpha, the sister-in-law of Ruth, Mara was connected with the family of David, from whom our Lord was descended. Sister Emmerich saw Jesus deliver Mara from four devils and grant her forgiveness of her sins on the 17th Elud (9th September) of the second year of his public life. She was living at Ainon, having been repudiated by her husband, a rich Jew, who had kept the children he had had by her with him. She had with her tree others, the offspring of her adulteries.

'I saw,' Sister Emmerich would say,—'I saw how the stray branch of the stock of David was purified within her by the grace of Jesus, and admitted into the bosom of the Church. I cannot express how many of these roots and offshoots I see become entwined with each other, lost to view, and then once more brought to light.']

Joseph of Arimathea returned home late from the supper-room, and he was sorrowfully walking along the streets of Sion, accompanied by a few disciples and women, when all on a sudden a band of armed men, who were lying in ambuscade in the neighbourhood of Caiphas's tribunal, fell upon them, and laid hands upon Joseph, whereupon his companions fled, uttering loud cries of terror. He was confined in a tower contiguous to the city wall, not far from the tribunal. These soldiers were pagans, and had not to keep the Sabbath, therefore Caiphas had been able to secure their services on this occasion. The intention was to let Joseph die of hunger, and keep his disappearance a secret.

Here conclude the descriptions of all that occurred on the day of the Passion of our Lord; but we will add some supplementary matter concerning Holy Saturday, the Descent into Hell, and the Resurrection.

CHAPTER LIV.

On the Name of Calvary.

Whilst meditating on the name of Golgotha, Calvary, the place of skulls, borne by the rock upon which Jesus was crucified, I became deeply absorbed in contemplation, and beheld in spirit all ages from the time of Adam to that of Christ, and in this vision the origin of the name was made known to me. I here give all that I remember on this subject.

I saw Adam, after his expulsion from Paradise, weeping in the grotto where Jesus sweated blood and water, on Mount Olivet. I saw how Seth was promised to Eve in the grotto of the manger at Bethlehem, and how she brought him forth in that same grotto. I also saw Eve living in some caverns near Hebron, where the Essenian Monastery of Maspha was afterwards established.

I then beheld the country where Jerusalem was built, as it appeared after the Deluge, and the land was all unsettled, black, stony, and very different from what it had been before. At an immense dept below the rock which constitutes Mount Calvary (which was formed in this spot by the rolling of the waters), I saw the tomb of Adam and Eve. The head and one rib were wanting to one of the skeletons, and the remaining head was placed within the same skeleton, to which it did not belong. The bones of Adam and Eve had not all been left in this grave, for Noah had some of them with him in the ark, and they were transmitted from generation to generation by the Patriarchs. Noah, and also Abraham, were in the habit, when offering sacrifice, of always laying some of Adam's bones upon the altar, to remind the Almighty of his promise. When Jacob gave Joseph his variegated robe, he at the same time gave him some bones of Adam, to be kept as relics. Joseph always wore them on his bosom, and they were placed with his own bones in the first reliquary which the children of Israel brought out of Egypt. I have seen similar things, but some I have forgotten, and the others time fails me to describe.

As regards the origin of the name of Calvary, I here give all I know. I beheld the mountain which bears this name as it was in the time of the Prophet Eliseus. It was not the same then as at the time of our Lord's Crucifixion, but was a hill, with many walls and caverns, resembling tombs, upon it. I saw the Prophet Eliseus descend into these caverns, I cannot say whether in reality or only in a vision, and I saw him take out a skull from a stone sepulchre in which bones were resting. Someone who was by his side—I think an angel— said to him, 'This is the skull of Adam.' The prophet was desirous to take it away, but his companion forbade him. I saw upon the skull some few hairs of a fair colour.

I learned also that the prophet having related what had happened to him, the spot received the name of Calvary. Finally, I saw that the Cross of Jesus was placed vertically over the skull of Adam. I was informed that this spot was the exact centre of the earth; and at the same time I was shown the numbers and measures proper to every country, but I have forgotten them, individually as well as in general. Yet I have seen this centre from above, and as it were from a bird's-eye view. In that way a person sees far more clearly than on a map all the different countries, mountains, deserts, seas, rivers, towns, and even the smallest places, whether distant or near at hand.

CHAPTER LV.

The Cross and the Winepress.

As I was meditating upon these words or thoughts of Jesus when hanging on the Cross: 'I am pressed like wine placed here under the press for the first time; my blood must continue to flow until water comes, but wine shall no more be made here,' an explanation was given me by means of another vision relating to Calvary.

I saw this rocky country at a period anterior to the Deluge; it was then less wild and less barren than it afterwards became, and was laid out in vineyards and fields. I saw there the Patriarch Japhet, a majestic dark-complexioned old man, surrounded by immense flocks and herds and a numerous posterity: his children as well as himself had dwellings excavated in the ground, and covered with turf roofs, on which herbs and flowers were growing. There were vines all around, and a new method of making wine was being tried on Calvary, in the presence of Japhet. I saw also the ancient method of preparing wine, but I can give only the following description of it. At first men were satisfied with only eating the grapes; then they pressed them with pestles in hollow stones, and finally in large wooden trenches. Upon this occasion a new wine-press, resembling the holy Cross in shape, had been devised; it consisted of the hollow trunk of a tree placed upright, with a bag of grapes suspended over it. Upon this bag there was fastened a pestle, surmounted by a weight; and on both sides of the trunk were arms joined to the bag, through openings made for the purpose, and which, when put in motion by lowering the ends, crushed the grapes. The juice flowed out of the tree by five openings, and fell into a stone vat, from whence it flowed through a channel made of bark and coated with resin, into the species of cistern excavated in the rock where Jesus was confined before his Crucifixion. At the foot of the winepress, in the stone vat, there was a sort of sieve to stop the skins, which were put on one side. When they had made their winepress, they filled the bag with grapes, nailed it to the top of the trunk, placed the pestle, and put in motion the side arms, in order to make the wine flow. All this very strongly reminded me of the Crucifixion, on account of the resemblance between the winepress and the Cross. They had a long reed, at the end of which there were points, so that it looked like an enormous thistle, and they ran this through the channel and trunk of the tree when there was any obstruction. I was reminded of the lance and sponge. There were also some leathern bottles, and vases made of bark and plastered with resin. I saw several young men, with nothing but a cloth wrapped round their loins like Jesus, working at this winepress. Japhet was very old; he wore a long beard, and a dress made of the skins of beasts; and he looked at the new winepress with evident satisfaction. It was a festival day, and they sacrificed on a stone altar some animals which were running loose in the vineyard, young asses, goats, and sheep. It was not in this place that Abraham came to sacrifice Isaac; perhaps it was on Mount Moriah. I have forgotten many of the instructions regarding the wine, vinegar, and skins, and the different ways in which everything was to be distributed to the right and to the left; and I regret it, because the veriest trifles in these matters have a profound symbolical meaning. If it should be the will of God for me to make them known, he will show them to me again.

CHAPTER LVI.

Apparitions on Occasion of the Death of Jesus.

Among the dead who rose from their graves, and who were certainly a hundred in number, at Jerusalem, there were no relations of Jesus. I saw in various parts of the Holy Land others of the dead appear and bear testimony to the divinity of Jesus. Thus I saw Sadoch, a most pious man, who had given all his property to the poor and to the Temple, appear to many persons in the neighbourhood of Hebron. This Sadoch had lived a century before Jesus, and was the founder of a community of Essenians: he had ardently sighed for the coming of the Messias, and had had several revelations upon the subject. I saw some others of the dead appear to the hidden disciples of our Lord, and give them different warnings.

Terror and desolation reigned even in the most distant parts of Palestine, and it was not in Jerusalem only that frightful prodigies took place. At Thirza, the towers of the prison in which the captives delivered by Jesus had been confined fell down. In Galilee, where Jesus had travelled so much, I saw many buildings, and in particular the houses of those Pharisees who had been the foremost in persecuting our Saviour, and who were then all at the festival, shaken to the ground, crushing their wives and children. Numerous accidents happened in the neighbourhood of the Lake of Genazareth. Many buildings fell down at Capharnaum; and the wall of rocks which was in front of the beautiful garden of the centurion Zorobabel cracked across. The lake overflowed into the valley, and its waters descended as far as Capharnaum, which was a mile and a half distant. Peter's house, and the dwelling of the Blessed Virgin in front of the town, remained standing. The lake was strongly convulsed; its shores crumbled in several places, and its shape was very much altered, and became more like what it is at the present day. Great changes took place, particularly at the south-eastern extremity, near Tarichea, because in this part there was a long causeway made of stones, between the lake and a sort of marsh, which gave a constant direction to the course of the Jordan when it left the lake. The whole of this causeway was destroyed by the earthquake. Many accidents happened on the eastern side of the lake, on the spot where the swine belonging to the inhabitants of Gergesa cast themselves in, and also at Gergesa, Gerasa, and in the entire district of Chorazin. The mountain where the second multiplication of the loaves took place was shaken, and the stone upon which the miracle had been worked split in two. In Decapolis, whole towns crumbled to the earth; and in Asia, in several localities, the earthquake was severely felt, particularly to the east and north-east of Paneas. In Upper Galilee, many Pharisees found their houses in ruins when they returned from keeping the feast. A number of them, while yet at Jerusalem, received the news of what had happened, and it was on that account that the enemies of Jesus made such very slight efforts against the Christian community at Pentecost.

The Dolorous Passion of Our Lord Jesus Christ

A part of the Temple of Garizim crumbled down. An idol stood there above a fountain, in a small temple, the roof of which fell into the fountain with the idol. Half of the synagogue of Nazareth, out of which Jesus had been drive, fell down, as well as that part of the mountain from which his enemies had endeavoured to precipitate him. The bed of the Jordan was much changed by all these shocks, and its course altered in many places. At Macherus, and at the other towns belonging to Herod, everything remained quiet, for that country was out of the sphere of repentance and of threats, like those men who did not fall to the ground in the Garden of Olives, and, consequently, did not rise again.

In many other parts where there were evil spirits, I saw the latter disappear in large bodies amid the falling mountains and buildings. The earthquakes reminded me of the convulsions of the possessed, when the enemy feels that he must take to flight. At Gergesa, a part of the mountain from which the devils had cast themselves with the swine into a marsh, fell into this same marsh; and I then saw a band of evil spirits cast themselves into the abyss, like a dark cloud.

It was at Nice, unless I am mistaken, that I saw a singular occurrence, of which I have only an imperfect remembrance. There was a port there with many vessels in it; and near this port stood a house with a high tower, in which I saw a pagan whose office was to watch these vessels. He had often to ascend this tower, and see what was going on at sea. Having heard a great noise over the vessels in the port, he hurriedly ascended the tower to discover what was taking place, and he saw several dark figures hovering over the port, and who exclaimed to him in plaintive accents: 'If thou desirest to preserve the vessels, cause them to be sailed out of this port, for we must return to the abyss: the great Pan is dead.' They told him several other things; laid injunctions upon him to make known what they were then telling him upon his return from a certain voyage which he was soon to make, and to give a good reception to the messengers who would come to announce the doctrine of him who had just died. The evil spirits were forced in this manner by the power of God to inform this good man of their defeat, and announce it to the world. He had the vessels put in safety, and then an awful storm arose: the devils cast themselves howling into the sea, and half the city fell down. His house remained standing. Soon afterwards he went on a great journey, and announced the death of the great Pan, if that is the name by which our Saviour had been called. Later he came to Rome, where much amazement was caused by what he related. His name was something like Thamus or Thramus.

CHAPTER LVII.

Guards are placed around the Tomb of Jesus.

Late on Friday night, I saw Caiphas and some of the chief men among the Jews holding a consultation concerning the best course to pursue with regard to the prodigies which had taken place, and the effect they had had upon the people. They continued their deliberations quite into the morning, and then hurried to Pilate's house, to tell him that, as that seducer said, while he was yet alive, 'After three days I will rise again,' it would be right to command the sepulchre to be guarded until the third day, as otherwise his disciples might come and steal him away, and say to the people, 'He is risen from the dead,' and the last error would be worse that the first. Pilate was determined to have nothing more to do with the business, and he only answered: 'You have a guard; go, guard it as you know.' However, he appointed Cassius to keep a watch over all that took place, and give him an exact account of every circumstance. I saw these men, twelve in number, leave the town before sunrise, accompanied by some soldiers who did not wear the Roman uniform, being attached to the Temple. They carried lanterns fastened to the end of long poles, in order that they might be able to see every surrounding object, in spite of the darkness of the night, and also that they might have some light in the dark cave of the sepulchre.

No sooner had they reached the sepulchre than, having first seen with their own eyes that the body of Jesus was really there, they fastened one rope across the door of the tomb, and a second across the great stone which was placed in front, sealing the whole with a seal of half-circular shape. They then returned to the city, and the guards stationed themselves opposite the outer door. They were five or six in number, and watched three and three alternately. Cassius never left his post, and usually remained sitting or standing in front of the entrance to the cave, so as to see that side of the tomb where the feet of our Lord rested. He had received many interior graces, and been given to understand many mysteries. Being wholly unaccustomed to this state of spiritual enlightenment, he was perfectly transported out of himself, and remained nearly all the time unconscious of the presence of exterior things. He was entirely changed, had become a new man, and spent the whole day in penance, in making fervent acts of gratitude, and in humbly adoring God.

CHAPTER LVIII.

A Glance at the Disciples of Jesus on Holy Saturday.

The faithful disciples of our Lord assembled together in the Cenaculum, to keep the eve of the Sabbath. They were about twenty in number, clothed in long white dresses, and with their waists girded. The room was lighted up by a lamp; and after their repast they separated, and for the most part returned home. They again assembled on the following morning, and sat together reading and praying by turns; and if a friend entered the room, they arose and saluted him cordially.

In that part of the house inhabited by the Blessed Virgin there was a large room, divided into small compartments like cells, which were used by the holy women for sleeping in at night. When they returned from the sepulchre, one of their number lighted a lamp which was hanging in the middle of the room, and they all assembled around the Blessed Virgin, and commenced praying in a mournful but recollected manner. A short time afterwards, Martha, Maroni, Dina, and Mara, who were just come with Lazarus from Bethania, where they had passed the Sabbath, entered the room. The Blessed Virgin and her companions gave them a detailed account of the death and burial of our Lord, accompanying each relation with many tears. The evening was advancing, and Joseph of Arimathea came in with a few other disciples, to ask whether any of the women wished to return to their homes, as they were ready to escort them. A few accepted the proposition, and set off immediately; but before they reached the tribunal of Caiphas, some armed men stopped Joseph of Arimathea, arrested, and shut him up in an old deserted turret.

Those among the holy women who did not leave the Cenaculum retired to take their rest in the cell-like compartments spoken of above: they fastened long veils over their heads, seated themselves sorrowfully on the floor, and leaned upon the couches which were placed against the wall. After a time they stood up, spread out the bedclothes which were rolled up on the couches, took off their sandals, girdles, and a part of their clothing, and reclined for a time in order to endeavour to get a little sleep. At midnight, they arose, clothed themselves, put up their beds, and reassembled around the lamp to continue their prayer with the Blessed Virgin.

When the Mother of Jesus and her pious companions had finished their nocturnal prayer (that holy duty which has been practised by all faithful children of God and holy souls, who have either felt themselves called to it by a special grace, or who follow a rule given by God and his Church), they heard a knock at the door, which was instantly opened, and John and some of the disciples who had promised to conduct them to the Temple, entered, upon which the women wrapped their cloaks about them, and started instantly. It was then about three in the morning, and they went straight to the Temple, it being customary among many Jews to get there before day dawned, on the day after they had eaten the Paschal lamb; and for this reason the Temple was open from midnight, as the sacrifices commenced very early. They started at about the same hour as that at which the priests had put their seal upon the sepulchre. The aspect of things in the Temple was, however, very different from what was usually the case at such times, for the sacrifices were stopped, and the place was empty and desolate, as everyone had left on account of the events on the previous day which had rendered it impure. The Blessed Virgin appeared to me to visit it for the sole purpose of taking leave of the place where she had passed her youth.

The Temple was, however, open; the lamps lighted, and the people at liberty to enter the vestibule of the priests, which was the customary privilege of this day, as well as of that which followed the Paschal supper. The Temple was, as I said before, quite empty, with the exception of a chance priest or server who might be seen wandering about; and every part bore the marks of the confusion into which all was thrown on the previous day by the extraordinary and frightful events that had taken place; besides which it had been defiled by the presence of the dead, and I reflected and wondered in my own mind whether it would be possible ever to purify if again.

The sons of Simeon, and the nephew of Joseph of Arimathea, were much grieved when they heard of the arrest of their uncle, but they welcomed the Blessed Virgin and her companions, and conducted them all over the Temple, which they did without difficulty, as they held the offices of inspectors of the Temple. The holy women stood in silence and contemplated all the terrible and visible marks of the anger of God with feelings of deep awe, and then listened with interest to the many stupendous details recounted by their guides. The effects of the earthquake were still visible, as little had been done towards repairing the numerous rents and cracks in the floor, and in the walls. In that part of the Temple where the vestibule joined the sanctuary, the wall was so tremendously shaken by the shock of the earthquake, as to produce a fissure wide enough for a person to walk through, and the rest of the wall looked unsteady, as if it might fall down at any moment. The curtain which hung in the sanctuary was rent in two and hung in shreds at the sides; nothing was to be seen around but crumbled walls, crushed flagstones, and columns either partly or quite shaken down.

The Blessed Virgin visited all those parts which Jesus had rendered sacred in her eyes; she prostrated, kissed them, and with tears in her eyes explained to the others her reasons for venerating each particular spot, whereupon they instantly followed her example. The greatest veneration was always shown by the Jews for all places which had been rendered sacred by manifestations of the Divine power, and it was customary to place the hands reverently on such places, to kiss them, and to prostrate to the very earth before them. I do not think there was anything in the least surprising in such a custom, for they both knew, saw, end felt that the God of Abraham, of Isaac, and of Jacob, was a living God, and that his dwelling among his people was in the Temple at Jerusalem; consequently it would have been infinitely more astonishing if they had not venerated those holy parts where his power had been particularly demonstrated, for the Temple and the holy places were to them what the Blessed Sacrament is to Christians.

Deeply penetrated with these feelings of respect, the Blessed Virgin walked trough the Temple with her companions, and pointed out to them the spot where she was presented when still a child, the parts where she passed her childhood, the place where she was affianced to St. Joseph, and the spot where she stood when she presented Jesus and heard the prophecy of Simeon: the remembrance of his words made her weep bitterly, for the prophecy was indeed fulfilled, and the sword of grief had indeed transfixed her heart; she again stopped her companions when she reached the part of the Temple where she found Jesus teaching when she lost him at the age of twelve, and she respectfully kissed the ground on which he then stood. When the holy women had looked at every place sanctified by the presence of Jesus, when they had wept and prayed over them, they returned to Sion.

The Blessed Virgin did not leave the Temple without shedding many tears, as she contemplated the state of desolation to which it was reduced, an aspect of desolation which was rendered still more depressing by the marked contrast it bore to the usual state of the Temple on the festival day. Instead of songs and hymns of jubilee, a mournful silence reigned throughout the vast edifice, and in place of groups of joyful and devout worshippers, the eye wandered over a vast and dreary solitude. Too truly, alas, did this change betoken the fearful crime which had been perpetrated by the people of God, and she remembered how Jesus had wept over the Temple, and said, 'Destroy the Temple and in three days I will build it up again.' She thought over the destruction of the Temple of the Body of Jesus which had been brought about by his enemies, and she sighed with a longing desire for the dawning of that third day when the words of eternal truth were to be accomplished.

It was about daybreak when Mary and her companions reached the Cenaculum, and they retired into the building which stood on its right-hand side, while John and some of the disciples re-entered the Cenaculum, where about twenty men, assembled around a lamp, were occupied in prayer. Every now and then new-comers drew nigh to the door, came in timidity, approached the group round the lamp, and addressed them in a few mournful words, which they accompanied with tears. Everyone appeared to regard John with feelings of respect; because he had remained with Jesus until he expired; but with these sentiments of respect was mingled a deep feeling of shame and confusion, when they reflected on their own cowardly conduct in abandoning their Lord and Master in the hour of need. John spoke to everyone with the greatest charity and kindness; his manner was modest and unassuming as that of a child, and he seemed to fear receiving praise. I saw the assembled group take one meal during that day, but its members were, for the most part, silent; not a sound was to be heard throughout the house, and the doors were tightly closed, although, in fact, there was no likelihood of anyone disturbing them, as the house belonged to Nicodemus, and he had let it to them for the time of the festival.

The holy women remained in this room until nightfall; it was lighted up by a single lamp; the doors were closed, and curtains drawn over the windows. Sometimes they gathered round the Blessed Virgin and prayed under the lamp;

at other times they retired to the side of the room, covered their heads with black veils, and either sat on ashes (the sign of mourning), or prayed with their faces turned towards the wall; those whose health was delicate took a little food, but the others fasted.

I looked at them again and again, and I saw them ever occupied in the same manner, that is to say, either in prayer or in mourning over the sufferings of their beloved Master. When my thoughts wandered from the contemplation of the Blessed Virgin to that of her Divine Son, I beheld the holy sepulchre with six or seven sentinels at the entrance—Cassius standing against the door of the cave, apparently in deep meditation, the exterior door closed, and the stone rolled close to it. Notwithstanding the thick door which intervened between the body of our Saviour and myself I could see it plainly; it was quite transparent with a divine light, and two angels were adoring at the side. But my thoughts then turned to the contemplation of the blessed soul of my Redeemer, and such an extensive and complicated picture of his descent into hell was shown to me, that I can only remember a small portion of it, which I will describe to the best of my power.

CHAPTER LIX.

A Detached Account of the Descent into Hell.

When Jesus, after uttering a loud cry, expired, I saw his heavenly soul under the form of a bright meteor pierce the earth at the foot of the Cross, accompanied by the angel Gabriel and many other angels. His Divine nature continued united to his soul as well as to his body, which still remained hanging upon the Cross, but I cannot explain how this was, although I saw it plainly in my own mind. The place into which the soul of Jesus entered was divided into three parts, which appeared to me like three worlds; and I felt that they were round, and that each division was separated from the other by a hemisphere.

I beheld a bright and beautiful space opposite to Limbo; it was enamelled with flowers, delicious breezes wafted through it; and many souls were placed there before being admitted into Heaven after their deliverance from Purgatory. Limbo, the place where the souls were waiting for the Redemption, was divided into different compartments, and encompassed by a thick foggy atmosphere. Our Lord appeared radiant with light and surrounded by angels, who conducted him triumphantly between two of these compartments; the one on the left containing the patriarchs who lived before the time of Abraham, and that on the right those who lived between the days of Abraham and St. John the Baptist. These souls did not at first recognise Jesus, but were filled nevertheless with sensations of joy and hope. There was not a spot in those narrow confines which did not, as it were, dilate with feelings of happiness. The passage of Jesus might be compared to the wafting of a breath of air, to a sudden flash of light, or to a shower of vivifying dew, but it was swift as a whirlwind. After passing through the two compartments, he reached a dark spot in which Adam and Eve were standing; he spoke to them, they prostrated and adored him in a perfect ecstasy of joy, and they immediately joined the band of angels, and accompanied our Lord to the compartment on the left, which contained the patriarchs who lived before Abraham. This compartment was a species of Purgatory, and a few evil spirits were wandering about among the souls and endeavouring to fill them with anxiety and alarm. The entrance through a species of door was closed, but the angels rapped, and I thought I heard them say, 'Open these doors.' When Jesus entered in triumph the demons dispersed, crying out at the same time, 'What is there between thee and us? What art thou come to do here? Wilt thou crucify us likewise?' The angels hunted them away, having first chained them. The poor souls confined in this place had only a slight presentiment and vague idea of the presence of Jesus; but the moment he told them that it was he himself, they burst out into acclamations of joy, and welcomed him with hymns of rapture and delight. The soul of our Lord then wended its way to the right, towards that part which really constituted Limbo; and there he met the soul of the good thief which angels were carrying to Abraham's bosom, as also that of the bad thief being dragged by demons into Hell. Our Lord addressed a few words to both, and then entered Abraham's bosom, accompanied by numerous angels and holy souls, and also by those demons who had been chained and expelled from the compartment.

This locality appeared to me more elevated than the surrounding parts; and I can only describe my sensations on entering it, by comparing them to those of a person coming suddenly into the interior of a church, after having been for some time in the burial vaults. The demons, who were strongly chained, were extremely loth to enter, and resisted to the utmost of their power, but the angels compelled them to go forwards. All the just who had lived before the time of Christ were assembled there; the patriarchs, Moses, the judges, and the kings on the left-hand side; and on the right side, the prophets, and the ancestors of our Lord, as also his near relations, such as Joachim, Anna, Joseph, Zacharias, Elizabeth, and John. There were no demons in this place, and the only discomfort that had been felt by those placed there was a longing desire for the accomplishment of the promise; and when our Lord entered they saluted him with joyful hymns of gratitude and thanksgiving for its fulfilment, they prostrated and adored him, and the evil spirits who had been dragged into Abraham's bosom when our Lord entered were compelled to confess with shame that they were vanquished. Many of these holy souls were ordered by our Lord to return to the earth, re-enter their own bodies, and thus render a solemn and impressive testimony to the truth. It was at this moment that so many dead persons left their tombs in Jerusalem; I regarded them less in the light of dead persons risen again than as corpses put in motion by a divine power, and which, after having fulfilled the mission entrusted to them, were laid aside in the same manner as the insignia of office are taken off by a clerk when he has executed the orders of his superiors.

I next saw our Lord, with his triumphant procession, enter into a species of Purgatory which was filled with those good pagans who, having had a faint glimmering of the truth, had longed for its fulfilment: this Purgatory was very deep, and contained a few demons compelled to confess the deception they had practised with regard to these idols, and the souls of the poor pagans cast themselves at the feet of Jesus, and adored him with inexpressible joy: here, likewise, the demons were bound with chains and dragged away. I saw our Saviour perform many other actions; but I suffered so intensely at the same time, that I cannot recount them as I should have wished.

Finally, I beheld him approach to the centre of the great abyss, that is to say, to Hell itself; and the expression of his countenance was most severe.

The exterior of Hell was appalling and frightful; it was an immense, heavy-looking building, and the granite of which it was formed, although black, was of metallic brightness; and the dark and ponderous doors were secured with such terrible bolts that no one could behold them without trembling. Deep groans and cries of despair might be plainly distinguished even while the doors were tightly closed; but, O, who can describe the dreadful yells and shrieks which burst upon the ear when the bolts were unfastened and the doors flung open; and, O, who can depict the melancholy appearance of the inhabitants of this wretched place!

The form under which the Heavenly Jerusalem is generally represented in my visions is that of a beautiful and well-regulated city, and the different degrees of glory to which the elect are raised are demonstrated by the magnificence of their palaces, or the wonderful fruit and flowers with which the gardens are embellished. Hell is shown to me under the same form, but all within it is, on the contrary, close, confused, and crowded; every object tends to fill the mind with sensations of pain and grief; the marks of the wreath and vengeance of God are visible everywhere; despair, like a vulture, gnaws every heart, and discord and misery reign around. In the Heavenly Jerusalem all is peace and eternal harmony, the beginning, fulfilment, and end of everything being pure and perfect happiness; the city is filled with splendid buildings, decorated in such a manner as to charm every eye and enrapture every sense; the inhabitants of this delightful abode are overflowing with rapture and exultation, the gardens gay with lovely flowers, and the trees covered with delicious fruits which give eternal life. In the city of Hell nothing is to be seen but dismal dungeons, dark caverns, frightful deserts, fetid swamps filled with every imaginable species of poisonous and disgusting reptile. In Heaven you behold the happiness and peaceful union of the saints; in Hell, perpetual scenes of wretched discord, and every species of sin and corruption, either under the most horrible forms imaginable, or represented by different kinds of dreadful torments. All in this dreary abode tends to fill the mind with horror; not a word of comfort is heard or a consoling idea admitted; the one tremendous thought, that the justice of an all-powerful God inflicts on the damned nothing but what they have fully deserved is the absorbing tremendous conviction which weighs down each heart. Vice appears in its own grim disgusting colours, being stripped of the mask under which it is hidden in this world, and the infernal viper is seen devouring those who have cherished or fostered it here below. In a word, Hell is the temple of anguish and despair, while the kingdom of God is the temple of peace and happiness. This is easy to understand when seen; but it is almost impossible to describe clearly.

The tremendous explosion of oaths, curses, cries of despair, and frightful exclamations which, like a clap of thunder, burst forth when the gates of Hell were thrown open by the angels, would be difficult even to imagine; our Lord spoke first to the soul of Judas, and the angels then compelled all the demons to acknowledge and adore Jesus. They would have infinitely preferred the most frightful torments to such a humiliation; but all were obliged to submit. Many were chained down in a circle which was placed round other circles. In the centre of Hell I saw a dark and horrible-looking abyss, and into this Lucifer was cast, after being first strongly secured with chains; thick clouds of sulphureous black smoke arose from its fearful depths, and enveloped his frightful form in the dismal folds, thus effectually concealing him from every beholder. God himself had decreed this; and I was likewise told, if I remember right, that he will be unchained for a time fifty or sixty years before the year of Christ 2000. The dates of many other events were pointed out to me which I do not now remember; but a certain number of demons are to be let loose much earlier than Lucifer, in order to tempt men, and to serve as instruments of the divine vengeance. I should think that some must be loosened even in the present day, and others will be set free in a short time.

It would be utterly impossible for me to describe all the things which were shown to me; their number was so great that I could not reduce them sufficiently to order to define and render them intelligible. Besides which my sufferings are very great, and when I speak on the subject of my visions I behold them in my mind's eye portrayed in such vivid colours, that the sight is almost sufficient to cause a weak mortal like myself to expire.

I next saw innumerable bands of redeemed souls liberated from Purgatory and from Limbo, who followed our Lord to a delightful spot situated above the celestial Jerusalem, in which place I, a very short time ago, saw the soul of a person who was very dear to me. The soul of the good thief was likewise taken there, and the promise of our Lord, 'This day thou shalt be with me in Paradise,' was fulfilled.

It is not in my power to explain the exact time that each of these events occurred, nor can I relate one-half of the things which I saw and heard; for some were incomprehensible even to myself, and others would be misunderstood if I attempted to relate them. I have seen our Lord in many different places. Even in the sea he appeared to me to sanctify and deliver everything in the creation. Evil spirits fled at his approach, and cast themselves into the dark abyss. I likewise beheld his soul in different parts of the earth, first inside the tomb of Adam, under Golgotha; and when he was there the souls of Adam and Eve came up to him, and he spoke to them for some time. He then visited the tombs of the prophets, who were buried at an immense depth below the surface; but he passed through the soil in the twinkling of an eye. Their souls immediately re-entered their bodies, and he spoke to them, and explained the most wonderful mysteries. Next I saw him, accompanied by a chosen band of prophets, among whom I particularly remarked David, visit those parts of the earth which had been sanctified by his miracles and by his sufferings. He pointed out to them, with the greatest love and goodness, the different symbols in the old law expressive of the future; and he showed them how he himself had fulfilled every prophecy. The sight of the soul of our Lord, surrounded by these happy souls, and radiant with light, was inexpressibly grand as he glided triumphantly through the air, sometimes passing, with the velocity of lightning, over rivers, then penetrating though the hardest rocks to the very centre of the earth, or moving noiselessly over its surface.

I can remember nothing beyond the facts which I have just related concerning the descent of Jesus into Limbo, where he went in order to present to the souls there detained the grace of the Redemption which he had merited for them by his death and by his sufferings; and I saw all these things in a very short space of time; in fact, time passed so quickly that it seemed to me but a moment. Our Lord, however, displayed before me, at the same time, another picture, in which I beheld the immense mercies which he bestows in the present day on the poor souls in Purgatory; for on every anniversary of this great day, when his Church is celebrating the glorious mystery of his death, he casts a look of compassion on the souls in Purgatory, and frees some of those who sinned against him before his crucifixion. I this day saw Jesus deliver many souls; some I was acquainted with, and others were strangers to me, but I cannot name any of them.

Our Lord, by descending into Hell, planted (if I may thus express myself), in the spiritual garden of the Church, a mysterious tree, the fruits of which—namely, his merits—are destined for the constant relief of the poor souls in Purgatory. The Church militant must cultivate the tree, and gather its fruit, in order to present them to that suffering portion of the Church which can do nothing for itself. Thus it is with all the merits of Christ; we must labour with him if we wish to obtain our share of them; we must gain our bread by the sweat of our brow. Everything which our Lord has done for us in time must produce fruit for eternity; but we must gather these fruits in time, without which we cannot possess them in eternity. The Church is the most prudent and thoughtful of mothers; the ecclesiastical year is an immense and magnificent garden, in which all those fruits for eternity are gathered together, that we may make use of them in time. Each year contains sufficient to supply the wants of all; but woe be to that careless or dishonest gardener who allows any of the fruit committed to his care to perish; if he fails to turn to a proper account those graces which would restore health to the sick; strength to the weak, or furnish food to the hungry! When the Day of Judgment arrives, the Master of the garden will demand a strict account, not only of every tree, but also of all the fruit produced in the garden.

CHAPTER LX.

The Eve of the Resurrection.

Towards the close of the Sabbath-day, John came to see the holy women. He endeavoured to give some consolation, but could not restrain his own tears, and only remained a short time with them. They had likewise a short visit from Peter and James the Greater, after which they retired to their cells, and gave free vent to grief, sitting upon ashes, and veiling themselves even more closely.

The prayer of the Blessed Virgin was unceasing. She ever kept her eyes fixed interiorly on Jesus, and was perfectly consumed by her ardent desire of once more beholding him whom she loved with such inexpressible love. Suddenly an angel stood by her side, and bade her arise and go to the door of the dwelling of Nicodemus, for that the Lord was very near. The heart of the Blessed Virgin leaped for joy. She hastily wrapped her cloak about her, and left the holy women, without informing them where she was going. I saw her walk quickly to a small entrance which was cut in the town wall, the identical one through which she had entered when returning with her companions from the sepulchre.

It was about nine o'clock at night, and the Blessed Virgin had almost reached the entrance, when I saw her stop suddenly in a very solitary spot, and look upwards in an ecstasy of delight, for on the top of the town wall she beheld the soul of our Lord, resplendent with light, without the appearance of a wound, and surrounded by patriarchs. He descended towards her, turned to his companions, and presenting her to them, said, 'Behold Mary, behold my Mother.' He appeared to me to salute her with a kiss, and he then disappeared. The Blessed Virgin knelt down, and most reverently kissed the ground on which he had stood, and the impression of her hands and knees remained imprinted upon the stones. The sight filled her with inexpressible joy, and she immediately rejoined the holy women, who were busily employed in preparing the perfumes and spices. She did not tell them what she had seen, but her firmness and strength of mind was restored. She was perfectly renovated, and therefore comforted all the rest, and endeavoured to strengthen their faith.

All the holy women were sitting by a long table, the cover of which hung down to the floor, when Mary returned; bundles of herbs were heaped around them, and these they mixed together and arranged; small flasks, containing sweet unctions and water of spikenard, were standing near, as also bunches of natural flowers, among which I remarked one in particular, which was like a streaked iris or a lily. Magdalen, Mary the daughter of Cleophas, Salome, Johanna, and Mary Salome, had bought all these things in the town during the absence of Mary. Their intention was to go to the sepulchre before sunrise on the following day, in order to strew these flowers and perfumes over the body of their beloved Master.

CHAPTER LVI.

Joseph of Arimathea miraculously set at large.

A short time after the return of the Blessed Virgin to the holy women, I was shown the interior of the prison in which the enemies of Joseph of Arimathea had confined him. He was praying fervently, when suddenly a brilliant light illuminated the whole place, and I heard a voice calling him by name, while at the same moment the roof opened, and a bright form appeared, holding out a sheet resembling that in which he had wrapped the body of Jesus. Joseph grasped it with both hands, and was drawn up to the opening, which closed again as soon as he had passed through; and the apparition disappeared the instant he was in safety at the tope of the tower. I know not whether it was our Lord himself or an angel who thus set Joseph free.

He walked on the summit of the wall until he reached the neighbourhood of the Cenaculum, which was near to the south wall of Sion, and then climbed down and knocked at the door of that edifice, as the doors were fastened. The disciples assembled there had been much grieved when they first missed Joseph, who they thought had been thrown into a sink, a report to that effect having become current. Great, therefore, was their joy when they opened the door and found that it was he himself; indeed, they were almost as much delighted as when Peter was miraculously delivered from prison some years after. When Joseph had related what had taken place, they were filled with astonishment and delight; and after thanking God fervently gave him some refreshment, which he greatly needed. He left Jerusalem that same night, and fled to Arimathea, his native place, where he remained until he thought he could return safely to Jerusalem.

I likewise saw Caiphas towards the close of the Sabbath-day, at the house of Nicodemus. He was conversing with him and asking many questions with pretended kindness. Nicodemus answered firmly, and continued to affirm the innocence of Jesus. They did not remain long together.

CHAPTER LXII.

The Night of Resurrection.

I soon after beheld the tomb of our Lord. All was calm and silent around it. There were six soldiers on guard, who were either seated or standing before the door, and Cassius was among them. His appearance was that of a person immersed in meditation and in the expectation of some great event. The sacred body of our Blessed Redeemer was wrapped in the winding-sheet, and surrounded with light, while two angels sat in an attitude of adoration, the one at the head, and the other at the feet. I had seen them in the same posture ever since he was first put into the tomb. These angels were clothed as priests. Their position, and the manner in which they crossed their arms over their breasts, reminded me of the cherubim who surrounded the Ark of the covenant, only they were without wings; at least I did not see any. The whole of the sepulchre reminded me of the Ark of the Covenant at different periods of its history. It is possible that Cassius was sensible of the presence of the angels, and of the bright light which filled the sepulchre, for his attitude was like that of a person in deep contemplation before the Blessed Sacrament.

I next saw the soul of our Lord accompanied by those among the patriarchs whom he had liberated enter into the tomb through the rock. He showed them the wounds with which his sacred body was covered; and it seemed to me that the winding-sheet which previously enveloped it was removed, and that Jesus wished to show the souls the excess of suffering he had endured to redeem them. The body appeared to me to be quite transparent, so that the whole depth of the wounds could be seen; and this sight filled the holy souls with admiration, although deep feelings of compassion likewise drew tears from their eyes.

My next vision was so mysterious that I cannot explain or even relate it in a clear manner. It appeared to me that the soul and body of Jesus were taken together out of the sepulchre, without, however, the former being completely reunited to the latter, which still remained inanimate. I thought I saw two angels who were kneeling and adoring at the head and feet of the sacred body, raise it—keeping it in the exact position in which it was lying in the tomb—and carry it uncovered and disfigured with wounds across the rock, which trembled as they passed. It then appeared to me that Jesus presented his body, marked with the stigmas of the Passion, to his Heavenly Father, who, seated on a throne, was surrounded by innumerable choirs of angels, blissfully occupied in pouring forth hymns of adoration and jubilee. The case was probably the same when at the death of our Lord, so many holy souls re-entered their bodies, and appeared in the Temple and in different parts of Jerusalem; for it is not likely that the bodies which they animated were really alive, as in that case they would have been obliged to die a second time, whereas they returned to their original state without apparent difficulty; but it is to be supposed that their appearance in human form was similar to that of our Lord, when he (if we may thus express it) accompanied his body to the throne of his Heavenly Father.

At this moment the rock was so violently shaken, from the very summit to the base, that three of the guards fell down and became almost insensible. The other four were away at the time, being gone to the town to fetch something. The guards who were thus thrown prostrate attributed the sudden shock to an earthquake; but Cassius, who, although uncertain as to what all this might portend, yet felt an inward presentiment that it was the prelude to some stupendous event, stood transfixed in anxious expectation, waiting to see what would follow next. The soldiers who were gone to Jerusalem soon returned.

I again beheld the holy women: they had finished preparing the spices, and were resting in their private cells; not stretched out on the couches, but leaning against the bedclothes, which were rolled up. They wished to go to the sepulchre before the break of day, because they feared meeting the enemies of Jesus; but the Blessed Virgin, who was perfectly renovated and filled with fresh courage since she had seen her Son, consoled and recommended them to sleep for a time, and then go fearlessly to the tomb, as no harm would come to them; whereupon they immediately followed her advice, and endeavoured to sleep.

It was towards eleven o'clock at night when the Blessed Virgin, incited by irrepressible feelings of love, arose, wrapped a grey cloak around her, and left the house quite alone. When I saw her do this, I could not help feeling anxious, and saying to myself, 'How is it possible for this holy Mother, who is so exhausted from anguish and terror, to venture to walk all alone through the streets at such an hour?' I saw her go first to the house of Caiphas, and then to the palace of Pilate, which was at a great distance off; I watched her through the whole of her solitary journey along that part which had been trodden by her Son, loaded with his heavy Cross; she stopped at every place where our Saviour had suffered particularly, or had received any fresh outrage from his barbarous enemies. Her appearance, as she walked slowly along, was that of a person seeking something; she often bent down to the ground, touched the stones with her hands, and then inundated them with kisses, if the precious blood of her beloved Son was upon them. God granted her at this time particular lights and graces, and she was able without the slightest degree of difficulty to distinguish every place sanctified by his sufferings. I accompanied her through the whole of her pious pilgrimage, and I endeavoured to imitate her to the best of my power, as far as my weakness would permit.

Mary then went to Calvary; but when she had almost reached it, she stopped suddenly, and I saw the sacred body and soul of our Saviour standing before her. An angel walked in front; the two angels whom I had seen in the tomb were by his side, and the souls whom he had redeemed followed him by hundreds. The body of Jesus was brilliant and beautiful, but its appearance was not that of a living body, although a voice issued from it; and I heard him describe to the Blessed Virgin all he had done in Limbo, and then assure her that he should rise again with his glorified body; that he would then show himself to her, and that she must wait near the rock of Mount Calvary, and that part where she saw him fall down, until he appeared. Our Saviour then went towards Jerusalem, and the Blessed Virgin, having again wrapped her veil about her, prostrated on the spot which he had pointed out. It was then, I think, past midnight, for the pilgrimage of Mary over the Way of the Cross had taken up at least an hour; and I next saw the holy souls who had been redeemed by our Saviour traverse in their turn the sorrowful Way of the Cross, and contemplate the different places where he had endured such fearful sufferings for their sakes. The angels who accompanied them gathered sacred flesh which had been torn off by the frequent blows he received, as also the blood with which the ground was sprinkled on those spots where he had fallen.

I once more saw the sacred body of our Lord stretched out as I first beheld it in the sepulchre; the angels were occupied in replacing the garments they had gathered up of his flesh, and they received supernatural assistance in doing this. When next I contemplated him it was in his winding-sheet, surrounded with a bright light and with two adoring angels by his side. I cannot explain how all these things came to pass, for they are far beyond our human comprehension; and even if I understand them perfectly myself when I see them, they appear dark and mysterious when I endeavour to explain them to others.

As soon as a faint glimmering of dawn appeared in the east, I saw Magdalen, Mary the daughter of Cleophas, Johanna Chusa, and Salome, leave the Cenaculum, closely wrapped up in their mantles. They carried bundles of spices; and one of their number had a lighted candle in her hand, which she endeavoured to conceal under her cloak. I saw them direct their trembling steps towards the small door at the house of Nicodemus.

CHAPTER LXIII.

The Resurrection of our Lord.

I beheld the soul of our Lord between two angels, who were in the attire of warriors: it was bright, luminous, and resplendent as the sun at mid-day; it penetrated the rock, touched the sacred body, passed into it, and the two were instantaneously united, and became as one. I then saw the limbs move, and the body of our Lord, being reunited to his soul and to his divinity, rise and shake off the winding-sheet: the whole of the cave was illuminated and lightsome.

At the same moment I saw a frightful monster burst from the earth underneath the sepulchre. It had the tail of a serpent, and it raised its dragon head proudly as if desirous of attacking Jesus; and had likewise, if I remember correctly, a human head. But our Lord held in his hand a white staff, to which was appended a large banner; and he placed his foot on the head of the dragon, and struck its tail three times with his staff, after which the monster disappeared. I had had this same vision many times before the Resurrection, and I saw just such a monster, appearing to endeavour to hide itself, at the time of the conception of our Lord: it greatly resembled the serpent which tempted our first parents in Paradise, only it was more horrible. I thought that this vision had reference to the prophetic words, that 'by the seed of the woman the head of the serpent should be crushed,' and that the whole was intended to demonstrate the victory of our Lord over death, for at the same moment that I saw him crush the head of the monster, the tomb likewise vanished from my sight.

I then saw the glorified body of our Lord rise up, and it passed through the hard rock as easily as if the latter had been formed of some ductile substance. The earth shook, and an angel in the garb of a warrior descended from Heaven with the speed of lightning, entered the tomb, lifted the stone, placed it on the right side, and seated himself upon it. At this tremendous sight the soldiers fell to the ground, and remained there apparently lifeless. When Cassius saw the bright light which illuminated the tomb, he approached the place where the sacred body had been placed, looked at and touched the linen clothes in which it had been wrapped, and left the sepulchre, intending to go and inform Pilate of all that had happened. However, he tarried a short time to watch the progress of events; for although he had felt the earthquake, seen the angel move the stone, and looked at the empty tomb, yet he had not seen Jesus.

At the very moment in which the angel entered the sepulchre and the earth quaked, I saw our Lord appear to his holy Mother on Calvary. His body was beautiful and lightsome, and its beauty was that of a celestial being. He was clothed in a large mantle, which at one moment looked dazzlingly white, as it floated through the air, waving to and fro with every breath of wind, and the next reflected a thousand brilliant colours as the sunbeams passed over it. His large open wounds shone brightly, and could be seen from a great distance: the wounds in his hands were so large that a finger might be put into them without difficulty; and rays of light proceeded from them, diverging in the direction of his fingers. The souls of the patriarchs bowed down before the Mother of our Saviour, and Jesus spoke to her concerning his Resurrection, telling her many things which I have forgotten. He showed her his wounds; and Mary prostrated to kiss his sacred feet; but he took her hand, raised her, and disappeared.

When I was at some distance from the sepulchre I saw fresh lights burning there, and I likewise beheld a large luminous spot in the sky immediately over Jerusalem.

CHAPTER LXIV.

The holy Women at the Sepulchre.

The holy women were very near the door of Nicodemus's house at the moment of our Lord's Resurrection; but they did not see anything of the prodigies which were taking place at the sepulchre. They were not aware that guards had been placed around the tomb, for they had not visited it on the previous day, on account of its being the Sabbath. They questioned one another anxiously concerning what would have to be done about the large stone at the door, as to who would be the best person to ask about removing it, for they had been so engrossed by grief that they had not thought about it before. Their intention was to pour precious ointments upon the body of Jesus, and then to strew over it flowers of the most rare and aromatic kinds, thus rendering all the honour possible to their Divine Master in his sepulchre. Salome, who had brought more things than anyone else, was a rich lady, who lived in Jerusalem, a relation of St. Joseph, but not the mother of John. The holy women came to the determination of putting down their spices on the stone which closed the door of the monument, and waiting until someone came to roll it back.

The guards were still lying on the ground, and the strong convulsions which even then shook them clearly demonstrated how great had been their terror, and the large stone was cast on one side, so that the door could be opened without difficulty. I could see the linen cloth in which the body of Jesus had been wrapped scattered about in the tomb, and the large winding-sheet lying in the same place as when they left it, but doubled together in such a manner that you saw at once that it no longer contained anything but the spices which had been placed round the body, and the bandages were on the outside of the tomb. The linen cloth in which Mary had enveloped the sacred head of her Son was still there.

I saw the holy women coming into the garden; but when they perceived the light given by the lamps of the sentinels, and the prostrate forms of the soldiers round the tomb, they for the most part became much alarmed, and retreated towards Golgotha. Mary Magdalen was, however, more courageous, and, followed by Salome, entered the garden while the other women remained timidly on the outside.

Magdalen started, and appeared for a moment terrified when she drew near the sentinels. She retreated a few steps and rejoined Salome, but both quickly recovered their presence of mind, and walked on together through the midst of the prostrate guards, and entered into the cave which contained the sepulchre. They immediately perceived that the stone was removed, but the doors were closed, which had been done in all probability by Cassius. Magdalen opened them quickly, looked anxiously into the sepulchre, and was much surprised at seeing that the cloths in which they had enveloped our Lord were lying on one side, and that the place where they had deposited the sacred remains was empty. A celestial light filled the cave, and an angel was seated on the right side. Magdalen became almost beside herself from disappointment and alarm. I do not know whether she heard the words which the angel addressed to her, but she left the garden as quickly as possible, and ran to the town to inform the Apostles who were assembled there of what had taken place. I do not know whether the angel spoke to Mary Salome, as she did not enter the sepulchre; but I saw her leaving the garden directly after Magdalen, in order to relate all that had happened to the rest of the holy women, who were both frightened and delighted at the news, but could not make up their minds as to whether they would go to the garden or not.

In the mean time Cassius had remained near the sepulchre in hopes of seeing Jesus, as he thought he would be certain to appear to the holy women; but seeing nothing, he directed his steps towards Pilate's palace to relate to him all that had happened, stopping, however, first at the place where the rest of the holy women were assembled, to tell them what he had seen, and to exhort them to go immediately to the garden. They followed his advice, and went there at once. No sooner had they reached the door of the sepulchre than they beheld two angels clothed in sacerdotal vestments of the most dazzling white. The women were very much alarmed, covered their faces with their hands, and prostrated almost to the ground; but one of the angels addressed them, bade them not fear, and told them that they must not seek for their crucified Lord there, for that he was alive, had risen, and was no longer an inhabitant of the tomb. He pointed out to them at the same moment the empty sepulchre, and ordered them to go and relate to the disciples all that they had seen and heard. He likewise told them that Jesus would go before them into Galilee, and recalled to their minds the words which our Saviour had addressed to them on a former occasion: 'The Son of Man will be delivered into the hands of sinners, he will be crucified, and the third day rise again.' The angels then disappeared, and left the holy women filled with joy, although of course greatly agitated; they wept, looked at the empty tomb and linen clothes, and immediately started to return to the town. But they were so much overcome by the many astounding events which had taken place, that they walked very slowly, and stopped and looked back often, in hopes of seeing our Lord, or at least Magdalen.

In the mean time Magdalen reached the Cenaculum. She was so excited as to appear like a person beside herself, and knocked hastily at the door. Some of the disciples were still sleeping, and those who were risen were conversing together. Peter and John opened the door, but she only exclaimed, without entering the house, 'They have taken away the body of my Lord, and I know not where they have laid him,' and immediately returned to the garden. Peter and John went back into the house, and after saying a few words to the other disciples followed her as speedily as possible, but John far outstripped Peter. I then saw Magdalen reenter the garden, and direct her steps towards the sepulchre; she appeared greatly agitated partly from grief, and partly from having walked so fast. Her garments were quite moist with dew, and her veil hanging on one side, while the luxuriant hair in which she had formerly taken so much pride fell in dishevelled masses over her shoulders, forming a species of mantle. Being alone, she was afraid of entering the cave, but stopped for a moment on the outside, and knelt down in order to see better into the tomb. She was endeavouring to push back her long hair, which fell over her face and obscured her vision, when she perceived the two angels who were seated in the tomb, and I heard one of them address her thus: 'Woman, why weepest thou?' She replied, in a voice choked with tears (for she was perfectly overwhelmed with grief at finding that the body of Jesus was really gone), 'Because they have taken away my Lord, and I know not where they have laid him.' She said no more, but seeing the empty winding-sheet, went out of the sepulchre and began to look about in other parts. She felt a secret presentiment that not only should she find Jesus, but that he was even then near to her; and the presence of the angels seemed not to disturb her in the least; she did not appear even to be aware that they were angels, every faculty was engrossed with the one thought, 'Jesus is not here! Where is Jesus?' I watched her wandering about like an insane person, with her hair floating loosely in the wind: her hair appeared to annoy her much, for she again endeavoured to push it from off her face, and having divided it into two parts, threw it over her shoulders.

She then raised her head, looked around, and perceived a tall figure, clothed in white, standing at about ten paces from the sepulchre on the east side of the garden, where there was a slight rise in the direction of the town; the figure was partly hidden from her sight by a palm-tree, but she was somewhat startled when it addressed her in these words: 'Woman, why weepest thou? Whom seekest thou?' She thought it was the gardener; and, in fact, he had a spade in his hand, and a large hat (apparently made of the bark of trees) on his head. His dress was similar to that worn by the gardener described in the parable which Jesus had related to the holy women at Bethania a short time before his Passion. His body was not luminous, his hole appearance was rather that of a man dressed in white and seen by twilight. At the words, 'Whom seekest thou?' she looked at him, and answered quickly, 'Sir, if thou hast taken him hence, tell me where thou hast laid him; and I will take him away.' And she looked anxiously around. Jesus said to her, 'Mary.' She then instantly recognised his beloved voice, and turning quickly, replied, 'Rabboni (Master)!' She threw herself on her knees before him, and stretched out her hands to touch his feet; but he motioned her to be still, and said, 'Do not touch me, for I am not yet ascended to my Father; but go to my brethren and say to them: I ascend to my Father and to your Father, to my God and your God.' He then disappeared.

The reason of the words of Jesus, 'Do not touch me,' was afterwards explained to me, but I have only an indistinct remembrance of that explanation. I think he made use of those words because of the impetuosity of Magdalen's feelings, which made her in a certain degree forget the stupendous mystery which had been accomplished, and feel as if what she then beheld was still mortal instead of a glorified body. As for the words of Jesus, 'I am not yet ascended to my Father,' I was told that their meaning was that he had not presented himself to his Father since his Resurrection, to return him thanks for his victory over death, and for the work of the redemption which he had accomplished. He wished her to infer from these words, that the first-fruits of joy belong to God, and that she ought to reflect and return thanks to him for the accomplishment of the glorious mystery of the redemption, and for the victory which he had gained over death; and if she had kissed his feet as she used before the Passion, she would have thought of nothing but her Divine Master, and in her raptures of love have totally forgotten the wonderful events which were causing such astonishment and joy in Heaven. I saw Magdalen arise quickly, as soon as our Lord disappeared, and run to look again in the sepulchre, as if she believed herself under the influence of a dream. She saw the two angels still seated there, and they spoke to her concerning the resurrection of our Lord in the same words as they had addressed the two other women. She likewise saw the empty winding-sheet, and then, feeling certain that she was not in a state of delusion, but that the apparition of our Lord was real, she walked quickly back towards Golgotha to seek her companions, who were wandering about to and fro, anxiously looking out for her return, and indulging a kind of vague hope that they should see or hear something of Jesus.

The whole of this scene occupied a little more than two or three minutes. It was about half-past three when our Lord appeared to Magdalen, and John and Peter entered the garden just as she was leaving it. John, who was a little in advance of Peter, stopped at the entrance of the cave and looked in. He saw the linen clothes lying on one side, and waited until Peter came up, when they entered the sepulchre together, and saw the winding-sheet empty as has been before described. John instantly believed in the Resurrection, and they both understood clearly the words addressed to them by Jesus before his Passion, as well as the different passages in Scripture relating to that event, which had until then been incomprehensible to them. Peter put the linen clothes under his cloak, and they returned hastily into the town through the small entrance belonging to Nicodemus.

The appearance of the holy sepulchre was the same when the two Apostles entered as when Magdalen first saw it. The two adoring angels were seated, one at the head, and the other at the extremity of the tomb, in precisely the same attitude as when his adorable body was lying there. I do not think Peter was conscious of their presence. I afterwards heard John tell the disciples of Emmaus, that when he looked into the sepulchre he saw an angel. Perhaps he was startled by this sight, and therefore drew back and let Peter enter the sepulchre first; but it is likewise very possible that the reason of his not mentioning the circumstance in his gospel was because humility made him anxious to conceal the fact of his having been more highly favoured than Peter.

The guards at this moment began to revive, and rising, gathered up their lances, and took down the lamps, which were on the door, from whence they cast a glimmering weak light on surrounding objects. I then saw them walk hastily out of the garden in evident fear and trepidation, in the direction of the town.

In the mean time Magdalen had rejoined the holy women, and given them the account of her seeing the Lord in the garden, and of the words of the angels afterwards, whereupon they immediately related what had been seen by themselves, and Magdalen wended her way quickly to Jerusalem, while the women returned to that side of the garden where they expected to find the two Apostles. Just before they reached it, Jesus appeared to them. He was clothed in a long white robe, which concealed even his hands, and said to them, 'All hail.' They started with astonishment, and cast themselves at his feet; he spoke a few words, held forth his hand as if to point out something to them, and disappeared. The holy women went instantly to the Cenaculum, and told the disciples who were assembled there that they had seen the Lord; the disciples were incredulous, and would not give credence either to their account or to that of Magdalen. They treated both the one and the other as the effects of their excited imaginations; but when Peter and John entered the room and related what they likewise had seen, they knew not what to answer, and were filled with astonishment.

Peter and John soon left the Cenaculum, as the wonderful events which had taken place rendered them extremely silent and thoughtful, and before long they met James the Less and Thaddeus, who had wished to accompany them to the sepulchre. Both James and Thaddeus were greatly overcome, for the Lord had appeared to them a short time before they met Peter and John. I also saw Jesus pass quite close to Peter and John. I think the former recognised him, for the started suddenly, but I do not think the latter saw him.

CHAPTER LXV.

The Relation which was given by the Sentinels who were placed around the Sepulchre.

Cassius hastened to the house of Pilate about an hour after the Resurrection, in order to give him an account of the stupendous events which had taken place. He was not yet risen, but Cassius was allowed to enter his bedroom. He related all that had happened, and expressed his feelings in the most forcible language. He described how the rock had been rent, and how an angel had descended from Heaven and pushed aside the stone; he also spoke of the empty winding-sheet, and added that most certainly Jesus was the Messiah, the Son of God, and that he was truly risen. Pilate listened to this account; he trembled and quivered with terror, but concealed his agitation to the best of his power, and answered Cassius in these words: 'Thou art exceedingly superstitious; it was very foolish to go to the Galilean's tomb; his gods took advantage of thy weakness, and displayed all these ridiculous visions to alarm thee. I recommend thee to keep silence, and not recount such silly tales to the priests, for thou wouldst get the worst of it from them.' He pretended to believe that the body of Jesus had been carried away by his disciples, and that the sentinels, who had been bribed, and had fallen asleep, or perhaps been deceived by witchcraft, had fabricated these accounts in order to justify their conduct. When Pilate had said all he could on the subject, Cassius left him, and he went to offer sacrifice to his gods.

The four soldiers who had guarded the tomb arrived shortly after at Pilate's palace, and began to tell him all that he had already heard from Cassius; but he would listen to nothing more, and sent them to Caiphas. The rest of the guards were assembled in a large court near the Temple which was filled with aged Jews, who, after some previous consultation, took the soldiers on one side, and by dint of bribes and threats endeavoured to persuade them to say that they fell asleep, and that while they were asleep the disciples came and carried away the body of our Lord. The soldiers, however, demurred, because the statement which their comrades were gone to make to Pilate would contradict any account which they could now fabricate, but the Pharisees promised to arrange everything with the governor. Whilst they were still disputing, the four guards returned from their interview with Pilate, and the Pharisees endeavoured to persuade them to conceal the truth; but this they refused to do, and declared firmly that they would not vary their first statement in the smallest degree. The miraculous deliverance of Joseph of Arimathea from prison was become public, and when the Pharisees accused the soldiers of having allowed the Apostles to carry off the body of Jesus, and threatened them with the infliction of the most severe punishment if they did not produce the body, they replied, that it would be as utterly impossible for them to produce the body of Jesus, as it was for the soldiers who had charge of Joseph of Arimathea to bring him back into his prison again. They spoke with the greatest firmness and courage; promises and menaces were equally ineffectual. They declared that they would speak the truth and nothing but the truth; that the sentence of death which had been passed upon Jesus was both unjust and iniquitous; and that the crime which was perpetrated in putting him to death was the sole cause of the interruption in the Paschal solemnity. The Pharisees, being perfectly furious, caused the four soldiers to be arrested and thrown into prison, and the others, who had accepted the bribes they offered, then affirmed that the body of Jesus had been carried off by the disciples while they slept; and the Pharisees, Sadducees, and Herodians endeavoured to disseminate this lie to the utmost of their power, not only in the synagogue but also among the people; and they accompanied this false statement by the most slanderous lies concerning Jesus.

All these precautions, however, availed but little, for, after the Resurrection, many persons who had been long dead arose from their graves, and appeared to those among their descendants who were not sufficiently hardened to be impervious to grace, and exhorted them to be converted. These dead persons were likewise seen by many of the disciples, who, overcome with terror, and shaken in faith, had fled into the country. They both exhorted and encouraged them to return, and restored their drooping courage. The resurrection of these dead persons did not in the slightest degree resemble the Resurrection of Jesus. He arose with a glorified body, which was no longer susceptible of either corruption or death, and ascended into heaven with this glorified body in the sight of all his disciples; but the dead bodies of which we spoke above were motionless corpses, and the souls which once inhabited them were only allowed to enter and reanimate them for a time, and after performing the mission given them, the souls again quitted these bodies, which returned to their original state in the bowels of the earth, where they will remain until the resurrection at the day of judgment. Neither could their return to life be compared to the raising of Lazarus from the dead; for he really returned to a new life, and died a second time.

CHAPTER LXVI.

The End of the Lenten Meditations.

On the following Sunday, if I remember right, I saw the Jews washing and purifying the Temple.[13] They offered up expiatory sacrifices, cleared away the rubbish, and endeavoured to conceal the effects of the earthquake by placing planks and carpets over the chasms and fissures made by it in the walls and on the pavement; and they recommenced the Paschal solemnities, which had been interrupted in the midst, declared that the disturbance had been caused by the presence of impure persons, and endeavoured to explain away the apparition of the dead. They referred to a vision of Ezechiel, but how I can no longer remember. They threatened all who dared to say a syllable concerning the events which had taken place, or who presumed to murmur, with excommunication and other severe punishments. They succeeded in silencing some few hardened persons who, conscious of their own guilt, wished to banish the subject from their minds, but they made no impression on those whose hearts still retained some remains of virtue; they remained silent for a time, concealing their inward belief, but later, regaining courage, proclaimed their faith in Jesus loudly to the world. The High Priests were much disconcerted, when they perceived how rapidly the doctrines of Christ spread over the country. When Stephen was deacon, the whole of Ophel and the eastern side of Sion was too small to contain the numerous Christian communities, and a portion were obliged to take up their residence in the country between Jerusalem and Bethania.

I saw Annas in such a state of frenzy as to act like one possessed; he was at last obliged to be confined, and never again to make his appearance in public. Caiphas was outwardly less demonstrative, but he was inwardly devoured with such rage and extreme jealousy that his reason was affected.

I saw Pilate on Easter Thursday; he was instituting a search for his wife in every part of the city, but his efforts for her recovery were fruitless; she was concealed in the house of Lazarus, in Jerusalem. No one thought of looking there, as the house contained no other female; but Stephen carried food to her there, and let her know all that was going on in the city. Stephen was first-cousin to St. Paul. They were the sons of two brothers. On the day after the Sabbath, Simon of Cyrene went to the Apostles and begged to be instructed and to receive baptism.

The visions of Sister Emmerich, which had continued from the 18th of February to the 6th of April 1823, here came to a conclusion.

---

[13] The above relation was given later, and it is impossible to say whether it relates to the day of the Resurrection or to the following Sunday.

APPENDIX.

Detached Account of Longinus.

On the 15th of March 1821, Sister Emmerich gave the following detached account of parts of a vision which she had had the previous night concerning St. Longinus, whose festival happened to fall upon that very day, although she did not know it.

Longinus, who had, I think, another name, held an office, partly civil and partly military, in the household of Pilate, who entrusted him with the duty of superintending all that passed, and making a report of it to him. He was trustworthy and ready to do a service, but previous to his conversion was greatly wanting in firmness and strength of character. He was excessively impetuous in all that he did, and anxious to be thought a person of great importance, and as he squinted and had weak eyes, he was often jeered at and made the laughing-stock of his companions. I have seen him frequently during the course of this night, and in connection with him I have at the same time seen all the Passion, I do not know in what manner; I only remember that it was in connection with him.

Longinus was only in a subordinate position, and had to give an account to Pilate of all that he saw. On the night that Jesus was led before the tribunal of Caiphas he was in the outer court among the soldiers, and unceasingly going backwards and forwards. When Peter was alarmed at the words of the maid-servant standing near the fire, it was he who said once: 'Art thou not also one of this man's disciples?'

When Jesus was being led to Calvary, Longinus, by Pilate's orders, followed him closely, and our Divine Lord gave him a look which touched his heart. Afterwards I saw him on Golgotha with the soldiers. He was on horseback, and carried a lance; I saw him at Pilate's house, after the death of our Lord, saying that the legs of Jesus ought not to be broken. He returned at once to Calvary. His lance was made of several pieces which fitted one into the other, so that by drawing them out, the lance could be made three times its original length. He had just done this when he came to the sudden determination of piercing the side of our Saviour. He was converted upon Mount Calvary, and a short time afterwards expressed to Pilate his conviction that Jesus was the Son of God. Nicodemus prevailed upon Pilate to let him have Longinus's lance, and I have seen many things concerning the subsequent history of this lance. Longinus, after his conversion, left the army, and joined the disciples. He and two other soldiers, who were converted at the foot of the cross, were among the first baptised after Pentecost.

I saw Longinus and these two men, clothed in long white garments, return to their native land. They lived there in the country, in a barren and marshy locality. Here it was that the forty martyrs died. Longinus was not a priest, but a deacon, and travelled here and there in that capacity, preaching the name of Christ, and giving, as an eye-witness, a history of his Passion and Resurrection. He converted a large number of persons, and cured many of the sick, by allowing them to touch a piece of the sacred lance which he carried with him. The Jews were much enraged at him and his two companions because they made known in all parts the truth of the Resurrection of Jesus, and the cruelty and deceits of his enemies. At their instigation, some Roman soldiers were dispatched to Longinus's country to take and judge him on the plea of his having left the army without leave, and being a disturber of public peace. He was engaged in cultivating his field when they arrived, and he took them to his house, and offered them hospitality. They did not know him, and when they had acquainted him with the object of their journey, he quietly called his two companions who were living in a sort of hermitage at no great distance off, and told the soldiers that they and himself were the men for whom they were seeking. The same thing happened to the holy gardener, Phocas. The soldiers were really distressed, for they had conceived a great friendship for him. I saw him led with his two companions to a small neighbouring town, where they were questioned. They were not put in prison, but permitted to go whither they pleased, as prisoners on their word, and only made to wear a distinctive park on the shoulder. Later, they were all three beheaded on a hill, situated between the little town and Longinus's house, and there buried. The soldiers put the head of Longinus at the end of a spear, and carried it to Jerusalem, as a proof that they had fulfilled their commission. I think I remember that this took place a very few years after the death of our Lord.

Afterwards I had a vision of things happening at a later period. A blind countrywoman of St. Longinus went with her son on a pilgrimage to Jerusalem, in hopes of recovering her sight in the holy city where the eyes of Longinus had been cured. She was guided by her child, but he died, and she was left alone and disconsolate. Then St. Longinus appeared to her, and told her that she would recover her sight when she had drawn his head out of a sink into which the Jews had thrown it. This sink was a deep well, with the sides bricked, and all the filth and refuse of the town flowed into it through several drains. I saw some persons lead the poor woman to the spot; she descended into the well up to her neck, and drew out the sacred head, whereupon she recovered her sight. She returned to her native land, and her companions preserved the head. I remember no more upon this subject.

Detached Account of Abenadar.

On the 1st of April 1823, Sister Emmerich said that that day was the feast of St. Ctesiphon, the centurion who had assisted at the Crucifixion, and that she had seen during the night various particulars concerning his life. But she had also suffered greatly, which, combined with exterior distractions, had caused her to forget the greatest part of what she had seen. She related what follows:

Abenadar, afterwards called Ctesiphon, was born in a country situated between Babylon and Egypt in Arabia Felix, to the right of the spot where Job dwelt during the latter half of his life. A certain number of square houses, with flat roofs, were built there on a slight ascent. There were many small trees growing on this spot, and incense and balm were gathered there. I have been in

Abenadar's house, which was large and spacious, as might be expected of a rich man's house, but it was also very low. All these houses were built in this manner, perhaps on account of the wind, because they were much exposed. Abenadar had joined the garrison of the fortress Antonia, at Jerusalem, as a volunteer. He had entered the Roman service for the purpose of enjoying more facilities in his study of the fine arts, for he was a learned man. His character was firm, his figure short and thick-set, and his complexion dark.

Abenadar was early convinced, by the doctrine which he heard Jesus preach, and by a miracle which he saw him work; that salvation was to be found among the Jews, and he had submitted to the law of Moses. Although not yet a disciple of our Lord, he bore him no illwill, and held his person in secret veneration. He was naturally grave and composed, and when he came to Golgotha to relieve guard, he kept order on all sides, and forced everybody to behave at least with common decency, down to the moment when truth triumphed over him, and he rendered public testimony to the Divinity of Jesus. Being a rich man, and a volunteer, he had no difficulty in resigning his post at once. He assisted at the descent from the Cross and the burial of our Lord, which put him into familiar connection with the friends of Jesus, and after the day of Pentecost he was one of the first to receive baptism in the Pool of Bethsaida, where he took the name of Ctesiphon. He had a brother living in Arabia, to whom he related the miracles he had beheld, and who was thus called to the path of salvation, came to Jerusalem, was baptised by the name of Cecilius, and was charged, together with Ctesiphon, to assist the deacons in the newly-formed Christian community.

Ctesiphon accompanied the Apostle St. James the Greater into Spain, and also returned with him. After a time, he was again sent into Spain by the Apostles, and carried there the body of St. James, who had been martyred at Jerusalem. He was made a bishop, and resided chiefly in a sort of island or peninsula at no great distance from France, which he also visited, and where he made some disciples. The name of the place where he lived was rather like Vergui, and it was afterwards laid waste by an inundation. I do not remember that Ctesiphon was ever martyred. He wrote several books containing details concerning the Passion of Christ; but there have been some books falsely attributed to him, and others, which were really from his pen, ascribed to different writers. Rome has since rejected these books, the greatest part of which were apocryphal, but which nevertheless did contain some few things really from his pen. One of the guards of our Lord's sepulchre, who would not let himself be bribed by the Jews, was his fellow countryman and friend. His name was something like Sulei or Suleii. After being detained some time in prison, he retired into a cavern of Mount Sinai, where he lived seven years. God bestowed many special graces upon this man, and he wrote some very learned books in the style of Denis the Areopagite. Another writer made use of his works, and in this manner some extracts from them have come down to us. Everything concerning these facts was made known to me, as well as the name of the book, but I have forgotten it. This countryman of Ctesiphon, afterwards followed him into Spain. Among the companions of Ctesiphon in that country were this brother Cecilius, and some other men, whose name were Intalecius, Hesicius, and Euphrasius. Another Arab, called Sulima, was converted in the very early days of the Church, and a fellow countryman of Ctesiphon, with a name like Sulensis, became a Christian later, in the time of the deacons.

THE END.

Made in the USA
San Bernardino, CA
27 November 2016